GLOBAL
SOUTH
ASIA

Padma Kaimal
K. Sivaramakrishnan
Anand A. Yang
SERIES EDITORS

The Rebirth of Bodh Gaya

Buddhism and the Making of a World Heritage Site

DAVID GEARY

UNIVERSITY OF WASHINGTON PRESS

Seattle and London

Copyright © 2017 by the University of Washington Press
Printed and bound in the United States of America
Composed in Minion Pro, typeface designed by Robert Slimbach
21 20 19 18 17   5 4 3 2 1

Photos by the author unless otherwise credited
Map by Ben Pease, Pease Press Cartography

University of Washington Press
www.washington.edu/uwpress

Library of Congress Cataloging-in-Publication Data on file

ISBN 978-0-295-74236-6 (hardcover), ISBN 978-0-295-74237-3 (pbk),
ISBN 978-0-295-74238-0 (ebook)

For my parents,
Lorne and Angela Geary

Contents

Acknowledgments

This book has been a long journey and would not have been possible without an extensive community of support. Its inspiration began well over a decade ago when I first undertook research in India, and it would not have been possible without the direction and mentoring of John Barker at the University of British Columbia. Anand Yang at the University of Washington volunteered his time and shared his extensive knowledge of India and Bihar history over the years. I am also grateful for the intellectual support provided by David Gellner at the University of Oxford, who helped refocus the book toward a deeper engagement with Buddhism in South Asia. Numerous colleagues across the academy have supported this project and offered guidance and encouragement at critical phases: Gaston Gordillo, Harjot Oberoi, Simon Coleman, Ian Harris, Katherine Hacker, Millie Creighton, Shravasti Dhammika, Tapati Guha-Thakurta, Shantum Seth, Rohan D'Souza, Herb Stovel, Ian Prattis, Brian Given, and Sraman Mukherjee. I also owe an enormous debt to my supportive anthropology colleagues, graduate and undergraduate students at the University of British Columbia Okanagan in the Community, Culture and Global Studies Department: Sue Frohlick, John Wagner, Hugo de Burgos, Robin Dods, Diana French, Christine Schreyer, Sandra Peacock, Mike Evans, Matt Husain, Michelle Bjornson, Kristen Batty, and Joanne Gervais.

As will become apparent in the pages that follow, this book is embedded in a rich and growing scholarship on Bodh Gaya that has shaped the direction of my work on several fronts. Many of these scholars were brought together during the XVth International Association of Buddhist Studies Conference held at Emory University in 2008 and provided the inspiration for our coedited book *Bodh Gaya Jataka*: Tara Doyle, Alan Trevithick, Janice Leoshko, Robert Pryor, Fred Asher, Noel Salmond, Abhishek Singh Amar, Jessica Falcone, Kory Goldberg, Matthew Sayers, and Jason Rodriguez. I am truly grateful for the intellectual engagement and friendship that has developed out of our shared passion for Bodh Gaya over the years. This monograph also benefited enormously from the opportunity to participate in a writing workshop offered by the Theravada Civilizations Project in

Toronto, March 2012, where generous attention and feedback were provided by such an insightful group of scholars, especially Juliane Schober and Steven Collins. In 2012 I was incredibly fortunate to serve as a faculty member for the Carleton-Antioch Buddhist Studies program in Bodh Gaya. Spending four months at the Burmese *vihara* with such a wonderful group of students and faculty gave me a deeper appreciation for the place and the importance of seeing Bodh Gaya from an educational and monastic perspective. Over the years I have benefited from many conversations with faculty members in the Carleton-Antioch program, especially Robert Pryor, who has been a real mentor for me; his knowledge and assistance over the years have been invaluable.

Most of the stories and encounters that animate Bodh Gaya's bazaar are the result of friendships that have developed since my first pilgrimage to India during the winter of 2002–2003. I remain truly humbled by all those who have shared their lives with me. Although I have provided pseudonyms for many in this book, there are number of people I need to acknowledge for their contributions at various stages: P. C. Roy, Naresh Banerjee, Dr. Ansari, Ram Swarup Singh, Ali Ashgar, Mr. Shabuddin, Priyapal Bhante, Kiran Lama, Kabir Saxena, Seewalee Thero Bhante, Sister Mary, Kailash Prasad, Nangzey Dorjee, U Nyaneinda, and Richard and Wangmo Dixey. I am also grateful to all the generous friends and field assistants in Bodh Gaya who made this research possible. In particular, I want to thank my host family in Pacchetti, especially my dear friend Bhalwant and his parents, *mera chachiji* and *chacha*, for their love and support over the years. From early on in this research I was extremely fortunate to be affiliated with the Indian National Trust for Arts and Cultural Heritage (INTACH) and Hazaribagh Convenor Bulu Imam. Visiting Sanskriti and the Imam family in Jharkhand has always been a source of inspiration and joy. I am forever grateful for their kindness and hospitality.

This study would not have been possible without the generous financial support from a number of sources: the Social Sciences and Humanities Research Council (Government of Canada), University of British Columbia; the Shastri Indo-Canadian Institute; and the International Institute for Asian Studies in Leiden. Some of the material included here has been previously published elsewhere. I would like to thank Wiley and the Royal Anthropological Institute for allowing me to reprint portions of "Destination Enlightenment: Branding Buddhism and Spiritual Tourism in Bodhgaya, Bihar," an article published in *Anthropology Today* (2008). A slightly revised version of an article published in *Modern Asian Studies*

(2014) is included here in chapter 2 with permission from Cambridge University. Some of chapter 3 derives from an article published in *South Asian History and Culture* (2013a). Material published in *The Making of Heritage: Seduction and Disenchantment*, edited by C. Del Marmol, M. Morell, and J. Chalcraft (2014) appears in chapter 5 and is reproduced by permission of Taylor and Francis Group, LLC, a division of Informa PLC.

I also want to thank the editorial staff at the University of Washington Press, the Global South Asia series editors, and executive editor Lorri Hagman for her enthusiastic support and encouragement for this project.

Many family and friends in Vancouver have been a vital source of support throughout this endeavor. I owe my deepest gratitude to my parents, Lorne and Angela Geary, for their unconditional love and unwavering encouragement all these years. Last, but certainly not least, I wish to thank my wife Erika, son James, and daughter Nina—our little bodhisattva. I am deeply and enduringly grateful for your patience, love, and companionship.

Note on Translation and Transliteration

This book was written with the general reader in mind. For this reason I have removed diacritics from foreign terms, and I have tried to transliterate Hindi, Bhojpuri, Pali, and Sanskrit terms in a way that most closely approximates their local pronunciation. I have italicized these words throughout. Key terms can be found in the glossary. Bodh Gaya is spelled various ways, including Bodhgaya, Buddha Gaya, Budh-Gaya, and Bodh Gya. For the purpose of standardization, except in quotations or to reflect historical use, I use "Bodh Gaya" throughout the text.

All the statements and conversations reported in this book derive from recorded interviews and informal conversations recorded in field notes. Most of the interviews with Buddhist monks, nuns, laypeople, government officials, and tourists were conducted in English. A few of the interviews were conducted in Hindi and Tibetan with the help of a translator.

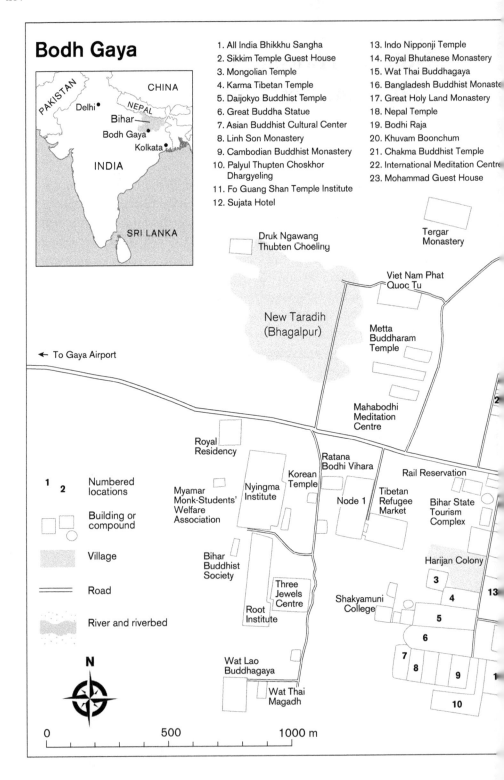

Bodh Gaya

1. All India Bhikkhu Sangha
2. Sikkim Temple Guest House
3. Mongolian Temple
4. Karma Tibetan Temple
5. Daijokyo Buddhist Temple
6. Great Buddha Statue
7. Asian Buddhist Cultural Center
8. Linh Son Monastery
9. Cambodian Buddhist Monastery
10. Palyul Thupten Choskhor Dhargyeling
11. Fo Guang Shan Temple Institute
12. Sujata Hotel
13. Indo Nipponji Temple
14. Royal Bhutanese Monastery
15. Wat Thai Buddhagaya
16. Bangladesh Buddhist Monaste
17. Great Holy Land Monastery
18. Nepal Temple
19. Bodhi Raja
20. Khuvam Boonchum
21. Chakma Buddhist Temple
22. International Meditation Centre
23. Mohammad Guest House

CHINA
PAKISTAN
Delhi
NEPAL
Bihar
Bodh Gaya
Kolkata
INDIA
SRI LANKA

Druk Ngawang Thubten Choeling

Tergar Monastery

Viet Nam Phat Quoc Tu

New Taradih (Bhagalpur)

Metta Buddharam Temple

← To Gaya Airport

Mahabodhi Meditation Centre

Royal Residency

Korean Temple

Ratana Bodhi Vihara

Rail Reservation

1   2   Numbered locations

Myamar Monk-Students' Welfare Association

Nyingma Institute

Node 1

Tibetan Refugee Market

Bihar State Tourism Complex

Building or compound

Village

Bihar Buddhist Society

Harijan Colony

Three Jewels Centre

Shakyamuni College

Road

Root Institute

River and riverbed

Wat Lao Buddhagaya

N

Wat Thai Magadh

0   500   1000 m

3
4
5
6
7
8
9
10
13

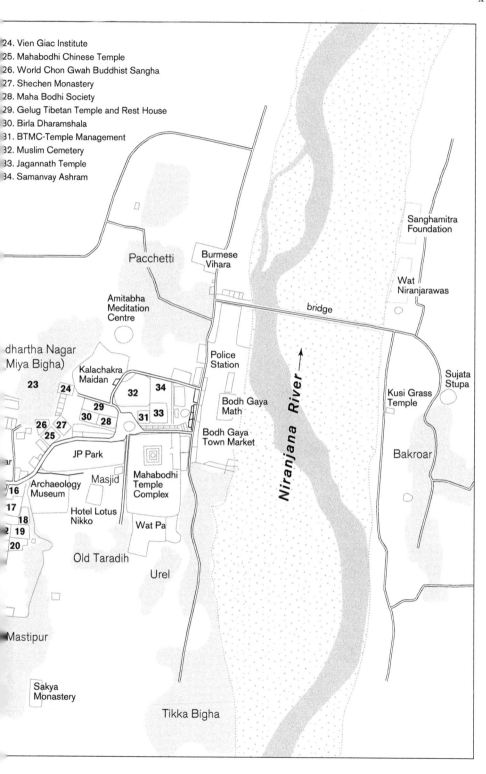

24. Vien Giac Institute
25. Mahabodhi Chinese Temple
26. World Chon Gwah Buddhist Sangha
27. Shechen Monastery
28. Maha Bodhi Society
29. Gelug Tibetan Temple and Rest House
30. Birla Dharamshala
31. BTMC-Temple Management
32. Muslim Cemetery
33. Jagannath Temple
34. Samanvay Ashram

Sanghamitra
Foundation

Pacchetti

Burmese
Vihara

Wat
Niranjarawas

bridge

Amitabha
Meditation
Centre

dhartha Nagar
Miya Bigha)

23   24

Kalachakra
Maidan

Police
Station

Sujata
Stupa

Kusi Grass
Temple

32   34

29

30   28   31   33

Bodh Gaya
Math

26 27
25

JP Park

Bodh Gaya
Town Market

Bakroar

ar

16

Archaeology
Museum

Masjid

Mahabodhi
Temple
Complex

17

18

Hotel Lotus
Nikko

19

Wat Pa

20

Old Taradih

Urel

Mastipur

Sakya
Monastery

Tikka Bigha

Niranjana River

The Rebirth of Bodh Gaya

Introduction

ALTHOUGH IT NEVER COMPLETELY LEFT, BUDDHISM HAS RETURNED to India in a big way. Nowhere is this more evident than in Bodh Gaya, which is fast becoming a global destination attracting hundreds of thousands of Asian Buddhist pilgrims and visitors each year.[1] According to the data collected by the Union Tourism Ministry in 2009, the North Indian state of Bihar, where Bodh Gaya is located, attracted 4.2 lakh (420,000) foreign tourists that year, eclipsing the popular tourist destination Goa. "Celebrated as the party destination in India, Goa appears to have lost its 'happening' tag to the humble Bihar," reports a *Times of India* article (Dhawan 2011). By 2011, the number of visitors to Bihar had nearly doubled to 972,487 overseas tourists, earning its place as one of the top ten Indian states to attract foreign travelers, according to India's tourism ministry (Guha 2013).

With the rebranding of India's third most populous state as "Blissful Bihar," clearly a remarkable metamorphosis is under way—one that looks to shed Bihar's beleaguered reputation as an uncivilized place marked by poverty, illiteracy, caste warfare, Maoist guerillas, political corruption, and "backwardness." In fact, looking backward and capitalizing on heritage has become an integral strategy for an "enlightened" administration with vast cultural resources for increased commerce, including spiritually motivated tourism. During a public appearance on May 28, 2008, at opening of the Nalanda Multimedia Museum, Chief Minister Nitish Kumar asked the audience, "What is there in Bihar? It is people. It is the soil, and its heritage. After the separation of Jharkhand [in 2000], all the industry went there and we got the heritage. But the one who has heritage is the most powerful in the world today."[2]

This is a study of heritage and place: heritage as a spatial practice and a contested social field that lends meaning to place. I began this research over ten years ago with the assumption that Bodh Gaya and other revived Buddhist pilgrimage sites were important material vectors for growing inter-Asian connections and networks that would play a significant role in redefining Asia in the early twenty-first century. Heritage concerns that which is handed down from the past. As a record of human achievement

"Say with pride I am Bihari"—signage near front
entrance of Mahabodhi Temple

and a legacy of the physical and intangible attributes of a group, society, or
nation, cultural heritage has become a key concept of the modern era as
both a resource for social integration and an indelible force in the proliferation of identity claims. Commonly manifested in monuments, artifacts, and
other forms of material culture, the contemporary valorization of Buddhist
heritage and the evocations around India's Buddhist past are inseparable
from the significance a society attaches to it. So, what makes Buddhist heritage so important to India and Bihar in the early twenty-first century?

The spread of the Buddha *sasana* (teachings of the Buddha) beyond India
has long underlined the concept of Asia as an interlinked historical and
geographic formation. Although globalization and the flow of people, ideas,
and goods across regional and nation-state boundaries are often treated
as a recent historical phenomenon, pilgrimage and the circulation of
religious ideas, texts, and images have always been central to the practice
of Buddhism. Ever since Emperor Ashoka (ca. 268–232 BCE) patronized
and propagated Buddhism during the Mauryan Empire, Buddhist word and

praxis have crossed vast distances, enlarging the global scope of Buddhism and reinforcing its sacred ties to the Indian subcontinent. This transmission has not been unidirectional, but rather a multifaceted process involving intertwined networks of trade that set in motion a vibrant exchange of commercial and religious interactions that filtered back to the places of origin (Sen 2014). Thus, over the course of many centuries, the spread of Buddhist teachings has undergone complex cultural, doctrinal, and ritual adaptations that have given unique shape to the teachings of the Buddha as they adapt to local cultural and social conditions throughout Asia.

Popular historical and public discourse frequently claims that Buddhism went through a period of decline during the early medieval period (ca. 600–1200 CE), when it was appropriated by popular Hindu devotional cults and eventually extinguished by Turkish Muslim invaders in the twelfth and thirteenth centuries. Thus, prior to the late nineteenth-century Buddhist revival, Indian Buddhism is said to have died out, but continued to thrive outside the subcontinent as an export religion across much of Asia. This oversimplified narrative of Indian history has come under increasing scrutiny in light of growing textual, epigraphic, and archaeological evidence showing there were several intra- and inter-site connections well past the twelfth century, especially with respect to traffic along the peninsular region of South India, Bengal, and both the Western and Eastern Himalayas (Singh 2010, Ray 2014, Sen 2014). Tibetan and Chinese biographies of Sariputra also show that in North India as well, Buddhism was far from extinct, as Buddhist pilgrims continued to visit and reside in Bodh Gaya until the early 1400s (McKeown forthcoming). This growing corpus of scholarship has provided a much-needed revision of the colonial paradigms and assumptions that have framed the history of Buddhism in the India subcontinent. But this is not to deny that colonial knowledge production, especially with the development of post-Enlightenment disciplines such as archaeology and history, played a pivotal role in the reinvention of Buddhism in the late nineteenth and twentieth centuries.

Although the main ethnographic focus of this book is on the rapid growth in Bodh Gaya within the last few decades, it is important to situate this research within the broader historical, political, and economic transformations of modern South Asia. With the rise and expansion of colonial powers, many ancient Buddhist sites were restored by the British Indian government and charged with new potentialities. As part of the larger archaeological and textual "rediscovery" of Buddhism by Orientalist scholars (Almond 1988,

Lopez 1995), these material remains of ancient Buddhism have become important anchors for Buddhist communities of practice as well as catalysts for sacred reclamation and reform.

In *The Holy Land Reborn*, Tibet scholar Toni Huber (2008) examines the changing Tibetan relationship with India's Buddhist geography and provides a compelling critique of the modern conceptualization and reimagining of India's Buddhist sites as part of an original network of ancient pilgrimage places. Although his invocation of a fluid geography and "shifting terrain of the Buddha" may have applied to premodern Tibetan Buddhist pilgrimage culture, there is no denying the immutable character of this pilgrimage schema in the global Buddhist imaginary today and the growing connectivity between them as part of an international Buddhist circuit in North India and Nepal. This "locus classicus" for the tradition of Buddhist pilgrimage (Huber 2008) mirrors the widely cited Great Final Enlightenment Sutra (Mahaparinirvana Sutra), in which the Buddha encouraged his disciples to undertake pilgrimage and visit the places associated with the pivotal events in his spiritual and biographical life. As objects of memorialization reconfigured by modern European textual scholarship and monumental archaeology under the British Raj, these sites are Lumbini, the birthplace of the Buddha; Bodh Gaya, the site of his enlightenment; Sarnath, the place of Buddha's first discourse; and Kushinagar, the place of his death, as well as satellite sites such as Shravasti, Sankassa, and Rajgir-Nalanda.

Although this "revived" ancient network of Buddhist pilgrimage owes a great deal to modern conditions, more important to this project is how these prominent Buddhist centers, in the past and present, have functioned as an important intercultural sphere and gateway for Asian Buddhist connections and interactions. These transnational Buddhist networks rapidly multiplied in the latter part of the twentieth century as different Asian communities of practice began seeking a foothold in Bodh Gaya and other revived Buddhist sacred centers. Although these developments are also taking place in other parts of India and Nepal, as well as throughout the Buddhist world, the sheer acceleration of religious infrastructure that underlies Bodh Gaya's pan-Asian Buddhist enclave is unique. Given the extra-national reach of Buddhism and the popular appeal of charismatic Buddhist leaders wishing to reconnect with the land of origins, India's Buddhist sites provide an important social laboratory as a global Buddhist ethnoscape and melting pot for the dissemination and exchange of Buddhist ideas, practices, teachers, and institutions.

Monasteries and temples reflecting diverse Buddhist lineages and communities of practice are being built at Bodh Gaya with significant interest and investment from countries such as Japan, Korea, China, Thailand, Cambodia, Vietnam, Myanmar, and Sri Lanka. The inter-Asian revival of these Buddhist sacred centers raises a number of important questions about the political and economic potential of Indian cultural heritage in the formation of what is frequently described as the "new Asian century." How is the growing connectivity of Buddhist pilgrimage sites in India tied to transnational memory and growing inter-Asian aspirations? How are the material remains of India's Buddhist past used to forge a pan-Asian Buddhist identity and unite both secular and sacred interests? How is such extra-national interfacing and interfinancing driven by Asian elite actors, the state, religious communities, and the circulation of ideas surrounding "Asian civilization?" How do converging interests and conflicting agendas involving pilgrimage, tourism, and heritage come to shape the development of Bodh Gaya as an international destination? And, how do religious, economic, and social aspirations intermingle and connect people across national boundaries?

Perhaps there is no better example of this historical reimagining than the current revitalization of Nalanda University—a postgraduate institution modeled on the famous Buddhist monastic university that flourished between the fifth and twelfth centuries. The revival effort is part of a joint undertaking between the Indian government and a consortium of Asian countries, led predominantly by Singapore and Japan. As a site of multinational diplomacy and extensive financial investment involving millions of dollars, the university aims to serve as an icon of Asian renaissance, with the explicit goal of advancing the concept of an "Asian community" through its rediscovery of ancient educational and religious ties (Pinkney 2015). As the example of Nalanda University illustrates, the Indian state's reframing of Buddhist cultural heritage as a wider Asian phenomenon is part of a broader trend in contemporary Asian diplomacy that evokes precolonial transnational connections, memory, and cultural flows.

Similarly, the emerging field of global heritage incorporates a broader diversity of cultural forms, values, and expressions, including the role of religious practice and communities of faith (UNESCO 2010) as opposed to a narrow view of the built environment based on European preoccupations with architecture and monumental archaeology. Although heritage conservation remains embedded in regimes of European power/knowledge and state-dominated approaches to cultural nationalism, there is a growing interest in the politics of heritage from a transregional and global perspective, in line with growing inter-Asian connections and interactions.[3] In this respect, the Buddhist pilgrimage sites of India provide an important context for heritage diplomacy that mirrors wider political, cultural, and economic linkages between Asian countries.

While a considerable body of scholarly literature exists on the modern revival of Buddhism in India, especially under British colonial rule, the goal of this book is to provide a multi-layered historical ethnography of Bodh Gaya's modern rebirth as the place of Buddha's enlightenment and the spatial politics that underlie its designation as a UNESCO World Heritage Site today. This is not to deny the veneration of the place where Shakyamuni attained enlightenment in the past, but to draw attention to the interests and motivations of a range of Western and Asian actors that continue to play a significant role in reimagining India as the "homeland" of Buddhism over the last 150 years. Also central to the argument of this book is that Bodh Gaya is much more than a destination and a Buddhist place. Following Buddhist scholar David McMahan (2008, 18) and his study of Buddhist modernism, in using the term *enlightenment* rather than *Bodhi*, I recognize both the significance attached to the Buddha's awakening and how this term intersects with a complex set of meanings and values associated with the European Enlightenment and conjoined notions of responsible governance that are inseparable from the making of heritage. The modern category of religion also owes a considerable debt to certain Enlightenment presuppositions that have given rise to the discursive formation of "world religions" organized around a pilgrimage tradition and universalist claims toward a sacred center (Masuzawa 2005).

In this complex and rapidly changing cultural landscape, modern categories and spatial practices associated with the heritage complex in Bodh Gaya are brought into accordance with UNESCO's standard of "outstanding universal value." But who decides what constitutes the "official" history of a place and how it is to be regulated and managed? Who decides what pasts and memories should be "preserved" and what should be "forgotten?" Since the Mahabodhi Temple Complex was formally declared a UNESCO World Heritage Site in 2002, this recent historical layering has given rise to a series of conflicts that foreground the politics of space and meaning among Bodh Gaya's diverse set of publics. For these reasons it is important to draw attention to both the "multilocality" and "multivocality" that underlie World Heritage designation and to delineate the historical and spatial meanings that place holds for different people (Rodman 1992). In recognizing the polyphony of voices that constitute ethnographic field-work and moving beyond the ways in which anthropologists have incarcerated "the native" within specific spatial and cultural locales (Appadurai 1988), one can begin to address some of the power differentials and inequalities that are produced within a transnational meeting ground like Bodh Gaya.

Foregrounding the varying ways Bodh Gaya is constructed through overlapping and multiple points of production also allows us to move beyond some of the theoretical limitations in the fields of pilgrimage and tourism studies. Rather than asking whether or not Bodh Gaya is a pilgrimage or tourist site, for example, we can examine the tensions between these multifaceted social forms as an integral part of place construction. The limitations around the conceptual and theoretical approaches to the study of pilgrimage have been described as constraining metaphors: the Turnerian (1973, Turner and Turner 1978) depiction of *anti-structure* and *communitas*, and Eade and Sallnows's (1991) emphasis on the sacred as a *contested* process at pilgrimage sites (Coleman 2002). Although both communitas and especially contestation have shaped Bodh Gaya in the past and present (see Geary et al. 2012), these models have created intellectual straitjackets that have prevented other forms of analysis (Coleman 2002). The spatial environment at Bodh Gaya holds a diverse set of meanings and continues to be shaped by complex and overlapping forces that do not reflect clear-cut dichotomies and rigid separations between communitas and contestation, pilgrimage and tourism, structure and process, sacred and profane, and faith and markets. In an effort to disrupt these binary oppositions, including the all-too-familiar chorus of global integrative forces and local reactions, I am drawn to the work of anthropologist Anna Tsing (2005, 4) and her proposal for a more nuanced ethnographic appreciation of global connection and how it comes to life in "friction": "the awkward, unequal, unstable, and creative quality of interconnection across difference."

Like other pilgrimage and tourist destinations that are undergoing rapid social change, the transformation of Bodh Gaya into a World Heritage Site can be interpreted as a by-product of globalization resulting from the transnational movement of people, capital, ideas, and images that links the memory of the space with a particular event in the history of Buddhism. Within the last few decades, in particular, there has been a surge of extranational Buddhist groups acquiring land, new networks of international aid and assistance, improved transportation, and both tourism and urban development initiatives, all of which have accelerated the profile of Bodh

Gaya and India's Buddhist circuit on the global map. For anthropologist Anna Tsing, the term *global* is not a claim to explain everything in the world at once (2005, ix–x). Instead, she approaches projects of universalism such as the supra-community logics of World Heritage and the reclamation of a sacred center of Buddhist faith as a way of thinking about the history of social projects that grow from spatially distant collaborations and interconnections. Although it is often assumed that globalization implies world homogenization and a loss of diversity, cultural and/or religious difference is not banished from these interconnections; rather, "it is what makes them possible, bringing a creative friction to global connections" (ix–x). In framing Bodh Gaya as a space of global connection, one must attend to the overlapping histories and relationships that underlie the aspirations for the universal and show how projects of world-making are embedded in specific settings where the contingency of encounters and particular historical conjunctures give them content and force (8). In seeking to unravel the social and spatial relations that derive from cultural encounters in Bodh Gaya, this historical ethnography utilizes ethnographic synchronic data to make diachronic inferences about historical change. While mediating a broader and diverse set of themes, each chapter is premised on interaction and connection, showing how history, memory, narratives, and groups are entangled in the productive friction between the local and the global, the particular and the universal.

FIELDWORK AND METHODOLOGY

The findings presented in this book derive from extensive fieldwork in Bodh Gaya between 2005 and 2007 and secondary fieldwork in 2011 and 2013. Participant observation, semistructured interviews, and surveys were my primary ethnographic methods.[4] Several months of archival research also took place at the London India Office (British Library), the Patna State Archives, and the Nehru Memorial Museum and Archives in New Delhi. For most of my fieldwork, I lived with an Indian family in the nearby village of Pacchatti, but also at the Burmese *vihara* in 2012–2013 as a faculty instructor in the Carlton-Antioch Buddhist Studies Program. I studied Hindi for two years at the University of British Columbia prior to my fieldwork, and a language teacher in Bodh Gaya assisted me with the Maghi dialect, which is common to the region. This training was integral to building social relations among the Indian residents, even though English and other languages are frequently spoken in Bodh Gaya.

My first experience with Bodh Gaya was a pilgrimage tour called "In the Footsteps of the Buddha," in which I traveled for three and half weeks with a group of North American and European Buddhists to all of the major Buddhist pilgrimage sites in the north-gangetic region. This pilgrimage tour was led by Shantum Seth, an Indian Buddhist and teacher in the tradition of Vietnamese Zen monk Thich Nhat Hanh. As part of an itinerary of transformation, our group traversed the North Indian countryside, exploring the Buddha's life through the ruins of the past and incorporating his profound insights into our daily practice and meditation.

The extent to which these prominent sacred sites are located in areas of extreme poverty was disquieting. Although Shantum Seth is a skillful guide who brought our group into contact with the everyday lives of peasant farmers, artisans, and nongovernmental organizations (NGOs) operating in the area, as part of the tour package we also had the comfort of residing in five-star hotels and feasting on gourmet Indian buffets. In the town of Rajgir, for example, our group stayed at the Indo Hokke Hotel in air-conditioned rooms with a distinctive Japanese aesthetic featuring teak floors and stocked with kimono robes, at US$128 per night. We had access to international channels, the internet, a spa bath, and Japanese food and beer. My romanticized and naïve Eurocentric view of Buddhism as a religion of renunciation was troubled by this blend of luxury spiritual tourism, and the strong impression of that trip in many ways informs this book.

Shortly after the pilgrimage tour I also spent one month in Bodh Gaya interviewing other Western Buddhist pilgrims and participating in the Kalachakra empowerment, led by the 14th Dalai Lama. During this time I learned about Bodh Gaya's 2002 UNESCO World Heritage designation and some of the underlying spatial tensions and conservation issues that had begun to emerge. For example, a major concern at the time was the so-called oil lamp controversy and the impact of Tibetan Buddhist ritual activities, which were allegedly causing damage to the Bodhi tree, under which the Buddha is believed to have attained enlightenment, and surrounding temple precincts. This and other tensions surrounding the ritual component of the sacred landscape and fresh demands for appropriate heritage management and archaeological intervention had intensified and expanded well beyond the walls of the Mahabodhi Temple Complex by the time I returned to Bodh Gaya in August 2005 for further fieldwork.

Interest in World Heritage designation, especially in terms of broader spatial issues and competing visions of place, was apparent, and there was a mounting fear that the Mahabodhi Temple Complex would be demoted

Signage for the Hotel Lord Buddha

to the List of World Heritage in Danger only three years after its official entry on the UNESCO list. A chief concern related to World Heritage designation was that the site was allegedly in "desperate need" of a one-kilometer buffer zone to meet the necessary international conservation requirements. However, implicit in the public discourse was another layer to this heritage management and conservation rhetoric that had little to do with safeguarding material culture for future generations. Rather, the spatial consequence of a one-kilometer buffer zone was seen as a necessary mechanism to "preserve the peace" and curtail the rampant commercialism and unchecked development that was now "encroaching" upon this famed Buddhist site.

Many of the Buddhist pilgrims and long-term visitors I interviewed over the course of my fieldwork expressed alarm that Bodh Gaya was fast becoming a bloated tourist site full of commercial activity and greed. I was told that previously one could rest in the shade of the Bodhi tree throughout the day and night without interruptions, restrictions, or obstructions. The temple complex was like an open-air museum and the bazaar was full of charming local hospitality. This sense of nostalgia and lament for the recent past was accompanied by frustration with and growing criticism of the

Beggars lined up along footpath near front entrance of Mahabodhi Temple

present, including the recent World Heritage designation. The town's inclusion on the World Heritage List became a symbol of mass tourism that was bringing rapid urban development and social change to this humble town in south Bihar. Unregulated development and a new international airstrip had brought an explosion of hotels, guesthouses, monasteries, seasonal NGOs, and shops, all within close proximity to the Mahabodhi Temple. There were concerns about the lack of public toilets, growing mountains of plastic garbage, contaminated swamps, inefficient water and electricity systems, and noise pollution. Alcohol, drugs, and other illegal activities were on the rise, and some locals feared it would not be long before sex tourism arrived.

Visitors seeking a moment of solace and quietude under the Bodhi tree had complained to the temple management about aggressive shopkeepers, hustlers, and beggars along the footpath. Even at the main temple precinct, so-called sly monks, or beggars-in-robes, requested money and food in their begging bowls only to remove their robes at the end of the tourist season. There was also talk of golf courses, chairlifts to the nearby Dhungeshwari caves (a site of the Buddha's former austerities), light-and-sound shows, and other major tourism initiatives that would bring further "contamination"

Tibetan monks leaving Mahabodhi Temple, next to image of Bollywood star Shahrukh Khan

to this hallowed site where the Buddha obtained ultimate bliss. Common to all the accusations, rumors, and finger pointing was a general discomfort and anxiety surrounding the accelerated pace of development at Bodh Gaya from a small rural town in south Bihar into a major global destination. The spatial conflicts produced and negotiated within this changing environment are the focus of this book.

1 The Light of Asia

From an obscure position as a small village of no interest, Uruvilvá rose to high distinction as the hermitage of one of the greatest religious reformers of the world—of one who exercised the most unbound influence on the mind of man. For over sixteen hundred years it was held to be the most sacred spot on earth by at least one-fifth of the human race. For centuries the stream of pilgrims flowed towards it without intermission. Princes from all parts of India vied with one another in enriching it with the highest treasures of art that they could command. (Mitra 1878, 21)

THE FOLLOWING PASSAGE IS A RECORD OF A NINETEENTH-CENTURY Burmese pilgrimage to the Maha Bodhi tree and the offerings made there. Although this is not the earliest evidence of Asian Buddhist pilgrimage to Bodh Gaya in the modern era, it is particularly important because it prompted the British Indian government to take greater control over the restoration of the Mahabodhi Temple and assert its historicist and archaeological jurisdiction over the space. It also sets the stage for an enduring set of disputes over proprietorship and rites of worship that reverberate to the present.

In the year 1236 (1875 A.C.E.) of the Burmese era, on the 2nd day on the waning month of Pyatho, Chief Clerk Mr. Tarlapo and General Palmer from the foreign department of the Government of India escorted four Burmese ambassadors to the Howrah Railway station, where they boarded a train destined to Budh Gya via Bankipore, the administrative centre of the Patna division of Bihar. Urged by deep reverence and devotion for the Maha Bodhi Tree, the King of Burma Mindon Min had sent a royal dispatch to make offerings to the central shrine of the Buddha and to assess restoration needs in the spirit of merit-making. Placed at the disposal of the General Governor and accompanying the special Burmese envoy was Secretary Maung Ponk Kyine, Babu Charu Chunder Mitra, messengers Nga Po Choe and Nga Po Han, clerks Nga Toe and Nga Shoon, and two servants. Before the train departed at 9 a.m., the Governor General honored the Burmese ambassadors with a special 15-gun salute.

After a journey of a day and night from Howrah on a cold winters day, the envoy arrived at Bankipore Station in the early morning at about 3:50 a.m. and was received by a Guard of Honor and over 100 men bearing torchlights. Together, the entire retinue was taken by conveyance to quarters prepared for temporary residence. The District Collector of Bankipore, in compliance with the telegram received by the Governor General informed the Burmese that every arrangement would be made for the comforts and needs of the group, including an escort of 3 *sepoys*, 6 carriages, and sufficient provisions to continue the journey. With a desire to reach the Maha Bodhi Tree as soon as possible, the Burmese ambassadors requested they leave for Gya that very morning.

Accompanied by the District Collector of Bankipore the retinue travelled south for a day and night to the town of Gya. After spending a night, the District Collector informed the group that the Maha Bodhi was 3 miles distant from Gya town but part of the journey was of sandy ground and very cumbersome by carriage. To aid in their journey, he provided the Burmese with two elephants for conveyance, an escort of 40-armed men and 8 *sepoys*. Leaving Gya at 9 a.m. they arrived at the Maha Bodhi Tree by 3 p.m. and were warmly greeted by the Mahantaji Yogi who was recognized as the principal caretaker of the Maha Bodhi Tree. He was dressed in a suit composed of a red turban round his head and a coat made of muslin embroidered with gold and silver filigree like those worn of Hindu Maharajas. For their comfort the ambassadors were provided with a three storied pucca building for temporary residence and a translator, Babu Radicar Prasad Das from Calcutta.

On the following morning and for the next three days, the Burmese ambassadors worshipped continually at the Maha Bodhi shrine and kept sabbath for majesty King Mindon Min and for his good merit. Every morning, food was offered to the central shrine and every evening 1000 flowers, 1000 candles and 1000 oil lamps were lit. As many bowlfuls of water as there are years in Mindon Min's life were poured from golden vessels on the shrine and each day prayers were dedicated to the King, the Queen, the Prince and Princes, royal relatives, ministers, and other state officials for their long life and for the propagation of the Buddha's *sasana*.

Having found various portions of the great temple to the east of the Maha Bodhi tree in disrepair, the ambassadors collected all the pieces of Buddha's images lying about and carefully stored them inside the hollow portion of the temple and the four cornered edifices attached to the temple. Not only did they worship several of Buddha's images over the course of three days, but they did so alongside the Hindu Brahmins who also made offerings of food, flowers and candles to various images of the Buddha who they recognized as Vishnu and Kacchayana. Although they found no one who declared themselves a follower of Gautama and who made use of the Three Ratna Gatha, on Saturdays they observed a large number of visitors from the surrounding area who came to worship the Bodhi tree.

Surrounding the Maha Bodhi Tree, they also came to know of a Hindu village of over 200 houses called "Taradira" that, like the Maha Bodhi temple and its images, was under the control of the Mahantaji Yogi. Out of the land dedicated to the Maha Bodhi temple, the Mahantaji enjoyed annual revenue of Rs. 7500. This prosperity was evident in the nearby four storied compound built of stone and marble where he and his 1000 Yogi disciples resided. Although they live a life of celibacy and devotion, the compound houses a vast accumulation of wealth that had been obtained and stored together from generation to generation, including golden *ptees* (umbrellas) and golden *tagoons* (streamers) that were offerings provided by King Bagyidaw, a predecessor of King Mindon Min. As a token of their appreciation and friendship, the Burmese ambassadors provided the Mahantaji with a small betel case, one small bowl to hold preserved let-pet (green tea leaves) and one drinking cup. They also informed him that Gautama Buddha's religion flourished in Burma and that the Burmese race were all descendants of the people of Majjhima Desa (middle land) in India, and thus in many respects the Burmese were similar to the Hindus.

After the exchange of gifts, the Chief Ambassador informed the Mahantaji Yogi of the King's desire to erect a monastery near the Maha Bodhi Tree with a view to make offerings at the Bodhi Tree daily and to aid in the restoration of the courtyard wall of the shrine that had fallen into disrepair. Expressing his great delight, the Mahantaji Yogi gave his consent to the Chief Ambassador for the restoration and provided a small parcel of rent-free land on which to build a monastery at a distance of 15 *laggas* (equivalent to about 40 yards) to the west of the Maha Bodhi Tree. On the occasion of the Mahantaji Yogi's delivery of possession of the land to the Burmese, the ambassadors and the whole retinue expressed their delight by distributing 1000 copper coins to the beggars and other destitute persons with a view to increase the King's good merit.

From that night a heavy rain fell continually for 3 days. The Hindus in the vicinity said that it was unusual to have rain in the month of Pyatho and that a heavy rain on that occasion was due to the fact that the Burmese King of the Rising Sun was provided a site to facilitate the making of offerings at the Maha Bodhi Tree, and the Great *Devas* of the Tree

being glad, caused a heavy downpour of rain. After the deluge of rain, in
the early morning they found the Maha Bodhi Tree, as green and as ten-
der as a newly grown young tree, unlike all others, evoking an insatiable
desire to worship at the tree.

With a view to increasing the merit of King Mindon Min, before departing, the Burmese ambassadors made over two messengers (Loobyandaw)
Nga Pocho and Nga Po Han to the Mahantaji Yogi, with a sum of Rs. 30, so
that daily offerings of food, flowers and lights could be made to the Maha
Bodhi Tree during the month of Tabodwe. (Maha Bodhi Society 1907)[1]

Following the Burmese pilgrimage to Bodh Gaya, the Mahabodhi
Temple became a highly sensitive custodial object and an important material signifier of India's Buddhist civilization. The process of restoring the
temple and disseminating knowledge around what came to be called "Buddhism" by the mid-nineteenth century also foregrounded the politics of
religious identity. Thus, during the nineteenth and twentieth centuries, we
see how the grand program of colonial archaeology intersects with the
modern revival of Asian Buddhist interest in the site. The archaeological
practice and layering of new regimes of value, ownership, and claims of
identity during British India also play a critical role in shaping the heritage
assemblage that is central to postcolonial state formations.

RECOVERING THE PAST: MONUMENTAL ARCHAEOLOGY
AND THE MAKING OF THE BRITISH RAJ

The sacredness of India haunts me like a passion. . . . To me the message is carved in granite, hewn in the rock of doom: that our work is
righteous and that it shall endure. (Viceroy George Nathaniel Curzon,
cited in Meyer and Brysac 1999, xxxvi)

With the disintegration of Mughal authority and the beginning of British rule
in the eighteenth and nineteenth centuries, a politically sensitive set of questions occupied the archaeological "discovery" of the Mahabodhi Temple: To
whom does the temple belong? To whom are the images dedicated? Who are
the proper heirs to Bodh Gaya's cultural patrimony? And whose rendering of
the past should have greater authority under British colonial jurisdiction?

The difficulty in answering these questions lies in the overlapping histories and competing religious claims to sacred property that came to define

Bodh Gaya's space in the late nineteenth century. On the one hand, for a period of at least six hundred years, the ruins of the Mahabodhi Temple were located in an area where no Buddhist residents were found and very few Buddhists ever visited (Trevithick 2016). On the other hand, the memory of the temple and its association with the central event in the life of the Buddha remained influential elsewhere in the Buddhist world (Leoshko 1988). The central position awarded to the place of Buddha's enlightenment is evident in numerous Buddhist texts, scriptures, and artworks, including the diffusion of Mahabodhi Temple replicas and models in Burma, Tibet, Nepal, Sri Lanka, China, and Thailand. Thus despite the virtual disappearance of a Buddhist institutional presence in Bodh Gaya at the time of the Burmese mission, many Buddhist groups continued to venerate and memorialize the place of Buddha's enlightenment from a distance.

As a result of the declining number of Buddhist pilgrims and patrons from the twelfth and thirteenth centuries onward, the physical site diminished and was appropriated by another religious sect. Central to this process was an ascetic named Gosain Ghamandi Giri, a Hindu follower of Shiva who settled in the area around the year 1590 (a date assigned by the ascetic group itself) during his penitent wanderings. This was by no means a forceful takeover of the temple, but rather the likely occupation of an abandoned sacred site, as often occurs with sites of longstanding sanctity (Asher 2008, 16–17). Thus, for over four hundred years a lineage of Giri *mahantas* (religious superiors) extended their authority over the temple and made Bodh Gaya the corporate headquarters for the Shaiva Dasanami renunciate order. The religious institution also wielded strong regional influence as a powerful *zamindar* (landlord) from the eighteenth century onward, when the Giri sect claimed to have received a rent-free grant of four villages from Emperor Shah Alam (1759–1806), including a deed of ownership on which the ruins of the Mahabodhi Temple lay.

Among the Indian pilgrims who frequented the site at the time of the Burmese pilgrimage, the Mahabodhi Temple and surrounding objects had taken on a distinctly Vaishnava character as monuments to "Buddha Dev," an *avatara* of Vishnu and a popular site in the larger network of Hindu pilgrimage linked to Gaya-*sraddha*. For these Hindu pilgrims, performing *sraddha* entailed visiting a wide circuit of sacred sites and completing final rites for dead family members that involved *pindadana* (offerings of balls of rice, wheat, or barley) and prayer.

Adding to this complex dynamic is the central place of the new British rulers and early Orientalists and antiquarians who held the site in high archaeological esteem and were engaged upon a quest to locate the "original" sites of the Buddha in India.[2] In recent years, several studies have chronicled the romantic expeditions of early British explorers and artists who traveled through the Indian subcontinent in search of the mystic East and India's picturesque ruins (e.g., Allen 2003, Almond 1988, Leoshko 1996, Lopez 1995). The early stages of Bodh Gaya's modern reinvention also occurred in a geopolitical context greatly influenced by British imperial interests in South Asia, in which Orientalist constructions of knowledge and history helped in the consolidation of colonial power (see Doyle 1997, King 1999, Ludden 1996, Said 1979). As part of the filtering of the Orient into Western consciousness, India was defined by its religious sensibilities, and the essence of Buddhism (and India's greatness) was located in a "golden era" of the past. This nostalgia for origins, accompanied by an aesthetic of ruination, was also integral to the sense of scientific self that the British imposed on India through the colonial project of retrieving and restoring the past (Asher 2004, Doyle 1997, Cohn 1996).

Commissioned by the directors of the East India Company as part of the newly expanded Bengal presidency, Scottish explorer and physician Francis Buchanan-Hamilton (1762–1829) was the first British-Indian government surveyor to undertake a significant mission to the area. Buchanan stands as an emblematic figure in the early stages of European constructions of knowledge around the "religion of Bouddha" given his extensive travel in Burma, Chittagong, and Nepal, which preceded his survey of the Patna and Gaya Districts in 1811–1812. Through his descriptive reports and detailed diary of the Gaya region, he highlighted the decrepit condition of the ancient temple in Bodh Gaya and indicated that there was no sign of Buddhist worship in the area except for that of his Rajput tour guide, an unnamed *sannyasin* renunciate who had been converted to the "doctrine of the Buddhs" some years prior by Burmese officers dispatched by the king of Ava.[3]

Although Buchanan describes the populace in Bodh Gaya as "Hindoo," with limited knowledge of Gautama Buddha, he was, as Doyle suggests, one of the first European surveyors to see and represent "Buddha Gaya" "as *originally*, and therefore *essentially*, a Buddhist place" (Doyle 1997, 80). For example, he described the Hindu mythic history as found in the Gaya-*mahatmya* tradition as a "monstrous legend" with no credibility and dismissed the Hindu practice of worshiping "Buddhist" statues as brahmanical gods, writing, "It is evident, that the [local] people are totally careless in this respect" as "the images which they worship, are actually Buddhas in the most unequivocal forms" (cited in Martin 2012, 77). Francis Buchanan and his contemporaries mark a pivotal moment in a chain of events from the early nineteenth century onward by which the physical landscape of Bodh Gaya was reconstituted and discursively inscribed with stories associated with the "historical" Buddha, even though the Mahabodhi Temple and its environs continued to be overseen by local Hindu *pandas* (Brahmin priests) and *sannyasins* with their own history and sacred narratives.

With the establishment of archaeology as a modern discipline, there was a growing interest in Buddhist monuments and sites by the mid-nineteenth century that conjoined historicism and imperial statecraft. Following the aftermath of the Great Mutiny of 1857 and growing anti-Hindu sentiment, exacerbated by the Indian uprising, the application of modern archaeological science by "enlightened" European scholars became wedded to a larger civilizing mission and imperial ethic designed to introduce Indian British subjects to their glorious past (Doyle 1997, 92–93). Furthermore, the investigation of a so-called "dead" religion would in no way compromise "the British government's purportedly neutral stance vis-à-vis India's living religious communities," namely, Hindus and Muslims (93).

One of the first British officials to generate significant archaeological interest in Bodh Gaya was Major-General Alexander Cunningham (1814–1893), the British army engineer who is frequently cited as the "father" of Indian archaeology.[4] Shortly after Cunningham's retirement in 1861, he sent a memorandum to the viceroy, Lord Canning, requesting a detailed investigation of India's ancient remains. This request was bolstered by a growing number of Buddhist-related epigraphic, archaeological, and textual material, including recent translations from the famous Chinese pilgrims Faxian and Xuanzang. In his letter to Lord Canning in 1861, he writes: "Hitherto the Government has been chiefly occupied with the extension and consolidation of empire." Therefore, "it would redound equally to the honor of the British Government to institute a careful and systematic investigation of all the existing monuments of ancient India" (cited in Asher 2004, 61). Lord Canning replied to Cunningham with undivided support and noted that it would be in the best interest of future generations and for an enlightened administration to "rescue from oblivion" India's forgotten past (62).

With the official backing of the viceroy, the Archaeological Survey of India (ASI) was formally established in 1861 and Cunningham was appointed the first director general. The first project undertaken by the ASI under Cunningham was a survey and field trip to the Hindu pilgrimage town of Gaya and the smaller satellite town of Bodh Gaya in the winter of

1861–1862 to take an inventory of Indian antiquities. He returned to Bodh Gaya several times up until the late 1880s, overseeing several excavations by his assistants—Major Mead, Rajendralala Mitra, and J. D. Beglar—all of whom greatly contributed to the physical and discursive construction of the site as the place of Buddha's enlightenment. The succession of archaeological surveys not only yielded significant treasures but also foregrounded the extent to which Hindus had assimilated the Buddhist imagery into their own ritual practices. For example, both Major Mead and Rajendralala Mitra indicate that Hindus had literally appropriated and desecrated the surrounding Buddhist objects, such as turning stupas into Shiva lingams. This concern about the Hindu absorption of Buddhist iconography was also evident in other material objects of devotion, such as sculptures, images, and footprints, where there was considerable interchange and a blurring of religious boundaries (Kinnard 1998, 2014). Although the restoration of ancient monuments was far beyond the desired expenditure of the British imperial government in its early years of formation, the arrival of the Burmese Royal Mission described at the beginning of this chapter prompted the British government to undertake restorative action and retain control over the archaeological process at Bodh Gaya.

Since the late eighteenth century, Burmese kings had begun to renew their interest in the sacred geography of the Buddha with the intent of restoring the Mahabodhi Temple as a form of ritual merit-making and to bolster their own government's political prestige in line with Theravada views of *dhamma-rajas* (Doyle 1997).[5] Found throughout South and Southeast Asia, this vision of an ideal Buddhist king linked merit-making practices such as the building, endowment, and restoration of temples with both the sociopolitical and spiritual welfare of the state (Doyle 1997). When the British Indian government received a request from the king of Burma, Mindon Min (1853–1878), to send a mission to Bodh Gaya, the main concern expressed by the colonial government at the time was that nothing should be done to "offend the prejudices of the Hindoos," in particular, the powerful Giri sect that inhabited the site (Trevithick 2006, 19).

Once the Burmese had obtained the right to rehabilitate the site, they returned to Bodh Gaya in January 1877 and spent the next six months repairing the enclosure of the Mahabodhi Temple and its environs. However, it was soon reported to the government of Bengal that from an archaeological standpoint the "Burmese workmen were making a mess of the old temple" through their haphazard renovations (Trevithick 2006, 36). Shortly after this notification, the government of Bengal deputed the noted Indian

philologist and high-ranking ASI member Rajendralala Mitra to report on
the authenticity of the Burmese restoration efforts. Rajendralala Mitra wrote:

> The Burmese gentlemen were doubtless very pious and enthusiastic in
> the cause of their religion, but they were working on no systematic or tra-
> ditional plan. They were ignorant of the true history of their faith, and
> perfectly innocent of all knowledge of architecture and the requirements
> of archaeology and history; and the mischief they have done by their mis-
> directed zeal has been serious. (Mitra 1878, 66)

Thus, prior to Mitra's account of Burmese mischief, the British (at least in
principle) were committed to upholding religious neutrality among their
colonized subjects and felt no need to impose their own program of archaeological jurisdiction over the site. But in light of these concerns, including
the deterioration of Anglo-Burmese relations following the death of Mindon Min in 1878, the British Indian government felt an obligation to con-
serve the ancient history of the Mahabodhi Temple by utilizing the
"appropriate" scientific methods and asserting its own monopoly over the
restoration process. Thus, for the first time at Bodh Gaya, as Guha-Thakurta
writes, "the traditional religious practices associated with the renovation of
a sacred monument found themselves at odds with a modern historical and
archaeological view of restoration" (2004, 288–289).

Leading the charge were Alexander Cunningham and his assistant
engineer, J. D. Beglar, who were appointed by the lieutenant governor of
Bengal, Sir Ashley Eden, with the task of restoring the ancient temple
between 1879 and 1884.[6] The large-scale restoration of the Mahabodhi
Temple cost the British government nearly Rs. 200,000 and involved
rebuilding much of the upper stories of the temple, constructing the front
pavilion and four corner towers, removing "non-original" additions, and
re-facing the entire temple structure (Doyle 1997, 100). The "old" Bodhi tree
had apparently been uprooted during the Burmese renovations and was
significantly damaged as a result of "excessive devotion" that included
watering the roots with "eau-de-cologne" (Sinha 1921, 45). Anticipating the
coming catastrophe, Cunningham had two saplings of the old tree planted,
one for Hindus to the north of the temple and the other set apart exclusively
for Buddhists.

Not surprisingly, these restoration efforts have not been without controversy. When Cunningham and his assistants began the restoration work,
they modeled the temple on the basis of a twelfth-century miniature stone

replica unearthed at the site that depicted the Bodhi tree, the railing, and the throne. This bias toward architectural form and early material traces at the Mahabodhi Temple by surveyors and archaeologists has produced an incomplete and deeply entrenched monolithic image of a pure, "original" Buddhism at the expense of a more complicated picture that involved repeated renovations and diverse appropriations of the site over time (Leoshko 1996). In other words, the present physical temple complex and the location of the Bodhi tree, which stand as testimony to the ancient history of Buddhism in India, involved a significant degree of reinvention or re-creation on behalf of the colonial archaeologists (Leoshko 1996). Moreover, as a natural consequence of having repaired and restored the temple at enormous costs, the British Indian government sought to take greater responsibility for the maintenance of the site by placing the building and its grounds under the government supervision of the Public Works Department.

Thus, prior to the restoration efforts, there appears to have been no recorded grievances aroused by Burmese Buddhists, who continued to reside in the nearby guesthouse of the Bodh Gaya Math (monastic center). So, at this early point in the modern recovery and reinvention of Bodh Gaya's ancient past, "Hindus" and "Buddhists" appear to have had no serious conflicts (Trevithick 2006, 39). The main contention was between a Western archaeological and historicist engagement that sought an "original" and thus "true" history of Buddhism versus a Burmese Theravada perspective that looked to Bodh Gaya as a living sacred center and a template for miraculous deeds and meritorious acts (Doyle 1997). This was the complex new reality—involving cooperation between the British, the Burmese, and the Hindu Giri sect—that confronted the Sinhalese Buddhist pilgrim Anagarika Dharmapala.

RECLAIMING THE PAST: "OH YE BUDDHISTS OF ASIA! ARISE"

An ordinary village zemindar [sic] dictating to a powerful Government principles of international policy is a sight even for the gods to weep! (Dharmapala 1925, 7)

The Saivite mahant of the Bodhgaya math plays the part of the dog in the manger in desecrating the hallowed spot whereon stands the Vajrasana. . . . Until then the unbelieving Saivite mahant with the connivance of the British Indian Machiavallis, shall continue

to desecrate the most hallowed spot associated with the life of the
Supreme Teacher of Wisdom . . . who has not more right to be the
custodian of the Buddhist shrine than the Roman Pope to the West-
minster Abbey. (Dharmapala, cited in Maha Bodhi Society 1924)

In spite of the considerable time and expenditure that went into the restoration of the Mahabodhi Temple between 1879 and 1884, some concerns were
being raised among British administrators in Gaya about the "very unsat-
isfactory state of affairs" relating to "the Bodh-Gaya Temple." For example,
G. A. Grierson, the officiating magistrate and collector of Gaya, had sent
several letters to the superintendent engineer in the late 1880s regarding the
lack of drainage, salt exudations destroying the plaster, and the encroach-
ment of villagers, who were in the habit of digging up sculpture and statuary
to be used for "curry-stones" and "well-levers."[7] Visitors to Bodh Gaya were
also actively plundering the ancient remains, carrying away valuable images
and carved stones they found lying about on the temple land. Grierson
reported that on one occasion, he had a difficult time recovering some
twenty to thirty stone objects that had been taken by an Austrian count who
was visiting Bodh Gaya. "This beautiful historic building the repair of
which have cost the Government thousands of rupees," Grierson wrote, was
now being overseen by a "venal chowkidar" (local guard) hired by the government on a salary of Rs. 5 per month.

Around the same time that G. A. Grierson was raising concerns about
the state of the Mahabodhi Temple, a new discourse of "world religions"
was emerging among some influential Asian Buddhist reformers surrounding the "forgotten" holy places associated with the historical biography of
the Buddha.[8] These rediscovered ancient sites of Buddhist pilgrimage were
increasingly understood and articulated in relation to other great religious
faiths such as Christianity, Judaism, and Islam (Huber 2008, 219). The
importance of this holy land discourse became part of a wider set of universal criteria that underscored and constituted what came to be known as
"world religions" from a predominantly European scholarly perspective.
For those influenced by this emerging discourse, the place of Buddha's
enlightenment was seen as equivalent to Mecca for the Muslims and Jerusalem for Christians—an object of modern crusade that could serve as a
focal point for the construction of pan-Asian Buddhist solidarity. Thus,
Bodh Gaya was a pilgrimage site commensurate with the holy places of
other world religions, and it was under threat of being controlled by people
of another religious sect (Kemper 2015, 426).

Sir Edwin Arnold (1832–1904), the celebrated author of *Light of Asia*, used this discourse masterfully, playing a pivotal role in the revival of Indian Buddhist holy places.[9] Published in 1879, Arnold's highly romanticized poetic rendition of the Buddha's life brought him considerable fame and international recognition. In the wake of his literary success, in January 1886 Edwin Arnold made his own pilgrimage to the town of Bodh Gaya, followed by a trip to Ceylon, where he met with high-ranking monks such as Hikkaduwe Sumangala (1827–1911). During his visit he was convinced by the Ceylonese monks to use whatever influence he might have to reclaim the Mahabodhi Temple for the Buddhists of Asia.

Returning to London, Arnold inundated British government officials with letters and wrote a number of editorials for the popular *Daily Telegraph* demanding that the British government take control of the temple and hand it over to the Buddhists. One such editorial, published in 1893 and entitled "East and West: A Splendid Opportunity," deserves to be quoted at length as it exemplifies Arnold's universalizing aspirations and this emerging discourse, which would help propel Bodh Gaya onto the world stage.

I think there never was an idea which took root and spread so far and fast as that thrown out thus in the sunny temple-court at Panadurè, amid the waving taliputs. Like those tropical plants which can almost be seen to grow, the suggestion quickly became a universal aspiration, first in Ceylon and next in other Buddhist countries. I was entreated to lay the plan before the Oriental authorities, which I did. I wrote to Sir Author Gordon, Governor of Ceylon, in these words: "I suggest a Governmental Act, which would be historically just, which would win the love and gratitude of all Buddhist populations, and would reflect enduring honour upon English administration. The temple and enclosure at Buddha-Gaya are, as you know, the most sacred spots in all the world for the Buddhists. . . .

To rectify this sad neglect, and to make the temple, what it should be, the living and learned centre of purified Buddhism, money was not, and is not, lacking. . . . Asia did not abandon its new desire. . . . [I] went at last to the then Indian Secretary of State, Lord Cross—always intelligent, kindly and receptive—and once more pleaded for the great restoration[.] "Do you wish, Lord Cross," I asked, "to have four hundred millions of Eastern peoples blessing your name night and day, and to be for ever remembered in Asia, like Alexander or Asoka, or Akbar the Great?" "God bless my soul, yes" answered the Minister; "how is that to be done?"

I was astonished and rejoiced to find how firmly the desire of this restoration had taken root, and how enkindled with the hope of it Ceylon,
Siam, Burmah, and Japan had become. The Maha Bodhi Society, established to carry out the scheme, was constituted. Thus is this new and great
idea spreading, and the world will not be very much older, I think, before
Buddhism by this gateway goes back to its own land, and India becomes the
natural centre of Buddhistic Asia. Some people who will ask, why should
the British public take any concern in such a movement? . . . Apart from
the immense historical, religious and social importance of Buddhism in
Asia, here is an opportunity for the Government of India to gratify and
concilate half the continent by the easiest and least costly exercise of goodwill. Buddhism would return to the place of its birth, to elevate, to spiri-
tualise, to help and enrich the population. It would be a new Asiatic crusade, triumphant without tears, or tyranny, or blood; and the Queen's
administration would have the glory and benefit of it. . . . The Hindu of
Madras, a leading native journal, writes: "If there is anything in the intellectual and moral legacies of our forefathers of which we may feel proud,
it is that sublime, pure and simple conception of a religious and moral
system which the world owes to Buddha. Educated Hindoos cannot hesi-
tate in helping Buddhism to find a commanding and permanent footing
once more in their midst, and to live in mutually purifying amity with our
Hinduism itself. Here is indeed, for an enlightened British Indian Minister, "a splendid opportunity."[10]

As evidenced by Sir Edwin Arnold's romantic and descriptive account,
Bodh Gaya, it was proposed, could provide the British colonial authorities
with a "a splendid opportunity," one that could bestow honor upon English
administration and unite some "four hundred millions of Asiatics." One
particular English-speaking Asian Buddhist who was greatly inspired by
the British author's Bible-like rendition of the Buddha's life and his provocative plea for the restoration of Bodh Gaya to the Buddhists was the Sinhalese
Buddhist modernist Anagarika Dharmapala (1864–1933).

A great deal has been written about this remarkable and complex figure
(see, e.g., Guruge 1965, Gombrich and Obeyesekere 1988, Bond 1992, McMahan 2008, Kemper 2014, Trevithick 2006, Sangharakshita 1980). Born Don
David Hewavitarne into a wealthy merchant family in Matara in 1864, he
grew up in a Sinhala Buddhist milieu that was part of wider attempt to
counteract centuries of European colonialism and Christian missionizing

activities. As a young man, Dharmapala was deeply influenced by the The-osophists, who, inspired in part by the famous 1873 Panadura debate, visited Colombo in 1880.[11] The leading proponents of the Theosophical movement—Madame Helena Petrovna Blavatasky (1831–1891) and her American colleague, Colonel Henry Steel Olcott (1832–1907)—traveled to Colombo to meet Sinhalese monastic leaders and establish a Buddhist branch for the Theosophical Society.[12] Their desire for universal brotherhood and their support for the Sinhalas in their struggle to revitalize the "noble heritage" of Buddhism appealed deeply to Dharmapala, and he soon became Olcott's young disciple, serving as manager of the Buddhist Theosophical Society. Inspired by the Theosophists as well as Edwin Arnold's *Light of Asia*, he decided to take up a life of renunciation, later changing his name to Anagarika (homeless or celibate wanderer) Dharmapala (protector of the True Law).

With the goal of establishing new outposts for the Buddhist Theosophical Society and popularizing Olcott's Buddhist catechism, Dharmapala set out as Olcott's assistant on a trip to Japan in 1889, where he spent most of his time at a government hospital in Kyoto recovering from an attack of rheumatism. While resting in his quarters, Dharmapala apparently had an epiphany reading one of Sir Edwin Arnold's romantic travel accounts—a plea for the Mahabodhi Temple that would prompt him to make his own pilgrimage to Bodh Gaya two years later in the company of two young Japanese—Shaku Kozen (also known as Kozen Gunaratana) and Chiezo Tokuzawa.[13] "The idea of restoring the Buddhist Jerusalem into Buddhist hands," Dharmapala wrote, "originated with Sir Edwin Arnold after having visited the sacred spot in 1886. It was he who gave me the impulse to visit the shrine, and since 1891 I have done all I could to make the Buddhists of all lands interested in the scheme of restoration" (cited in Guruge 1965, 336).

Following this formative trip to Bodh Gaya, Dharmapala made his aspirations for the recovery of the temple concrete with the establishment of the Maha Bodhi Society in Colombo on May 31, 1891 (originally named the Budh-Gaya Mahabodhi Society). The well-respected high priest of Ceylon, Hikkuduwa Sumangala, was elected president, Colonel Olcott was named director and chief advisor, and Dharmapala was named general secretary. The main objective of the Maha Bodhi Society was to revive Buddhism as a pan-Asian force and to internationalize the campaign: "to make known to all nations the sublime teachings of the Arya Dharma of Buddha Sakya Muni, and to rescue, restore and re-establish as the religious centre of this movement, the holy place Buddha Gaya, where our Lord attained supreme wisdom" (Maha Bodhi Society 1891, 1). From the very outset, Dharmapala had also made explicit his ecumenical and pan-Asian framework for recovering Bodh Gaya: "The society representing Buddhism in general, and not any single aspect of it, shall preserve absolute neutrality with respect to doctrines and dogmas taught by sections and sects among Buddhists. It is not lawful for anybody, whether a member or not, to attempt to make it responsible, as a body, for his own views" (cited in Trevithick 2006, 82).

After establishing the Maha Bodhi Society and acquiring four young Ramanna *nikaya* monks to reside at the Burmese Rest House in Bodh Gaya on a more permanent basis, Dharmapala set out on his mission to recover the temple and unite the Buddhist world.[14] One of the first activities Dharmapala organized was to stage the International Buddhist Conference in Bodh Gaya on October 31, 1892, a date selected to coincide with a visit by the lieutenant governor of Bengal.[15] Although the conference was a relatively small affair, it did bring together a handful of Buddhist participants from Japan, China, Ceylon, and the Chittagong region, and they passed a resolution that Bodh Gaya should be handed over to the Buddhists. The Japanese delegates also announced that the authorities of the Nishi Nonganji Temple were prepared to purchase the Mahabodhi Temple by paying an adequate price to the *mahant*.[16] Although the *mahant* declined the offer, the conference did set in motion a series of communications between Bengal's lieutenant governor, Gaya Collector G. A. Grierson, and the Maha Bodhi Society under Dharmapala.

While sympathetic to the Buddhist claims, the British government in Bengal had not established any formal rights of proprietorship concerning the temple, nor had it envisioned doing so (Trevithick 2006, 84). The government did not reject the notion that a group such as the Maha Bodhi Society might be able to express the aspirations of the Buddhist communities, but they were also concerned that the activities of "outsiders" might exacerbate existing religious tensions (96). The hoisting of a Japanese flag next to the Maha Bodhi flag during the conference also likely reminded the lieutenant governor of the Russo-Japanese problem and the possibility that the Japanese might be using Bodh Gaya as a spearhead for their imperial ambitions in India (Sangharakshita 1980). The British government thus believed that either formal government jurisdiction or private ownership by the Japanese and/or "unknown strangers from Ceylon or Burma" would be unwise at this juncture (Trevithick 2006, 86). It also became clear that the *mahant*, Hem Narayan Giri, while very friendly to Anagarika during his initial six-week visit, was loath to give up his lucrative jurisdiction over the site.[17]

Dismayed by the lack of official support and without any concrete rights to access the temple, Dharmapala immediately set out to cultivate Asian Buddhist networks and request financial support to acquire the temple and land in Bodh Gaya. During these formative years of the Maha Bodhi Society, both Olcott and Dharmapala toured a number of countries, where they lectured, established new branches, and appealed for funds to support the rescue efforts. During a lecture at the Sule Pagoda in Rangoon, for example, Dharmapala held out a picture of the Mahabodhi Temple and said to the audience, "Imagine Buddha Gaya with its grand majestic temples, a Buddhist University where the languages of all Buddhist countries shall be taught to the hundreds of students that would assemble there from distant Japan and China, Burma, Cambodia, Ceylon, Siam and Tibet, a centre of Buddhist activity whose influence would penetrate to the distant countries of the world" (Maha Bodhi Society 1952, 71). The Maha Bodhi Society, he concluded, could be the greatest medium of Buddhist propaganda in the world.

Central to Dharmapala's lobbying efforts was the need for a permanent headquarters and the launching of the *Journal of the Maha Bodhi Society and the United Buddhist World* in November 1892.[18] Through the journal, Dharmapala could keep his society members informed, present various literary and scholarly publications on Buddhism in English and Indian vernaculars, and promote the revival of Buddhism in India through the journal's wide circulation in Asia and the West. In a style reminiscent of Edward Arnold before him, his editorial writings are full of references comparing Bodh Gaya to Mecca and Jerusalem, and there is no denying that this holy land rhetoric helped to inspire devotional sentiment and elevate Bodh Gaya as an object of desire across the Buddhist world. At the same time, through this increasingly nuanced discourse, Dharmapala continued to sharpen the distinctions between Buddhism and a Hindu "Other," which may have further exacerbated tensions with the "theosophical piety" of Colonel Olcott, who continued to see the Maha Bodhi Society and Dharmapala's cause as merely a branch of the larger organization (Trevithick 2006, 88).

The Maha Bodhi Society headquarters were established in Calcutta, sharing space with the Theosophical Society—a location that conveyed certain advantages. Situated in the center of British colonial power amidst the latest developments in modern India, Dharmapala benefited greatly from elite Bengali supporters and friends who were sympathetic to the Buddhist revival movement. This included contact and collaboration with other vehicles of Buddhist revival such as the Bauddha Dharmankura Sabha

(Bengal Buddhist Association), founded in Calcutta in 1892 under the Kiripasaran Mahasthavir (1865–1926), a Buddhist monk from the Chittagong Hill tracts in far eastern Bengal who had also pledged his life to reviving Buddhism in India.

A turning point in the transnational career of Dharmapala was his participation in the famous 1893 World Parliament of Religions in Chicago, where he accepted an invitation as a representative of the "Southern Buddhist Church." His talk, entitled "The World's Debt to Buddha," was well received, which greatly bolstered his confidence. As Trevithick (2006, 98–99) explains, this excursion to the United States not only redefined Dharmapala's self-image as an international figure but also marked the beginning of a certain financial independence for the Maha Bodhi Society, as well as a renewed sense of possibility and purpose to his *dhammaduta* mission. Central to this independence was his fortuitous encounter in Honolulu with a wealthy Hawaiian philanthropist named Mary E. Foster (1844–1930). While en route to India through the Pacific, this chance meeting became the single most important contact for the financial backing of the Maha Bodhi Society and its Buddhist revival projects in South Asia.[19]

On this return visit, Dharmapala also made a detour through Japan, where he was given a seven-hundred-year-old wooden Amitabha Buddha statue by Shuko Asahi, the high priest of the Tentokuji Temple in Tokyo. Asahi hoped that the Amitabha Buddha would be installed in the upper-level chamber of the Mahabodhi Temple as a symbol of future amity between the northern and southern branches of Buddhism. Thus, when Dharmapala returned to India, he set out for Bodh Gaya, accompanied by two Sinhalese monks and a lay pilgrim, N. S. De Silva, to install the image.[20]

In his absence, relations between the young Sinhalese Buddhist monks assigned to Bodh Gaya and the *mahant* began to deteriorate (see Kemper 2015). Likely anticipating more conflict and seeing this as an opportunity to internationalize the situation, when Dharmapala and his companions reached Bodh Gaya on February 25 they climbed to the upper chamber of the Mahabodhi Temple and installed the Japanese Buddha on the altar.[21] Viewing this act as a provocation, the *mahant*'s henchmen quickly arrived on the scene and forcefully removed the statue. Shortly thereafter, Dharmapala filed a petition to District Magistrate D. J. Macpherson asking that a warrant be issued against the *sannyasins* and two *muktiars* who had directly interfered with their "rights of worship," thus bringing the issue of proprietorship and Buddhist claims to holy ground into the public domain.

This incident set in motion a longstanding legal contest that both polarized and concretized Buddhist and Hindu demands over rights of worship that has reverberations up to the present. Throughout his life, Dharmapala referred at length to this protracted litigation as the "Great Case" in an effort to galvanize support for the Maha Bodhi Society and his historical mission as leader of the pan-Asian Buddhist campaign to "rescue" the Buddhist Jerusalem. Throughout the long duration of the Great Case, the specific legal situation at Bodh Gaya remained largely undefined. The proprietorship of the temple was best characterized as "dual custodianship," shared between the *mahant* and to some extent the British government, which had spent Rs. 200,000 on the restoration and thus asserted some right to oversee its preservation and protection (Trevithick 2006, 121). The Great Case also went through a series of appeals, which revealed the challenges faced by the British Indian government in terms of "regulating, guaranteeing, or delimiting religious rights" around sacred space (131). In seeking a stance of religious neutrality, the extensive legal deliberations in many ways strengthened the general impression that the *mahant* was the actual owner or at least custodian of the Mahabodhi Temple and its sacred precincts. At the same time, it was acknowledged that Buddhists should have some right of worship and access to the temple, although the British government was reluctant to place the property in the hands of the Maha Bodhi Society.

For Dharmapala and his recently launched organization, the Great Case was in many ways a great failure. As the legal battle dragged on, Dharmapala was forced to pay upward of Rs. 22,500 in legal fees and lost significant credibility among many of his Buddhist supporters and patrons, including high-ranking British officials, who began to view him as a religious fanatic and troublemaker aggravating communal sentiment in the area and beyond. In 1916–1917, for example, he was interned by the government of Bengal for "pestering the King of Siam," who now desired to be protected from Dharmapala's "persistent annoyance" in his repeated endeavors to persuade the king to a take a leading part in the recovery of the Mahabodhi Temple (Anonymous 1923–1926). With his international reputation in need of much rehabilitation, and given the society's financial woes, over the next few decades Dharmapala focused most of his energy building new branches, such as the Dharmarajika Chaitya Vihara in Calcutta and the Mulagandhakuti Vihara in Sarnath, where he passed away.

Despite Dharmapala's difficulties in Bodh Gaya, the conservation of Buddhist heritage did receive significant attention under the policies of the viceroy, Lord Curzon, who sought to protect the Mahabodhi Temple under the Ancient Monuments Preservation Act of 1904. Along the lines of many Orientalist scholars before him, Lord Curzon held a strong sense of history and the place of the British Empire within it. As viceroy of India between 1899 and 1904, he placed great emphasis on a secular program of conservation as part of the civilizing mission of British imperialism. Lord Curzon first became aware of the contested nature of Bodh Gaya on a trip to Mandalay, where he visited the Kuthodaw Pagoda on November 29, 1901, and received a petition from the Burmese Buddhists expressing concern over the "fate of presents" sent by King Mindon to Mahabodhi Temple, which had allegedly been appropriated by the *mahant* (Trevithick 2006, 145). When Curzon learned of the legal disputes and competing claims of proprietorship over the temple, he took it upon himself to visit Bodh Gaya on January 13, 1903, and to quiz the *mahant* directly about his religious association with the place.

Following the meeting, Curzon later formed a special commission to explore the question of authority over the Mahabodhi Temple. Having collected and examined the available evidence, the commission recommended that more "government supervision [was] needed" to regulate and oversee appropriate religious conduct at the temple, especially to ensure that it was not damaging to the site's antiquarian value. A 1903 memorandum sent by Bengal lieutenant governor J. A. Boudillon to the viceroy further recommended that a supervisory board of "five respectable gentlemen"—excluding non-Indians and Buddhists, due to their sectarian influence—be established to oversee temple management (Trevithick 2006, 158). Despite the viceroy's efforts to press the government's jurisdictional claims, in the end the *mahant*, Krishna Dayal Giri, refused to accept the new terms, and once again the issue was dropped back to the level of regional administration. Under Lord Curzon and collector of Gaya C. E. A. Oldham, Dharmapala was at least able to obtain some land in Bodh Gaya for the construction of the Maha Bodhi Society Rest House. Although this was described as a major achievement for Dharmapala, complicated matters of custodianship and Buddhist sectarianism continued to strain the reputation of the society both locally and further afield.

The *mahant* was more welcoming of the Japanese intellectual Okakura Kakuzo (1862–1913), who arrived in 1903. Count Okakura was a friend of Hindu reformer Vivekananda and was greatly influenced by his neo-Vedanta philosophy as well as Rabindranath Tagore's humanism. With his pan-Asian view of Hindu-Buddhist cooperation and a broad appeal to "civilizational origins," Okakura entered into negotiations with the *mahant* over a land grant in Bodh Gaya for the purpose of building a rest house for Japanese pilgrims. From the *mahant*'s point of view, the prospect of "a distinguished representative of Japan" was most welcome, and he was more than willing to cooperate with Okakura's request for land—this despite his ongoing efforts to evict Dharmapala from his occupation of the Burmese Rest House (Trevithick 2006, 171). Due to reservations by the British government about the transfer of land to "an Asiatic alien," the Bengal government expressed two main concerns: "1) that foreign influence in the area might exacerbate existing tensions, and 2) that within the 'Buddhist Community' itself, dangerous rivalries obtained" (cited in Trevithick, 171). Thus, in an effort to avoid further international complications, the Bengal government denied the building permit for the rest house, offering the following statement: "[The] Government is not satisfied that there is any necessity for another resthouse at [Bodh] Gaya and, moreover is of the opinion that the multiplication of interest there is undesirable" (cited in Trevithick, 172).[22]

During the late nineteenth and early twentieth centuries, as colonial archaeology became interwoven with the demands of modern Buddhist revivalists, the Buddhist holy sites in India took on new affective meaning in the Asian world as markers of identity within an emerging public and scholarly discourse surrounding "world religions." In the evolving disputes over proprietorship and rites of worship at the Mahabodhi Temple, including Dharmapala's Great Case, British administrators were reluctant to disrupt the jurisdictional status of the temple under the Bodh Gaya *mahant* despite the integral involvement of the British colonial state in constructing and reinscribing Bodh Gaya's Buddhist past at an archaeological level. Upholding a position of religious neutrality and disengaging themselves from the administration of temple affairs, regional authorities focused on maintaining peace in the area. This does not mean that the Buddhist revivalists gave up. Until India's independence, the place of Buddhist heritage and Buddhism in India were important subjects of discussion within Indian legislative bodies and political organizations, especially among the vanguards of an emerging Indian nationalist movement.

RECONFIGURING THE PAST: THE BUDDHA AND THE NATION

Much as I should like to help you, it is not possible for me to do anything directly at the present moment. The question you raise can be solved in a moment when India comes into her own. (Gandhi, cited in Maha Bodhi Society 1922, 242)

I am sure it will be admitted by all Hindus who are true to their own ideals, that it is an intolerable wrong to allow the temple raised on the spot where Lord Buddha attained His enlightenment, to remain under the control of a rival sect which can neither have an intimate knowledge of, nor sympathy for, the Buddhist religion and its rites of worship. (Rabindranath Tagore, cited in Maha Bodhi Society 1922, 242.)

Beginning with the second partition of Bengal in 1911, Bodh Gaya and the claims of Buddhist groups were reconfigured as part of the provincial jurisdiction under the government of Behar and Orissa. "Secular" and "liberal" Hindus from the Indian National Congress and All-Indian Hindu Mahasabha were, unlike some British, sympathetic to the concerns of the Buddhists. As part of this new emerging national configuration, the universal claims of Buddhist revivalists and their demands for the Mahabodhi Temple became embedded in a larger Indian national context that required a strategy of compromise and mutual interest.

The Bodh Gaya question first came before an Indian nationalist representative body at the Thirty-Seventh Session of the Bihar Provincial Conference of the Indian National Congress, held in Gaya in 1922, which included over one hundred Buddhist delegates from Burma. The chairman of the conference, Nanda Kishore Lal, who was also the Maha Bodhi Society's chief legal advisor, proposed a legislative solution based on "Hindu-Buddhist veneration of a common sacred ground" (Trevithick 2006, 178). Having given up all hope of intervention by the British Indian government, Dharmapala had written to members of the Indian National Congress, including Mahatma Gandhi, seeking their support for the cause. Gandhi replied to Dharmapala from prison, after the violent Chauri Chaura incident in the Gorakhpur district in 1922, expressing his sympathies on the matter but also saying that little could be done until India gained its own freedom from the tyranny of British rule. Gandhi's foretelling would become reality two years after India's independence, but for the time being, the Bodh Gaya question and the discourse of mutual cooperation required further distillation through a series of Indian public forums and debates.

Shortly after the Indian National Congress conference at Gaya, the Bodh Gaya temple issue was referred to a "working committee" under the Bihari lawyer and future first president of India, Rajendra Prasad (1884–1963), who was authorized to gather suitable persons for the investigation. The members of the committee would include Braj Kishore Prasad, Dr. Kashi Prasad Jaiswal, Gunasinha, and Damodar Das (who later became Rahul Sankrityayan). Echoing British officials, the Punjabi author and politician Lala Lajpat Rai cautioned Prasad that "international complications might arise if the temple were given over to Buddhists of foreign nationality" (Prasad 1957, 232).

Meanwhile, Buddhist representatives at the Cocanada Conference, held in Andhra Pradesh in 1923, as well as those at the joint session of the All-Indian Congress and the All-Indian Hindu Mahasabha, held at Belgaum in 1924, continued to raise the Bodh Gaya question. Under the suzerainty of the British Raj, Buddhist delegates from Ceylon and Burma were particularly vocal at these conferences. Having for all purposes abandoned their attempt to gain exclusive control of the temple, the Buddhist delegation at Belgaum, in particular, was effective in garnering much conservative Hindu backing, especially with their support for the abolition of cow-killing and beef-eating (Trevithick 2006, 180). Thus, following the Belgaum conference, when Rajendra Prasad returned to Bihar, the working committee set out to explore the views of Hindus on the matter.

Based on the working committee investigation, a resolution was adopted during the Bihar Hindu Mahasabha session in Muzaffarpur in 1925 recommending the management of the temple by a joint committee of five Hindus and five Buddhists, with full liberty of worship according to their own methods. The resolution also stipulated that one of the Hindu positions would be hereditary and belong to the Bodh Gaya *mahant*, and another position would belong to a Hindu minister from the government of Behar and Orissa. Echoing Lala Lajpat Rai's concern for "international complications," the resolution also stipulated that the "Buddhist members would hail from within the British Empire (i.e., India, Burma, and Ceylon), and not, it was expressly noted, from Japan, China, or Tibet" (Doyle 1997, 175).

When Rajendra Prasad visited the *mahant* and tried to persuade him to relinquish the temple, assuring him reasonable compensation for his loss of income, the *mahant* outright refused, claiming that "it was a position of great honor and because of it he commanded great respect in India and abroad" (Prasad 1957, 233). Complicating matters was some resistance to the resolution by Buddhist groups themselves, especially those based in Rangoon. Headed by the devout Buddhist lawyer and future chief justice of the Burmese Union U Thein Maung (1890–1975), a group of seven Burmese "gentlemen" had formed their own "Buddha Gaya Temple Committee" and introduced a bill to the assembly demanding complete control of the temple for "Buddhist British Subjects" (Maha Bodhi Society 1923–1926). Given these differences of opinion and lacking consent from the Bodh Gaya *mahant*, Prasad recommended the postponement of the issue to a "more opportune time" (Prasad 1957, 233).

With Japan's entry into World War II and its conquest of Southeast Asia, those who had maintained religious and cultural ties with the country incurred the suspicion of British intelligence, which had ramifications for the Bodh Gaya question. Given the Maha Bodhi Society's longstanding collaboration with Japanese Buddhists, the new general secretary Devapriya Valisinha had his quarters searched in December 1941, and he was arrested for sedition. Although he was released after three weeks, he remained confined to the society's headquarters and was not allowed to go more than five miles from his residence. In British Burma the situation was more complex.

Burmese Buddhists continued to agitate for control of the Mahabodhi Temple on their own initiative, with some using Bodh Gaya as a negotiating tactic against the specter of Japanese conquest. Throughout the 1930s and early 1940s, for example, U Thein Maung Bar-at-Law and Dr. Thein Maung continued to press a Buddhagaya bill before the Legislative Assembly, making provisions for the management of the site. They also approached the *mahant* directly with the hope of purchasing the temple and its properties. A memorandum written to the British government suggests that

> all these mistakes can be avoided if we can approach the Mahant in
> a friendly way and buy up the place. This the government can do if
> they want to stop the accusation that the British cared for a landowner
> more than the millions of Buddhists. In this case I can secure the help
> of Dr. B. M. Barua, the Professor of Pali of the University of Calcutta. He
> is a Buddhist and a friend of the said Mahant and an influential figure
> in the Hindu Mahasabha circles. Once we can get Buddhagaya restored
> to the Buddhists the good will of the Buddhists in Burma towards the
> British is assured. Our propaganda can create marvels out [of] it. (Anonymous 1944)

While many Burmese subjects sided with the British under conditions of war, others looked east to imperial Japan and the prospect of Azad Hind (free India) for liberation.[25] For example, according to U Thein Pe, Burmese Buddhist U Maung Maung appealed to the Japanese authorities and the Ba Maw government to negotiate with Subhas Chandra Bose regarding the restoration of Bodh Gaya. Although I have been unable to verify this in the archives, U Thein Pe wrote: "I don't think the Japs would be slow to seize such a clever suggestion. It may be the Burmese cynicism of Japanese conquest of India that is holding back the plan" (Anonymous 1944).

During this period of considerable geopolitical upheaval—including the fracturing of the British Empire in South Asia—letters in the Public Relations Department of the Indian Government of Burma make clear that the British were willing to accede to Burmese demands for Buddhist control of the temple given the propaganda value in a time of much-needed endorsement. Although the bill transferring ownership to a committee was never debated seriously until after independence, there was clearly broad support among the British and India's emerging national leaders for at least some Buddhist control over the temple.

Leading this effort in the aftermath of India's independence was the first prime minister of India, Jawaharlal Nehru (1889–1964), who looked to the historical Buddha as one of India's greatest sons. For many of India's secular-leaning politicians, the Buddha provided an "all-India inclusive ethic" and a "symbol to declare that India's civilization was noble, culturally variegated, and intellectually respectable" on the international stage (Holt 2004, 23). As illustrated in his earlier writings, such as *Glimpses of World History* (2012 [1934]) and the *Discovery of India* (2004a [1946]), Nehru looked to India's past as a reservoir for an integrated vision of the nation. From his childhood, Nehru had a personal interest in the Buddha and was deeply inspired by Edwin Arnold's *Light of Asia*. In his *Autobiography,* he writes:

> The Buddha story attracted me even in early boyhood and I was drawn
> to the young Siddhartha who, after inner struggle and pain and torment,
> was to develop into the Buddha. Edwin Arnold's *The Light of Asia* became
> one of my favorite books. In the later years when I traveled about a great
> deal in my province, I liked to visit many places connected with the Bud-
> dha legend, sometimes making a detour for the purpose. (Nehru 2004b
> [1936], 130)

Nehru's appreciation for India's Buddhist heritage would also play an integral role in shaping the new nation's iconography, with the adoption of the lion capital from the Ashokan pillar and the *dharmachakra* wheel as official emblems in 1950.

Although these deliberations around the national symbols involved public debate and consensus, rather than individual choice per se (Ray

2014), many of the historical references adopted by the Indian National Congress rested on a construction of the Ashoka-Mauryan past. As a template for unification that transcended volatile religious and political sensibilities in the aftermath of partition, the Buddhist "golden era" of Ashoka provided a rich set of concepts in political philosophy, such as *dhamma-vijaya*, or victory/rule through *dharma*, that resonated with the ethos of Gandhi's nonviolence (Brown 2009). Foreshadowing Nehru's own construction of the non-alignment movement, the appropriation of Buddhism and the reign of Ashoka also provided a model for international relations and diplomacy that could be interpreted as the postcolonial equivalent of the "middle way" based on the five rules of conduct, or *panchasila*, a Buddhist term calling for peaceful coexistence between people, nations, and ideologies.

Throughout his career as prime minister, Nehru frequently invoked the Buddha's and Ashoka's compassionate ideals for a secular path of progress and national prosperity. For example, in his speeches and written correspondence with neighboring Asian countries, Nehru would celebrate the "message of the Buddha" to encourage a transregional cultural ethos that was as vital in his day as it was two thousand years ago.

> If a nation is to be great, she cannot afford to have any barriers between her and the outside world or between different sections of her own people. If such barriers do exist, such a nation cannot influence the world nor can she take advantage of the experiences and discoveries of each other's countries. After a continuous study of the history of India, I have noticed that whenever the nation has been at the peak of her greatness there have been few barriers between her and other nations. At such times her influence has spread far beyond her frontiers as ancient monuments at places like Angkor in Siam [*sic*] proved. India's strength had been cultural and did not arise from military strength. Her great men, too, like Gautama Buddha and Mahatma Gandhi belonged to the world. (Nehru 1948, 5)

Given the importance of Buddhist heritage in shaping national identity and cultural diplomacy in the region, the Bodh Gaya question still needed to be addressed. At the Asian Relations Conference, which took place in New Delhi in March–April 1947, for example, Nehru was urged by delegates from India, China, Tibet, Nepal, Burma, and Sri Lanka to bring a quick and satisfactory resolution to the problem. In his persuasive appeal, Indian *bhikkhu* Jagdish Kasyapa said:

In this history of Delhi it is an unprecedented event of unique importance that chosen men and women in so many countries in Asia have
met together to build an Asia culturally united as one. The problem that
needs immediate solution in the best interests of cultural unity of India
and the rest of Asia is that of handing over of Buddhagaya, the holiest of
our shrines[,] to the Buddhists. Let Pandit Jawaharlal Nehru, the leader
of our country, realize the gravity of the issue and hand over the management of the temple to us who compromise over one third of the population of Asia. (Maha Bodhi Society 1947, 150–151)

Responding to their concerns, Nehru promised to offer "all support for the
restoration of Bodh Gaya to Buddhists" (Maha Bodhi Society 1947, 150).

With the endorsement of Nehru and the Indian National Congress, the
first chief minister of Bihar, S. K. Sinha, introduced a draft bill to the Bihar
State Legislative Assembly in October 1948 endorsing joint management.
Building directly on the groundwork of Rajendra Prasad and his working
committee, the draft bill proposed a joint administration of the Mahabodhi
Temple comprised of an equal number of Hindu and Buddhist representatives elected by the state government. Although direct government control
became effectively nominal, the bill ensured that the district magistrate of
Gaya, "so long as the district magistrate is a Hindu," would serve as the ex-
officio chairperson, a move that tipped the balance of power toward a Hindu
majority.[26] The proposed legislation also ensured that Buddhist members of
the committee would be restricted largely to "Indian Buddhists."

Not surprisingly, when the draft bill was passed and circulated for public comment in 1948, the Maha Bodhi Society, led by Devapriya Valisinha,
was opposed to the "sectarian" legislation, calling it a "caricature of justice"
(Maha Bodhi Society 1948b, 342–344). Pressing for a number of changes,
Valisinha argued that there were few "genuine Indian Buddhists" that
could oversee the management of this international site of Buddhist worship and that the Maha Bodhi Society should be empowered to select the
Buddhist members of the managing committee. In order to satisfy the
demands of the Maha Bodhi Society, Bihar chief minister S. K. Sinha, in
collaboration with Nehru, made a few amendments to the bill, including
the establishment of a separate advisory board to allow for greater involvement among "non-Indian" Buddhist members and to help facilitate closer
relations with newly independent Asian countries, which might benefit
India economically and politically. Writing to his private secretary, Nehru
noted that "it would be desirable to give a certain international character

to this temple . . . [that] would have no executive authority or power but will nevertheless be helpful and will be a graceful gesture to the Buddhist world" (Nehru 1949, 607).

Another reason why Nehru strongly endorsed the Bodh Gaya Temple Act, according to Copland (2004, 559), was that S. K. Sinha wanted to reassure the state's Muslim population that the Indian National Congress was serious about protecting religious minorities. Unlike the British colonial rulers, who maintained a certain distance from the management of religious affairs, the newly elected democratic state government wanted to honor the Indian public and the promise of full freedom of worship under the new Indian Constitution. Thus, after several decades of public debate and legal deliberations, the Bihar state government assumed responsibility for the protection, management, and monitoring of the temple and its properties on June 19, 1949, under the Bodh Gaya Temple Act (Bihar XVII of 1949).[27]

Although the Maha Bodhi Society reluctantly accepted the Bodh Gaya Temple Act, the *mahant*, Harihar Giri (1932–1958), petitioned to the Supreme Court declaring the act a violation of the Indian Constitution. Refusing to give up possession, the *mahant* even succeeded in obtaining an injunction from the High Court preventing the government from taking control of the Mahabodhi Temple. As a result of these obstructive tactics, for nearly three years, the government of Bihar was blocked from taking the temple and entrusting it to the management committee, as envisaged in the act. This "defiant legal maneuvering" infuriated Nehru, who threatened the *mahant* that if he did not give up the temple, Nehru would "look quite closely" at the amount of land then owned by the Math (Doyle 1997, 181). "We have had too much shilly-shallying about this matter," he wrote to Chief Minister Krishna Sinha. "We are going to put an end to this" (Nehru 1952, 204). It was not until the end of 1952 that the *mahant* accepted the joint management scheme under a set of conditions that allowed him to retain the three *samadhis* of his ancestors, the *panch-pandava* shrines, and the former Burmese Rest House. With the *mahant* finally satisfied, preparation for the official transfer of the temple to the new management committee began.

The day chosen for transfer was May 28, 1953—the Buddha *purnima*, the full-moon day commemorating Sakyamuni's enlightenment at this site.[28] As Trevithick (2006, 201–202) points out, in many ways this highly ritualized ceremony served as a sort of "mnemonic device" encapsulating many of the underlying themes that characterized the dispute prior to the transfer of power to a joint committee. Drawing over five thousand people, the ceremony began with a colorful procession of Buddhist monks and laypeople from the Maha Bodhi Rest House to the temple grounds, led by a contingent of Tibetan monks playing cymbals, drums, and oboe-like instruments, followed by Ceylonese, Burmese, Cambodian, and Indian Buddhists (Maha Bodhi Society 1952, 249–256). Presiding over the ceremony was the governor of Bihar, R. R. Diwakar, and the chief minister of Bihar, S. K. Sinha. The chief minister recalled the glory the Buddha had bestowed on the land of Bihar and hoped that Buddhists from all over the world would come to revive the dry fountain of Buddhist culture and restore the link between India and the world. The *mahant* recited Sanskrit hymns, a Maha Bodhi Society *bhikkhu* recited Buddhist *tiratana* in Pali, a popular Indian singer (Malati Sarve) performed two *bhajans* (in Hindi) praising Vishnu, and prominent foreign and Indian dignitaries (including Jawaharlal Nehru) read several congratulatory messages. After the *mahant* presented the official declaration to the new chairperson of the Bodh Gaya Temple Management Committee, a Hindu employee of the Bihar Education Department brought the celebration to an end with several quotations from Edwin Arnold's *Light of Asia*.

CONCLUSION

European and Indian scholars and archaeologists, as well as Buddhist revivalists and national leaders, all have contributed in various ways to the modern rebirth of Bodh Gaya as the place of Buddha's enlightenment. Under the British curatorial state, the production and circulation of historical knowledge surrounding the Mahabodhi Temple and India's Buddhist past were part of a broader civilizing mission to introduce Indians to their own civilizational roots. These formations of the historical past and the networks of institutions charged with reclaiming evidence about the past intersected with modern Buddhist revival demands, especially under the Maha Bodhi Society, and an emerging discourse associated with "world religions" and the importance of sacred sites of collective memory. The assertion of Buddhist rights of worship over the temple gave rise to protracted legal proceedings and longstanding religio-political concerns about the management of sacred space that shaped the dual-custodianship model that emerged after India's independence.

In effect, the 1949 Bodh Gaya Temple Act shifted Bodh Gaya's position from that of an archaeological and art-historical object under the control of a local *zamindar* to a religious monument that would become the focus for the spatialization of heritage under the Indian nation-state. The ceremonial transfer of the Mahabodhi Temple to the new management committee marked the conclusion of some three centuries of Math jurisdiction and the commencement of increased international Buddhist and Bihar state influence over temple management and development (Doyle 1997, 194).

In the following chapters, we examine how various social actors and institutions have given rise to new regimes of value and claims of ownership in the twentieth and early twenty-first centuries, with particular attention to heritage, which is negotiated through complex postcolonial and transnational frames. While disputes over rights to worship and the politics of religious identity continue under the surface of this contested site of memory, other important relationships and spatial commitments surrounding pilgrimage, tourism, and heritage have also come into play.

2   Rebuilding the Navel of the Earth

Pasts become meaningful and usable only when they are activated by
the contemporary desires of individuals and communities, and, most
powerfully, by the will of the nations. (Guha-Thakurta 2004, xvii)

JUST A YEAR PRIOR TO HIS DEATH IN 1933, ANAGARIKA DHARMA-
pala wrote in his diary that at Bodh Gaya, "Burmese, Japanese, Chinese,
Siamese [and] Tibetans should have cottages built for each country" (Trevithick 2006, 205).[1] This prophetic description of Bodh Gaya as a Buddhist
colony surrounded by ethnic, national-sectarian monasteries across Asia is
today a reality. At Bodh Gaya there are upward of seventy Buddhist monasteries (*viharas*), temples, and pilgrim rest houses, with many representing
the unique aesthetic and architectural styles of different Buddhist traditions
and national forms. These religious landmarks, which range in size and
opulence, present a pronounced spatial and visual counterpoint to the rural
landscape, projecting an image and presence of international Buddhism
over the surrounding geography.

Bodh Gaya can be seen as a religious diasporic landscape, with transnational networks of Buddhism underlying the growing globalization of
this sacred site. *Transnational* refers here to those religious migrants who
live their lives across borders, maintaining various temples and monasteries
in their country of origin as well as abroad. The rooting of these diasporic
communities and the global dissemination and exchange of Buddhist ideas,
practices, teachers, and institutions have been a vital force in building a
pan-Asian Buddhist identity through collective reinvestment in a Buddhist
sacred site. Questions about the production of Buddhist sacred space in
relation to patrimonial claims over national and cultural heritage emerge:
How is the notion of Buddhism as a "world religion" formed in relation to
pilgrimage and sacred sites? How have Buddhist monasteries and transnational networks reconfigured Bodh Gaya's sacred space and inscribed the
landscape with religious meaning? Finally, how are Buddhist communities
connected and confined by national, linguistic, and cultural differences in
Bodh Gaya today?

Throughout the late twentieth century we saw far-reaching changes in the translocal cultural regimes known as "world religions," and there have been considerable attempts to map the new transnational terrain of religion, especially in relation to public politics and culture around the world (Hefner 1998). As an expression of "transnational transcendence" (Csordas 2009) and a key constituent in the propagation of religious forms of globalization, the practice of pilgrimage has historically been on the forefront of creating new networks of social identity that do not necessarily conform to territorial or nation-state boundaries. At the same time, it is important not to overestimate the continuing salience of the nation-state in defining religious identity and constraining religious practice (Borchert 2007).

This tension is evident in the sociospatial practices of monastic building in Bodh Gaya, in particular, the ways in which diasporic Buddhist communities interface with state agendas and cultural programs at the national level—where India's Buddhist heritage has emerged as a key symbol of the postcolonial nation-state. These underlying tensions in the reconfiguration of sacred space are evident in the national and regional networks of monastic growth involving prominent Buddhist leaders, specific institutions, and events that have transformed Bodh Gaya, especially following the landmark 2,500th Buddha Jayanti celebrations held in 1956. At the risk of reifying the nation-state, I view the historical growth of these monasteries along roughly national and cultural-linguistic lines in order to examine the multiple and overlapping developments that are currently taking place at Bodh Gaya.[2]

JOURNEYS TO THE DIAMOND THRONE

In the old days when the message of Buddha went out from India to far-off lands, pilgrims came here from those countries carrying that message. There was coming and going and there was confluence of spirit. Leaving aside all political contingencies and looking at ourselves with detachment we would find that we were all tied together by powerful silken ties. . . . Buddhism more than anything else laid the foundation of Greater India and established cultural unity of an abiding value between India and many parts of Asia. A free India can worthily strengthen and revitalize those contacts. (Nehru 1949, 102)

During the late colonial rule in India, the Buddhist revival movement greatly benefited from the development of more open and modern travel conditions, which greatly boosted international pilgrimage to the holy places of the Buddha and helped fuel a new understanding of India as the homeland of Buddhism (Huber 2008). During this period, the "eight places of the Buddha" scheme was increasingly circulated and invoked in a wide range of contexts "as the primary model for representing and understanding India as a sacred Buddhist terrain of pilgrimage and also as a basis for actual ritual practice among modern Buddhist converts" (32). Dharmapala and the Maha Bodhi Society certainly played a leading role in transforming this pilgrimage culture by facilitating tours and goodwill missions from Asian Buddhist delegates, gaining special concession fares on the Indian railway system, providing accommodation at *dharmashalas* (pilgrim rest houses), and displaying sacred relics (Huber 2008).[3]

A significant postindependence event that helped reinforce the universal significance of India's Buddhist geography was the nationwide celebration of the Buddha Jayanti, held in 1956. This year-long commemorative event marked the 2,500th anniversary of the Buddha's entry into *parinirvana*, or final liberation (based on a Theravada chronology), and was a historical landmark for the revival of Buddhism at Bodh Gaya, helping to revitalize key inter-Asian links and connections.[4] The event was particularly auspicious among many Theravada Buddhist communities because the Buddha is believed to have prophesied that his *sasana* would endure for five thousand years, and at the midpoint of that period would undergo great renewal and resurgence (Bond 1992). It was also significant because many Asian countries had recently achieved political independence, and Buddhism provided an important cultural and symbolic resource that strengthened their sense of unity. Not surprisingly, the main lobbying force behind the event was the Maha Bodhi Society, which alerted the government of India and its wide network of Asian Buddhist supporters to celebrate the event in a worthy manner.

The first prime minister of India, Jawaharlal Nehru (1889–1964) agreed that this event was important, and, in memory of "one of the greatest sons of India," should be celebrated on a grand scale.[5] He stipulated, however, that "so far as the government is concerned, our celebrations will not be of a religious character" but rather, would be predominantly "cultural" (Nehru 1955a, 450–451). Although the Buddha Jayanti was part of a larger, yearlong program held at several Buddhist sites throughout the country (and in other parts of the world), the celebration reached its zenith on the Buddha *purnima*, held over three days (May 22–25). On this occasion, thousands of visitors, including international Buddhists and prominent Asian elites, converged on Bodh Gaya's sacred landscape to honor the memory of the Buddha and reinforce the symbolic importance of Bodh Gaya as *the* navel of the earth and the center of the Buddhist world among emerging post-colonial Asian networks.[6]

In addition to the 2500th Buddha Jayanti celebrations, 1956 was significant for two other important reasons. First, the government-constituted Bodh Gaya Temple Advisory Board was established. This advisory board grew out of the 1949 legislature, which transferred jurisdiction of the Mahabodhi Temple to a joint Buddhist-Hindu management committee. Consisting of a Buddhist majority "not all . . . of Indian citizenship," this board provided an important transnational link for the representation of Buddhists groups outside of India.[7] As a gesture to the Buddhist world, the advisory board was closely aligned with Jawaharlal Nehru's national and political vision, which positioned India at the cultural center of a new post-colonial world order. Nehru said, "We have to give a sense of partnership to these foreign countries . . . [and] remember that this advisory body will have a larger significance than merely one for the Bodh Gaya temple. It really brings India into the international picture from another point of view" (Nehru 1955c, 453–454). During the advisory board's inaugural meeting, held at the Maha Bodhi Rest House on the March 17, members discussed the application for plots of land at Bodh Gaya for the construction of Buddhist monasteries and rest houses. Following India's independence, Devapriya Valisinha had pressed the first chief minister of Bihar, Krishna Sinha, to set aside twenty-five thousand acres of land for the establishment of a "Buddhist colony" to ensure that Bodh Gaya would develop into a great center of culture and education, as in ancient days (Maha Bodhi Society 1948a). A permanent international Buddhist presence in this sacred locality would enable India to establish friendly relations with other Asian countries and benefit financially from the pilgrim traffic.

The year of the Buddha Jayanti was also significant in terms of the development of "new Buddhism" (or neo-Buddhism), which emerged from the writings and legacy of the *dalit* political leader "Babasaheb"—Dr. B. R. Ambedkar. In Nagpur, Maharashtra, on October 14, the highly accomplished low-caste leader embraced the three refuges and five precepts and then proceeded to convert an additional four hundred thousand of his *dalit* followers—one of the largest mass conversions in modern history. He himself administrated an additional twenty-two vows, including an "emphatic repudiation" of Hinduism and Hindu practices rejecting the idea that the Buddha was an *avatara* (incarnation) of Visnu (Singh 2010, 215). Ambedkar's decision to reject Hinduism reaches as far back as 1935, when, on the occasion of the Provincial Conference of the Depressed Classes at Yeola, he publicly declared that although he was born a Hindu, he would not die one (Beltz and Jondhale 2004). Although Ambedkar attempted to engage with wider networks of international Buddhism, following his conversation, it was also clear that this "new hermeneutics of liberation" (Queen and King 1996) was directed toward (but not limited to) the scheduled castes and combined a strong element of social and political protest, especially against the Hindu religion, as illustrated in his magnum opus, *The Buddha and His Dhamma* (2011 [1959]).

Although it is beyond the scope of this chapter to examine the legacy of Ambedkar's highly symbolic conversion to Buddhism, it is sufficient to say that he hoped to revive and reinvent Buddhism as a living tradition in India that would go beyond a mere historical appreciation (Singh 2010; Doyle 1997).[8] The extent to which Ambedkar Buddhists and international interests coalesce around the politics of the Mahabodhi Temple today is a topic I discuss later in this chapter. In the sections that follow, I turn to a detailed survey of the transnational histories and regional networks of Buddhist institutions that have acquired land at Bodh Gaya both before and after the landmark 1956 Buddha Jayanti year.

SOUTHEAST ASIA

Over the last two hundred years, Burmese pilgrims have played a leading role in renewing sacred ties to the place of Buddha's enlightenment. Throughout the nineteenth century, at least a half-dozen Burmese royal missions visited Bodh Gaya with the aim of restoring and venerating religious structures such as the Mahabodhi Temple. The majority of these Burmese missions to Bodh Gaya took place during the reign of the Konbaung kings (ca. 1752–1885), which was integral to the identity of Royal Burmese rulers through its patronage of the most elevated events, actors, and institutions of Burma's Buddhist past (Doyle 1997). As in other Theravada Buddhist cultures, these pilgrimage activities were in line with traditional views of *dhamma-raja*, or dharmic kingship based on the Ashokan ideal of a galactic polity (Tambiah 1976). The performance of these state-sponsored religious and symbolic acts also helped to bolster the merit of the Burmese kingdom, especially during the late nineteenth century under heightened British encumbrance.

As described in the previous chapter, growing out of arrangements between the Bodh Gaya *mahant* and King Mindon Min between 1875 and 1877 was a brick-and-mortar rest house built eighty yards west of the Mahabodhi Temple for the purpose of worshiping the Bodhi tree and maintaining the sacred shrine. The Kuthodaw Rest House, named after the famous Burmese Pagoda in Mandalay, was the first Buddhist place to be built in Bodh Gaya in the modern era and played a pivotal role in the *mahant*'s litigation with Dharmapala and his efforts to wrest control of the temple. Shortly after Dharmapala established the Maha Bodhi Society in 1891, he installed four young *samaneras* from Ceylon, and later, the Burmese novice Shin Chandra (later known as U Chandramani) and Shin Thuriya, who looked after the Kuthodaw Rest House and Buddhist shrine during the formative years of the society.[9] Although the Kuthodaw Rest House was later demolished in preparation for the Buddha Jayanti celebrations in 1956 (Doyle 1997, 140), a second Burmese *vihara* was built in 1937, and this institution became a vital link for the propagation of Buddhism now taking root in the West.[10]

Initiating these developments was the first prime minister of the new Democratic Republic of Burma, U Nu (1905–1995). U Nu was a devout Buddhist and a popular nationalist leader who undertook a conscious policy of sponsoring Buddhism at the state level, following the traditional patterns of *dhamma-raja*. Linked to these efforts to reform the Buddhist *sangha* and reestablish religious contact with the sacred sites in India was his visit to Bodh Gaya in 1956, as part of the Buddha Jayanti celebrations. During this time, U Nu came into contact with Acharya Anagarika Munindra (1915–2003), a Bengali Buddhist and scholar from the Chittagong region (now Bangladesh) who was appointed first superintendent of the Bodh Gaya Temple Management Committee (1953–1957). Although Munindra and U Nu had previously crossed paths during a Buddhist relic tour organized by the Maha Bodhi Society, on this occasion, U Nu invited him to Burma for the purpose of receiving instruction in *vipassana*, a meditation technique that had been preserved among the great Burmese masters. Accepting this invitation to deepen his understanding and practice, Munindra relinquished his position as superintendent and departed for Burma in early 1957, where he spent nearly ten years training at the Sasana Yeiktha meditation center in Rangoon under the guidance of Mahasi Sayadaw (1904–1982), one of the great Burmese meditation masters of the twentieth century.

When Anagarika Munindra returned to Bodh Gaya in 1966, he was, in fact, also fulfilling a Burmese Buddhist prophecy anticipating a resurgence of Buddhism and *vipassana* meditation twenty-five hundred years after the Buddha, and these teachings had a tremendous impact on the Burmese *vihara* (Pryor 2006). Located on the Gaya riverside road a short distance from the police station, this *vihara* was the main center of Burmese Buddhist activity throughout the latter part of the twentieth century. The Burmese monks who ran the *vihara* were, however, vulnerable to the changing political landscape of postcolonial Burmese nationalism. For example, following the military coup led by General Ne Win, chairman of the Revolutionary Council of Burma from 1962 until the late 1980s, the Burmese Buddhist *sangha* was largely cut off from political life, and all vestiges of state support for Buddhism were eliminated (Matthews 1999). Although Indo-Burmese relations were more fluid under the British colonial empire, following the military coup, Burma was largely closed off to foreigners, visas were curtailed, and many Burmese monks living abroad were ordered back.[11] Filling the vacuum created by the military-imposed travel restrictions, the Burmese monastery found new forms of financial and spiritual support in the late 1960s, when it became a central institution in the revitalization of the *vipassana* movement, especially among young Western travelers seeking meditation training and cheap accommodations. Munindra, in particular, became a key resource for the transmission of *vipassana* during this time, offering personal instruction at both the Burmese *vihara* and the nearby Samanvay Ashram.[12] With his kind and gentle demeanor, Munindraji (as he was often called) was able to make Buddhist teachings and practical guidance accessible to a growing number of Western followers. From 1966 to 1969, Anagarika Munindra was the only English-speaking *vipassana* teacher available in India, and many of his former students from Europe and America, such as Surya Das, Joseph Goldstein, Sharon Salzberg, and Daniel Goleman, are all well-known Buddhist teachers in the West (Pryor 2006).

Another very important *vipassana* teacher during this period was Satya Narayan Goenka. Born in Mandalay to Indian parents in 1924, Goenka was a prominent industrialist and leader of the Burmese Indian community before receiving formal training in *vipassana* from the Burmese teacher Sayagyi U Ba Khin (1899–1971) beginning in 1955. After fourteen years of training, Goenka, like Munindra before him, returned to India and began leading ten-day *vipassana* meditation courses and camps throughout the country. In Bodh Gaya, Goenka's first meditation camp took place at the Samanvay Ashram in August 1970, and thereafter he offered several ten-day courses over the winter season at both the ashram and Burmese *vihara*. These popular courses were taught on the roof of the old *vihara* building or under large tents and could draw upward of two hundred participants, many of whom were from Western countries, and helped to support the *vihara* during a period of economic hardship. However, by the mid-1970s, S. N. Goenka was no longer returning to Bodh Gaya, and Munindra provided his last retreat in the 1977–1978 winter season. When I spoke with Tara Doyle about her firsthand experience of these changes, she noted that this was the "end of an era for Westerners," but a void that was eventually filled through new channels of meditation instruction.

One teacher in particular who helped fill this void was the late *bhikku* Dr. Rashtrapal (1930–2008). Like Munindra, Rashtrapal was a Barua Buddhist, a monk and scholar from the Chittagong region. Rashtrapal cofounded the International Meditation Centre (IMC) with Munindra on January 29, 1970. This institution claims to be the first registered Buddhist meditation center to be established in India, providing regular meditation instruction and budget accommodation for pilgrims throughout the year. Rashtrapal was also an active member of the Bodh Gaya Temple Management Committee from 1984 to 1994 and helped establish the annual Kathina Civara Dana ceremonies—a traditional Theravada practice that marks the end of the monsoon "rain retreat" season in which visiting pilgrims and lay Buddhists offer robes and other provisions to fully ordained monks as specified in the Mahavagga of the Vinaya Pitaka (The Book of Discipline). Several influential Western practitioners and teachers also became an established part of the winter season in Bodh Gaya from the mid-1970s onward.[13] One of these instructors is Christopher Titmuss (b. 1944) and the insight meditation group, which has been leading popular ten-day retreats at the Royal Wat Thai every January and February since 1975. There is also the Antioch University (now Carleton-Antioch) Buddhist Studies Program, which began in 1979. Robert Pryor and Tara Doyle are the founders of this popular American-based study abroad program, which runs each year from September to December. Building on this legacy of Burmese-Western infusion, the educational program is based at the Burmese *vihara*, where North American university students receive four months of intensive training in Buddhist philosophy, history, contemporary Buddhist culture, meditation traditions, and both Hindi and Tibetan language.

Over the course of the last thirty years, the head monk of the Burmese monastery, Sayadaw U Nyaneinda (b. 1935) has also been instrumental in fostering transnational connections and is recognized as one of the senior members of the International Buddhist Council in Bodh Gaya—an organization of head monks, nuns, and managers of foreign monasteries that look after the collective needs of the growing Buddhist diasporic community. Ever since U Nyaneinda arrived in Bodh Gaya at the age of forty-one, he has been active in the "Buddhification" of Bodh Gaya's landscape as a land adviser for incoming Buddhist organizations and for erecting images, signboards, and Buddhist structures in the surrounding landscape (Doyle 1997). In joint efforts with famous Burmese sculptor U Han Tin, over a half-dozen Buddhist images have been built in the surrounding landscape and reflect popular legends and stories of the Buddha's biographical life. One of the more prominent sculptures is of the Buddha sheltered by the king of serpents Muchalinda, which sits in the water tank adjacent to the Mahabodhi Temple. Thus despite the isolationist policies and foreign restrictions following the military coup in 1962, the Burmese *vihara* at Bodh Gaya has been a transnational meeting ground between East and West that served as a gateway for the early dissemination of the *vipassana* meditation technique.

With Burmese political reforms in recent decades, including a liberalization of travel restrictions, there has been a surge of Burmese pilgrims and state officials returning to Bodh Gaya on pilgrimage missions. For example, as part of the new face of Myanmar foreign policy, on April 1, 1990, there was a "Good Will Mission" to India by a twenty-member Myanmar delegation. During their stay in Bodh Gaya, the group met with a number of professors at the nearby Magadh University and set up a program of mutual co-operation in the form of an exchange of scholars and students between India and Myanmar.[14] As a result of changing diplomatic relations, in the mid-1990s, Burmese pilgrims and postgraduate monk students began to arrive in growing numbers, a trend that has continued and intensified in the last twenty years. These recent pilgrimage and educational developments have spawned a host of new Burmese institutions, such as the Great Holy Land Monastery, the Myanmar Monk-Students' Welfare Association of India, the Majjhimasuha Foundation, the Ramanyabhumi Buddha Vihara, the Anatta Meditation Monastery, and the Mahabodhi Meditation Centre. Linked to the earlier influence of S. N. Goenka is the Dhamma Bodhi Vipassana Centre, which was established in 1994 and runs a series of popular *vipassana* courses throughout the year.

Like the Burmese, Thai Buddhists have long played an important role in the restoration of Buddhist sacred sites in India, especially following the

Sayadaw U Nyaneinda,
abbot of the Burmese
vihara

landmark Buddha Jayanti celebrations. In January 1955, the Royal Thai
Embassy approached the government of Bihar and later the Ministry of
External Affairs asking to build a Buddhist temple at Bodh Gaya.[15] Although
Prime Minister Jawaharlal Nehru opined that a large accommodation hall
should be built at Bodh Gaya where foreign scholars and Buddhists could
stay irrespective of their country, he was also keenly aware of the symbolic
and diplomatic connections that Buddhism provided. For these reasons,
Nehru accepted a proposal by the king of Thailand, Bhumibol Adulyadej
(1927–2016), shortly after the Buddha Jayanti, and a large, 3.92-acre plot
of land was leased to the royal monarchy by the government of Bihar at a
limited annual rate for ninety-two years. Under the name the Royal Wat
Thai, this became the first Buddhist monastery and temple in the postindependence era to be built under the jurisdiction of a foreign head of state. To
celebrate the growing cultural exchange program between India and Thailand, a Golden Buddha statue was installed in the Royal Wat Thai on May 3,
1967, as a donation from the prime minister of Thailand, Thanom Kittika-
chorn (1911–2004). To ensure the safe travel of the Golden Buddha image, a
special United States military aircraft was chartered by the Thai government

to fly from Bangkok to the nearby Gaya aerodrome. This was followed by a series of circumambulations at the Mahabodhi Temple led by the Thai abbot Phra Deb Visuddhimoli, just before the formal installation of the statue at the Royal Wat Thai. On the occasion a message sent by the king of Thailand was read: "Let the installation of the Buddha image in the birth place of Lord Buddha and at the exact place where he attained Enlightenment symbolize the international friendship between India and Thailand" (Maha Bodhi Society 1967, 273).[16]

As a result of generous funding from the government of Thailand in the early 1970s, the Royal Wat Thai also received a significant makeover and was remodeled after the famous Marble Temple in Bangkok—*Wat Benchamabophit Dusitvanaram*—which was established by King Rama V in 1899. What is unique about the architectural mimesis and replication of the Marble Temple at Bodh Gaya is the extent to which this reconstruction is a reversal of the Mahabodhi Temple prototypes that were built between the early thirteenth and late fifteenth centuries in Burma, Thailand, Nepal, and China. As John Guy (1991) has suggested, one of the main reasons for the construction of Mahabodhi replicas beyond Buddhist India was the desire to create surrogate temples to allow veneration to continue when direct access to the navel of the earth became increasingly difficult from the twelfth century onward. Rather than serving as an architectural icon modeled after the Mahabodhi Temple, the Royal Wat Thai became a symbol of the Thai nation at the sacred power center of the Buddhist world.

Since the 1956 Buddha Jayanti, the Royal Wat Thai, in many ways, has been a benchmark for other national expressions of Buddhist architecture and aesthetic design. With its sloping curved roof and golden tiles, the beautifully adorned Royal Wat Thai remained the only Thai Buddhist institution in Bodh Gaya throughout most of the twentieth century. However, in the late 1990s, and especially with the commencement of direct international flights from Bangkok to Gaya in 2002, there was an upsurge of Thai Buddhist pilgrimage activities and a growing number of religious centers from Southeast Asia. One such center is the Wat Pa Buddha Gaya, which is associated with the Thai Bharat Society and Forest Monk tradition in Thailand. Stretched over several acres of land directly south of the Mahabodhi Temple, Wat Pa derives its name from its close association with Payap-Parutai Shinawatra, the younger brother of the now deposed Thai prime minister Thaksin Shinawatra. Across the Niranjana River is the Wat Niranjarawas, under the head monk Phrarajpipatanatorn (aka Luang Por Thavorn).

Royal Wat Thai

This Thai monk has honorary degrees from California and New York, as well as a large global network of supporters, including prominent American monastic branches in Houston and New York. Lastly, several other Buddhist centers from Southeast Asia have acquired land in recent years, with monasteries and temples currently under construction. These include the Cambodian Buddhist Monastery (Bodh Gaya and Uruvela), the Wat Thai Magadh Vipassana Centre, the Wat Thai Buddhabhumi, the Wat Pa Muchalinda, Metta Buddharam Temple, the Wat Lao Buddhagaya International, and the Buddha Sawika Bodh Gaya for Thai Nuns.

TIBETAN REFUGEES AND HIMALAYAN ZONE

As it was, the Tibetans were my salvation. They were poor, they were ragged, they were dirty, and the other pilgrims looked down on them, but they had walked all the way from Tibet, some of them with babies on their backs, and now they came shuffling in through the gate with their prayer-wheels and rosaries in their hands and expressions of ecstasy on their upturned faces. . . . As they circumambulated the Temple, as they prostrated themselves before the

Diamond Throne, as they lit butter-lamps round the Bodhi Tree,
they saw only the naked fact of the Buddha's Supreme Enlightenment, and through their eyes, even if not with my own, I could see
it too. (Sangharakshita 1988, 296–297)

There is a long history of Tibetans making pilgrimage to sacred sites in
India. An early pioneer in the transformation of Tibetan pilgrimage culture
in the twentieth century was the Amdo-born scholar and monk Gendün
Chöphel (1903–1951). Influenced by both European and Asian Orientalist
scholars and Buddhist modernists, Gendün Chöphel was the first Tibetan
pilgrim in history to systematically visit the major Buddhist sites and produce a popular modern pilgrimage guidebook (Stoddard 1985, Lopez 2006,
Huber 2008). This creative and controversial Tibetan monk developed close
ties with Indian Buddhist Rahul Sankrityayan (1893–1963) and members of
the Maha Bodhi Society after arriving in India in 1934. With his extensive
travel throughout the region, Gendün Chöphel became a catalyst for the
reconfiguration of Tibetan pilgrimage geography by reinforcing the modernist claims toward the "authentic" Buddhist sites and rejecting other
"popular" Tibetan Buddhist sites of veneration (Huber 2008). He also set a
ritual pattern for Tibetan pilgrims that would gain wider acceptance in the
coming decades.

Perhaps the most politicized Tibetan pilgrimage was the trip by the 14th
Dalai Lama, Tenzin Gyatso, and the 10th Panchen, Lama Lobsang Trinley
Lhündrub Chökyi Gyaltsen, as part of the 2,500th Buddha Jayanti held in
1956. This visit by the 14th Dalai Lama provided an opportunity to undertake direct diplomatic exchanges with the government of India, in particular, Jawaharlal Nehru, concerning the unfolding occupation of the Kham
and Amdo regions of Tibet by the Chinese army (PLA) (Huber 2008).
Departing Lhasa at the end of November with a small entourage that
included the Panchen Lama and his older brother, Lobsang Samten, they
traveled to Gangtok in Sikkim and later to New Delhi, alongside the Maha-
raj Kumar of Sikkim, Pelden Thondup Namgyal (1923–1982), who was then
president of the Maha Bodhi Society.

In the company of a large number of Tibetan devotees, the Dalai Lama
also initiated his first public religious act in India by undergoing pilgrimage
and offering teachings at a number of Buddhist holy sites, including Bodh
Gaya on December 27. On this special occasion, thousands of people
thronged the seven-mile route from Gaya to Bodh Gaya as the entourage
drove through numerous welcome arches that had been erected in honor

of their visit. Upon reaching the temple, with an international reception of Buddhist monks and visitors, the Dalai Lama and Panchen Lama presented sets of Tibetan Buddhist Scriptures to the temple management committee along with a gold lamp to be used in daily worship (Maha Bodhi Society 1957). In the Dalai Lama's (1990, 123) autobiography, *Freedom in Exile* he writes: "I was ecstatic. For us Tibetans, India is Aryabhumi, the Land of the Holy. All my life I had longed to make a pilgrimage there: it was the place that I most wanted to visit." At the age of twenty-one, the 14th Dalai Lama was visiting Bodh Gaya for the first but certainly not the last time. As Huber (2008, 350) remarks, the Dalai Lama was acutely aware of the "powerful symbolic resonance" of his activities at the ancient sites where Buddhism was founded, and these earlier instances of pilgrimage marked the beginning of a new ritual relationship with the Buddhist holy land and its increasingly deterritorialized Tibetan community.

The Chinese occupation of Tibet in 1959 dramatically changed both the meaning of and conditions for Tibetan pilgrimage. With the arrival of the Dalai Lama and over eighty-five thousand refugees, several generations have been born and raised in various settlements and cities throughout the country under diverse and extremely difficult circumstances. In addition to the government-in-exile headquarters in Dharamsala and the various refugee settlements, Bodh Gaya and other major Buddhist sites constitute a crucial locus of Tibetan exile geography and a "valued terrain in which to put down some temporary roots and rebuild their social and cultural lives" (Huber 2008, 351). The Tibetan veneration of India's sacred geography and their resettlement in the Buddhist holy land have also contributed to both the internationalization of Tibetan Buddhism and the revitalization of many Buddhist sites in India (Singh 2010). Nowhere is the Tibetan consecration of sacred space more evident than at Bodh Gaya, where several thousand Tibetans take up residence during the winter season and perform large-scale public ritual gatherings.

Although the pilgrimage season in Tibet was traditionally held during the summer months, the winter season has now become an integral part of the new ritual calendar for the Tibetan exile community and other Himalayan Buddhist groups. The Dalai Lama reinforced this ritual pattern in the winter of 1959, when he ordained, for the first time in his life, over a hundred Tibetan novices under the Bodhi tree at Bodh Gaya (Dalai Lama 1990, Huber 2008). Since that time, the frequent presence of the Dalai Lama and other renowned spiritual teachers at the place of Buddha's enlightenment enables pilgrims to receive personal blessings, accumulate merit, do prayers

14th Dalai Lama and Buddhist monks under the Bodhi tree

and virtuous acts, undertake seasonal work, and reunite with other Tibetan refugees throughout India and the surrounding Himalayan zone.

A major religious ceremony involving the 14th Dalai Lama was the Dukhor Wangchen, or the "Great Kalachakra Initiation," held directly in front of the Gelug Tibetan Temple and the Maha Bodhi Society in December 1974. Bringing an estimated hundred thousand Tibetan Buddhists together for the first time, the Kalachakra has since become the most widely known public Buddhist ritual to be held in the modern era and an important ritual medium for the revitalization-in-exile of Tibetan culture and religion.[17] Although many attendees follow the commitments and engage in the initiation practice, for others, especially those lay pilgrims from the Himalayan regions, the initiation has become an opportunity to accumulate merit and receive teachings and blessings from high-ranking lamas. This was certainly evident during the 1985 Kalachakra, which attracted a quarter of a million participants from over thirty-one countries and became the largest Kalachakra initiation ever performed by any Dalai

Lama in the history of Tibetan Buddhism. The organizers combined the celebration with a special staging of a six-day Monlam Chemno, or Prayer Festival, that began on December 16 and brought together thousands of monks and leading lamas from all of the four main schools of Tibetan Buddhism: the Gelug, Nyingma, Sakya, and Kagyu. First inaugurated in 1409 by the Gelug patriarch Tsongkhapa, the Monlam Chenmo is a popular New Year's festival and annual ritual event that has undergone significant innovation under conditions of exile (Doyle 1997, Huber 2008).

For example, on the final day of Kalachakra, Buddhist monks from Japan, Mongolia, Sri Lanka, Thailand, Vietnam, and India gathered under the Bodhi tree for a special prayer for world peace. The fact that the 1985 Monlam Chenmo was named Prayer for World Peace is highly significant, according to Huber, because it not only promotes Tibetan religiosity as a "significant resource of universal appeal" but also mirrors an increasingly sophisticated discourse that has been deliberately cultivated by the Tibetan government-in-exile and its supporters, projecting a nonviolent Tibetan national image and identity (Huber 2008, 363). The melding of Buddhism with a modernist discourse of world peace has obvious parallels with the universal claims by many religious groups in the contemporary era, but through the plight of the Dalai Lama and other charismatic Tibetan lamas, this relationship has certainly become more pronounced, especially among the growing network of supporters in the West.

Given the emphasis on world peace and the Tibetan use of ritual empowerment as a way of reviving sacred space at Bodh Gaya during the winter season, these large ritual festivals can have a significant impact on the host communities. For example, as part of the 1985 Kalachakra/Monlam, the government of Bihar deployed state agents to collect a tax of Rs. 5 on the main road into Bodh Gaya. Tara Doyle (1997, 352) writes that the understanding among the Bihar government officials and the Tibetan refugee community was that these funds were to be spent on basic facilities such as electricity, drinking water, latrines, and cooking oil. However, those pilgrims who participated in the gathering said that these services were not provided. Clean water and cooking fuel were almost impossible to find, and on the fringes of the vast tent city of Tibetan devotees a gigantic open sewer had formed. To make matters worse, on the final day of Kalachakra, a gale swept through and turned the whole area into a giant mud bath.

Although the event was in all likelihood a lucrative venture for state and district authorities, the neglect of basic amenities left many sick, including the Dalai Lama. According to one eyewitness, "The locals provided only four toilets so the Tibetans petitioned. . . . Shit was all around the river bank, there were so many flies, so we began to bury it. Immediately following the event, the Tibetans departed swiftly and this led to enormous resentment among the villagers." The foul smell and putrid conditions of the town remained for several months and even overlapped with the visit of a *Lonely Planet* writer who had this to say in his review about the place of enlightenment: "Bodh Gaya is small and quiet but, if you are not planning a longer study stay, a day is quite sufficient to see everything. Apart from the stupa and various monasteries Bodh Gaya is just a grubby little dump with an enormous population of flies" (Crowther 1985, 307).

The 1985 Kalachakra ceremony also involved a confrontation between Tibetan pilgrims, the government of Bihar, and municipal leaders concerning the public use of religious structures. Prior to the Tibetan gathering, a temporary *dais* and stage platform were constructed on the nearby (Kalachakra) *maidan* where the Dalai Lama could deliver his teachings to the audience. In spite of specific orders by the state to dismantle the religious structure at the ceremonies' conclusion, an image of the Buddha was allegedly installed by devotees. This spawned a backlash by several Bodh Gaya residents, who argued that if *all* public spaces were devoted to Buddhist religious functions, there would be no space for local congregations and meetings. This disquieting event was not easily resolved, and the matter was taken up in New Delhi (Banerjee 2000). As a result of these disputes and the heightened tension between the Tibetan exile community and both local and state authorities, the Dalai Lama temporarily stopped offering teachings at Bodh Gaya, shifting his base to the Central Higher Institute of Tibetan Studies in Sarnath (Doyle 1997).

Despite the 14th Dalai Lama's temporary break with Bodh Gaya, other prominent teachers have connected with the sacred space at Bodh Gaya and forged key transnational alliances abroad. One of these influential teachers is the prominent Nyingma lama Tarthang Tulku (b. 1934). As one of the last remaining lamas to have received a complete Buddhist education in pre-1959 Tibet, Tarthang Tulku taught Tibetan language at the Sanskrit University in Benares before migrating to the United States in 1969 with his wife, the poet Nazli Nour. Over the years, Tarthang Tulku sponsored several events in Bodh Gaya—all of which were financed by his Berkeley, California–based Tibetan Nyingma Institute and led by Nyingma teachers living in India, Bhutan, and Nepal (Doyle, 1997). Then, after spending twenty-one years in the United States, he returned to India in 1989 and began organizing the Nyingma Monlam Chenmo, or Great Prayer Festival for World Peace. With support from his California-based Dharma Publications and the Tibetan Aid project, Tarthang Tulku's annual event has grown significantly over the years, providing transportation, lodging, food, and texts for several thousand monastic participants.

Throughout the 1980s and 1990s, the other three main schools of Tibetan Buddhism each developed their own Monlam ceremonies dedicated to world peace at Bodh Gaya and at other major pilgrimage sites in India (Huber 2008). The Nyingma Monlam, for instance, was preceded by the smaller Kagyu Monlam Chemno, first held in 1983 from November 5 to 19. Under the leadership of Kalu Rinpoche (1905–1989) and Bokar Rinpoche (1940–2004), the Kagyu Monlam, like Tarthang Tulku's invention, reinforced the sacred and cultural ties of the Karmapa Kagyu lineage with the navel of the earth. The dramatic departure of Ugyen Trinley Dorje (b. 1985) from Tibet in 2000 also changed the appearance of the Monlam due to rival factions in the Kagyu school, each of which recognized his own Karmapa candidate.[18] For these reasons, the annual Kagyu Monlam has become an opportunity to legitimize Urgyen Trinley Dorje's sacred title for many devotees, including the Dalai Lama himself (Huber 2008). In 2002, for example, the Kagyu Monlam attracted over seven thousand Buddhist monks from different Kagyu subschools, including seventeen incarnate lamas. The Monlam was directly followed by the third Kalachakra initiation held in Bodh Gaya, an event that was attended by an estimated two hundred thousand devotees from over one hundred different countries.

Given the elevated importance of Bodh Gaya's sacred space among the Tibetan diaspora, other teachings, empowerment practices, and sponsored events are now part of Bodh Gaya's annual ritual cycle, catering to Tibetans, Western practitioners, and a growing number of East Asian Buddhists, especially from China, Taiwan, and Singapore. Some of these programs and events include the popular six-month spiritual program at the Root Institute for Wisdom Culture, the Shechen Monastery seminar series, annual teachings by the Karmapa before the Kagyu Monlam, lectures by the Nepal-based Chokyi Nyima Rinpoche as part of the Carleton-Antioch Buddhist Studies program, and a ten-day Phowa course taught by Ayang Rinpoche. In 2002, Wangmo Dixey (daughter of Tarthang Tulku) and her husband Richard established the California-based Light of Buddhadharma Foundation International (LBDFI) with the aim of restoring the Buddha *sasana* in India through four main activities: chanting ceremonies, development of pilgrimage, training monks, and the printing of *dharma* books. One of the principal activities organized by the LBDFI is the International Tipitaka Chanting Ceremony. Like the Monlam ceremonies, this annual event, first held in collaboration with the Maha Bodhi Society in 2006, brings several thousand monks and nuns from various Theravada Buddhist countries for the ten-day recitation of various sections of the Pali Canon.

Due to the great reverence bestowed upon the navel of the earth by Tibetan pilgrims, leaders from the four main schools of Tibet have established a *gompa* (monastery) to support their community in Bodh Gaya.[19] In his study of Boudhanath in *Buddhism Observed*, Peter Moran (2004, 62) writes that "for most Tibetan Buddhist masters in exile, building a monastery is not so much about *new* beginnings and innovation, but rather a rebuilding of their monasteries in Tibet, with the very specific aim of maintaining and spreading the ritual, philosophical, even artistic traditions of their *particular* Tibetan Buddhist lineages." Many of these monasteries were established after 1959, but the earliest Tibetan Buddhist *gompa* at Bodh Gaya predates the exiled community by some three decades. Founded by Lama Kanpo-Ngawang Samten of Ladakh, a small Tibetan temple from the Gelug school with attached lodging was built on land next to the Maha Bodhi Society in 1938. However, due to the lack of financial support and resources in Bodh Gaya during British India, the first head monk, Lobsang Samten, gifted the Tibetan temple to the Dalai Lama and the Gelug school in 1947. Since that time, the temple and monastery have been run by the Tibetan government, and provide accommodation and headquarters for the Dalai Lama when he undertakes pilgrimage to Bodh Gaya.[20] From an administrative point of view, the Gelug Tibetan Temple (also known as Gaden Phel Gay Ling Tibetan Mahayana Buddhist Monastery) is now an appendage of the Namgyal Private Monastery in Dharamsala, where the 14th Dalai Lama currently resides. Directly west of the main *gompa*, the temple also oversees the large Mahayana Tibetan Rest House, which was completed in 1983 and caters to Tibetan pilgrims throughout the year. Not surprisingly, in light of Bodh Gaya's revitalization as a locus of Tibetan Buddhist pilgrimage among the exile community, a number of high-ranking lamas have acquired land to build permanent lodgings and facilities.[21]

One of the latest Tibetan monasteries to be inaugurated in Bodh Gaya is the Pal Tergar Rigzin Khacho Dargye Ling (Yongey Tergar Monastery). Established in 2007 and known locally as the "Karmapa Temple," this monastery exemplifies the transnational transformation of Tibetan Buddhism today. The unveiling of the elaborately designed monastery was held on January 3, 2007, followed by a ten-day teaching program that was sponsored

Kagyupa Vajrayana Buddhist Monastery, "Karma" Tibetan Temple

by the Taiwan Hwayue Foundation. East Asian patrons are now some of the largest contributors to Tibetan ritual performances, and many of the new Tibetan monasteries in Bodh Gaya have been built by lamas with sponsors from Taiwan, Singapore, Hong Kong, and mainland China (Moran 2004). Although the head of the Tergar Monastery is Mingyur Rinpoche, the monastery is also the seat of the 17th Karmapa, Urgyen Trinley Dorje Rinpoche, who resides in private quarters above the main shrine while teaching in Bodh Gaya. Together, they are tied to Tergar International and Tergar Asia, which is a large religious transnational organization that supports *dharma* groups and social development projects in Bodh Gaya and around the world. In recent years, Urgyen Trinley Dorje Rinpoche has become an integral part of the winter pilgrimage season, attracting the largest number of devotees after the Dalai Lama and reinforcing his sacred ties with the Kagyu school and Tibetan Buddhism more broadly.

As Toni Huber (2008) explains in *The Holy Land Reborn*, the proliferation of monasteries and ritual events at Buddhist sacred sites both highlights the existence of the fragmented and dispersed Tibetan exile world and provides a vital cultural resource for the establishment of some socioreligious unity. The ecumenical spirit of these large-scale public rituals is certainly tied to the charismatic leadership of the Dalai Lama and other high-ranking religiopolitical elites, who have wisely adopted the navel of the earth and other Buddhist sites throughout India to foster good relations among the major Tibetan schools. As "intensive occasions" for a whole host of social relations, these huge rituals provide a crucial arena for the "negotiation of Tibetan 'national' identity in exile" while elevating their displaced refugee status within an increasingly globalized arena (Huber 2008, 373). It is for these reasons that Chinese authorities have tightened travel restrictions for those Tibetans looking to leave the PRC to receive instruction from teachers like the Dalai Lama in exile in recent years. According to some human rights organizations and Tibetan advocacy groups, many Tibetans were detained by Chinese officials and forced to undergo patriotic "re-education" programs upon return from the Kalachakra in 2012 and 2017 (Wong 2012).

For many Tibetans who reside in India, the state of exile has been the harbinger of new possibilities, but also a position of deep cultural constraint and uncertainty (Huber 2008). Around the world, Buddhism has become the dominant marker of Tibetan identity, and their economic survival as refugees hinges on their conformity to a notion of preserved and "authentic" Tibetan culture that almost always signifies Buddhism (Moran 2004, Prost 2006), making them key players in the internationalization of sacred Buddhist sites. It is precisely their extraneous position as refugees in the Buddhist holy land that has helped foster a growing transnational network of patronage ties toward their cultural survival and helped further their promotion of political independence. This, of course, has much to do with the current Dalai Lama, who has become the global saint of Tibetan Buddhism and a moral guide for many popular Buddhist followers around the world.

EAST ASIA

One of the oldest Buddhist centers in Bodh Gaya is the Mahabodhi Chinese Monastery and Temple, built in 1945.[22] Secondary literature attributes the Chinese temple to Si-Tingchen (or S. T. Chen), a Chinese Buddhist savant, and it was likely built on a plot of land donated by the industrial Birla family (Banerjee 2000). Although it is difficult to trace the origins of the Chinese temple, we do know that the Chinese professor Tan Yun-Shan (1898–1983), a close friend of Rabindranath Tagore and secretary of the Sino-Indian Cultural Association, played an important role in its establishment. After meeting Rabindranath Tagore in Malaysia in 1927, Tan Yun-Shan left for India and embarked on a lifelong journey to rebuild Sino-Indian cultural relations. Throughout his life, he maintained close ties with both the Santiniketan School and Jinaratana Mahathera from the Maha Bodhi Society in Calcutta. It was these connections with the Maha Bodhi Society that led Tan Yun-Shan to Bodh Gaya in 1931. With his deep-rooted interest in Buddhism, he played an instrumental role in fund-raising for the Chinese temple, overseeing several goodwill missions from Chinese delegates such as Taixu (president of the Chinese Buddhist Association) and Tai Chi Tao, and playing an active part in the wider Buddhist revival movement throughout the country. When Tan Yun-Shan passed away in Bodh Gaya in 1985, Prime Minister Indira Gandhi said in her condolence message, "Gurudeva and my father had affection and regard for him. . . . [He] contributed immensely to a better understanding between the civilisations of India and China."[23]

Vietnamese, Korean, and Japanese temples have also flourished in Bodh Gaya. Two kilometers west of the Mahabodhi Temple in Bhagalpur village is the Viet Nam Phat Quoc Tu, under head abbot Thay Huyen Dieu (aka Dr. Lam Trun Tu). Established in 1987, this was the first Vietnamese temple to be built in Bodh Gaya. Dr. Lam has played an active role in the revival of Vietnamese Buddhist pilgrimage activities in both Bodh Gaya as well as Nepal, where he heads a temple at the birthplace of the Buddha. Today, the Vietnamese temple is surrounded by a large, forested campus that includes a three-story rest house and a beautifully decorated, multi-tiered pagoda. Following the example set by Dr. Lam, several other Vietnamese temples have also been built in recent years, such as the Vien Giac Institute, which belongs to the Lin Tzi Zen tradition but practices Pure Land Buddhism; the Jona Data Temple and School, which is part of the Chua do Sanh Trust; the Linh Son Monastery, which is affiliated with the International Linh-Son Buddhist Association, headquartered in Joinville-le-pont (near Paris); the Tinh Xa Ky Vien, or Indian-Vietnamese Buddhist Trust; and the Vietnamese Mahaprajapati Nunnery, near Katorwa village.

Since the early 1990s, the Korean influence on Bodh Gaya's pilgrimage landscape has also grown significantly. Situated on a plot of land adjacent to the Nyingma Institute is the Hankuk Buddhist Society, popularly known as the Korean Temple, which was established in 1991. Both the president of the organization, Dr. Hyun Ki Hong, and the general secretary, Dr. Kim Kwang Tae, maintain close ties with the Korean National Centre of the Maha Bodhi Society. Another Korean organization that has had a significant social impact on the surrounding area of Bodh Gaya is the Join Together Society. Established in 1993, this international organization is headquartered in Seoul and has a growing number of field program offices in India, the Philippines, Afghanistan, and North Korea, as well as overseas chapters in the United States and Germany. According to its website, the society grew out of an encounter with *dalit* children in Bodh Gaya who were begging on the streets. After realizing the children had no school to attend, the Join Together Society decided to build a full school complex at the foothills of Prakbodhi hill in nearby Dungheswari (a popular pilgrimage site associated with the Buddha's austerities). The Sujata Academy provides education for upward of seven hundred students, mostly from scheduled castes/tribes, and also operates an additional seventeen preschools that have been built in the surrounding villages. In addition to these two societies, there is a Korean Buddhist Temple situated in Rati Bigha village; and the Buddha Dhamma Sangha Mula Arama—Pannarama Sati School—which involves close collaborations between Korean and Indian Buddhists.

Like many Asian Buddhist organizations in Bodh Gaya today, a number of Japanese Buddhist sects have maintained close ties with the Maha Bodhi Society and were active in India's Buddhist revival movement from its inception. Sponsored by Honganji, the largest school of Jodu Shinshu Buddhism, Kitabatake Doryu and Kurosaki reached Bodh Gaya in 1883 and provided one of the first pilgrim travel accounts of India's Buddhist sites. Alongside a growing textual and Orientalist discourse of Buddhism, these travel accounts helped to stimulate Japanese Buddhist interest in Shakyamuni Buddha as a historical figure and the importance of India's sacred geography as a focal point of an emerging world Buddhism (Jaffe 2004). These travel reports, as Jaffe illustrates, helped increase the awareness of Asian Buddhism and signaled growing Buddhist cooperation within the region.[24] Of particular importance to these growing Asian exchanges and networks in the late nineteeth century was Shaku Kozen (1849–1924), who accompanied Dharmapala to Bodh Gaya for the first time in 1891 and helped with the founding of the Maha Bodhi Society.

In the postindependence era, the first royal Japanese guests to visit Bodh Gaya were Crown Prince Akihito and the Crown Princess Michiko, who arrived by charter plane at the Gaya aerodome on December 5, 1960. This event marked the first time in history when the heir-apparent to the throne of Japan visited the seat of enlightenment. On this historic day a hundred welcome arches were erected along the main entrance road from the Gaya aerodome and upward of fifty thousand people were in attendance (Maha Bodhi Society 1961). Not surprisingly, the main coordinator of the event was the Maha Bodhi Society under Devapriya Valisinha, who formally welcomed the royal couple to the sacred site. In response, the crown prince delivered this speech:

Dear Friends,

It has been our long-cherished desire to visit India, especially this holy place of Lord Buddha. The spiritual and cultural tie which was created between India and Japan some 17 centuries ago through the Teachings of Lord Buddha is so deeply rooted and has been maintained up to this day when its revaluation is being ushered in under much changed modern situations, internal and as well as international.

My friends! When I stand here on the very spot where Lord Buddha attained His Supreme enlightenment two thousand and five hundred years ago, my heart is filled with pious respect, and those centuries seem to roll away like the mist. Lord Buddha is still alive in your hearts, and also in the hearts of tens of millions of Japanese. That is the solid spiritual foundation on which the most cordial co-operation between India and Japan might be built and strengthened. For this occasion we thank you most warmly, and wish your Society every success. (Maha Bodhi Society 1961, 22–23)

In light of the growing number of Japanese Buddhist delegates and missions to India throughout the 1960s, the government of Bihar leased a 4.6-acre plot of land to the International Buddhist Brotherhood Association, or Kokusai Bukkyo Koryu Kyokai, an independent organization founded by Buddhist sects in Japan. Under the direction of the chief priest, Reverend G. Tomatsu, the Japanese have since built a traditional Japanese-styled wooden pagoda modeled after a Buddhist temple in Kyoto, a pilgrim rest house with air-conditioned rooms and *ofuro* (hot baths), a library, and a meditation hall. The formal inauguration of the Indo Nipponji Temple took place on December 8, 1973—a date that coincides with the Japanese anniversary of Shakyamuni Buddha's enlightenment—and since that time, the International Buddhist Brotherhood Association has played a leading role in supporting Buddhist cultural events and establishing various philanthropic projects that continue today. These include the annual International Buddhist Conference, which commenced in 1975, a nursery and kindergarten, a medical dispensary, and an agricultural technology research center.

A second Japanese center also grew out of close transnational ties with the Maha Bodhi Society. From 1968 to 1983, Jinaratana Mahathera was the general secretary of the Maha Bodhi Society and, like many of his predecessors, he devoted his entire life to the progress of the society, forging strong links with Buddhist communities, especially in Japan. In keeping with these growing transnational ties, the general secretary gifted a portion of the

Buddha's relics at the request of the government of India to a Japanese Buddhist sect, the Daijokyo Sohonzan of Nagoya, on November 28, 1973 (Maha Bodhi Society 1973). *Daijokyo*, which means the "Great Vehicle of the Mahayana," was founded in 1914 by the late Reverend Tatsuko Sugiyama. Daijokyo is one of the newest lay sects in Japan; its members follow the Lotus doctrine and teachings propagated by St. Nichiren.

After receiving the Buddhist relics, members of the Daijokyo sect embarked on a pilgrimage tour through North India and Nepal in the late 1970s. During this time, the Daijokyo Association of Nagoya met with the Bodh Gaya Temple Management Committee and members of the Bihar state government to request land for the construction of a second Japanese temple and rest house. The request was granted and the Daijokyo Buddhist Temple, with its three-story pagoda, was inaugurated on February 13, 1983, in the company of former president of India Giani Zail Singh, Daijokyo president Reverend Y. Sugisaki, and vice president Mangal Subbha. Like the International Buddhist Brotherhood Association, the Japanese organization built a rest house for the benefit of Buddhist pilgrims and initiated several philanthropic programs, such as a vocational and agricultural training center.[25]

In addition to these social welfare projects, the Daijokyo Buddhist sect is particularly well known for its contribution to one of the greatest tourist attractions in Bodh Gaya—the "Great Buddha Statue." At approximately eighty feet high and nearly sixty feet wide, this image of the Buddha is one of the largest Buddha statues in India and towers over the rural landscape and surrounding monasteries. The consecration and unveiling of the Great Buddha Statue took place on November 18, 1989, in the company of the 14th Dalai Lama and depicts the Buddha sitting in the *dhyana mudra* position (or meditation pose) on a lotus flower with his eyes half closed. V. Ganapati Sthapati, one of the best-known contemporary sculptors of traditional images in India, spent five years designing the elaborate statue; Thakur & Sons, a prominent stone-working company, carved the entire statue out of blocks of pink chunar sandstone (Asher 2008). At the base is a solid concrete pedestal and inside is a hollow spiral staircase from the ground floor to the chest of the statue. Wooden shelves have also been built into the interior walls, wherein 16,300 small bronze Buddha images from Japan have been enshrined.

Evident in the description of Buddhist growth at Bodh Gaya thus far is the extent to which the rebuilding of the navel of the earth is highly gendered; most of the caretakers of the various monasteries are men. However, as a transnational meeting ground for Buddhist activity, Bodh Gaya was also the location for the first international gathering of Buddhist nuns,

Unveiling of the eighty-foot Great Buddha Statue on November 18, 1989, by the Daijokyo Buddhist sect. Photo courtesy of Daijokyo Buddhist Temple.

held on February 11–17, 1987 (Maha Bodhi Society 1987). This historic event, like the unveiling of the Great Buddhist Statue, was inaugurated by the 14th Dalai Lama, and brought together nuns, monks, and lay Buddhists from over twenty-six countries. This special occasion was also the first time in eight hundred years that a Bhikshuni *sangha* (a community of fully ordained nuns) in India performed the Bhikshuni *posadha*, the nuns' bimonthly purification and restoration of vows.[26] Although a lineage of fully ordained women had been maintained in China, Taiwan, Korea, and Vietnam, this was the first time, after many centuries, that a Bhikshuni *posadha* was conducted in the land where the Buddha's teachings originated (LeVine and Gellner 2005). The movement to establish full ordination for nuns was spearheaded by several women from both the Mahayana and Theravada Buddhist lineages, such as the American Karma Lekshe Tsomo (originally Patricia Zenn), founder of the Jamyang Foundation and professor of Buddhist Studies at the University of San Diego; Ayya Khema, meditation teacher and the first Western women to become a Theravada Buddhist nun; Dasa Sil Mata, a Buddhist laywoman in Sri Lanka; Sylvia Wetzel and Jampa Tsedroen (from Germany); Pema Chodron (Canada); Bhikkhuni Kusuma (formerly Dr. Kusuma Devendra from Sri Lanka); and Bhikkhuni Dhammananda (formerly Dr. Chatsumarn Kabilsingh from Thailand) (LeVine and Gellner 2005, Barnes 1996).

In addition to reviving the Bhikshuni *sangha*, this occasion was also the founding meeting of the Sakyadhita "Daughters of the Buddha"—a worldwide women's Buddhist organization. The Sakyadhita network was established at the end of the conference with a set of resolutions aimed at addressing gender inequality in Buddhist societies and Buddhist institutions more broadly. Since 1987, the Sakyadhita network—through its biannual conferences—has played a key role in building solidarity among Buddhist women worldwide and has worked to initiate ecumenical and interfaith exchanges across various cultural and educational backgrounds (Yu-Ling Chang 2017, Tsomo 2007).[27] One of the initial goals for Sakyadhita was to create opportunities for the full ordination of all Buddhist nuns and to (re)establish the Bhikshuni lineage in Buddhist traditions where it no longer existed. It was for these reasons that the Bodh Gaya International Full Ordination was held in February 1998.

Like the first international gathering of Buddhist nuns, this event brought together over fifteen hundred participants, including twelve hundred Taiwanese pilgrims and 134 nun candidates, from over twenty-two countries. There were translators in English, Hindi, Nepali, Tibetan, and Sinhala, and a series of ordinations took place over nine days. Leading the large-scale Bhikshuni ordination was Master Xingyun from the popular Fo Guang Shan Buddhist Order in Taiwan. This Chinese Buddhist monastic order represents a melding of Cha'n and Pure Land traditions with branches throughout the world. Fo Guang Shan (literal translation: "Buddha's Light Mountain") was founded in 1967 by Master Xingyun, a refugee from the Chinese mainland, and seeks to promote a humanistic approach to Buddhism in which gender equality is an important feature (LeVine and Gellner 2005). Following the meeting, the Taiwanese order also acquired land in Bodh Gaya and is currently building a Fo Guang Shan Buddhist studies institute and a home for children run by Buddhist nuns. In addition to the Fo Guang Shan Institute, there is an older monastery and rest house, built by the World Chon Ghwa Buddhist Sangha of Taiwan. The Sakyadhita network under Karma Lekshe Tsomo is also in the process of building a center across the Niranjana River that commemorates Ashoka's daughter Sanghamitra, who transmitted the Bhikshuni lineage from India to Sri Lanka.

SOUTH ASIA

As with the early missionary connections between the island kingdom and the Mauryan court, there is a long history of religious and cultural confluence between India and Sri Lanka. However, it was not until the arrival of Anagarika Dharmapala that these symbolic ties received a modern inflection with the establishment of the Maha Bodhi Society on May 31, 1891. Undoubtedly, Dharmapala's activity outside of Sri Lanka as a *dharmaduta* (messanger of dharma) set the course for modern Buddhist missionary work, and the Maha Bodhi Society can be described as the first modern transnational Buddhist organization (Kemper 2005). With its ecumenical orientation and modern organizational forms, the Maha Bodhi Society was founded on the moral imperative to revive Buddhism in India and restore the ancient pilgrimage sites, especially the Mahabodhi Temple. Under its charismatic leader, the organization founded numerous branches in India and overseas and was at the forefront of pilgrimage activities at Bodh Gaya throughout the twentieth century.

Although the main headquarters for the Maha Bodhi Society was first located on Creek Row in Calcutta (moving to College Square in 1915), after nearly ten years of perseverance, land was eventually acquired in Bodh Gaya from the District Board of Gaya in 1901 following a visit by Lieutenant Governor Woodburn, and the building was completed in 1903.[28] Like other Maha Bodhi Society rest houses (*dharamshalas*), the Buddha Gaya Centre was largely built through Burmese financial aid and serves as a receiving institution for foreign-looking Sinhalese monks who aim to educate Indian people about its Buddhist history, maintain *bhikkhus* at major pilgrimage sites, and provide accommodation and support for pilgrims abroad.[29] As a residue of the British colonial era, the architecture of the building still retains a British, turn-of-the-century colonial aesthetic, with its covered verandah and arched entrance ways (Asher 2008). Given the building's close proximity to the Mahabodhi Temple and the main bus loop, one might argue that the Buddha Gaya Centre has long served a dual function as both a watchtower for the navel of the earth and a magnet for international visitors, providing information to tourists and pilgrims.

Much scholarship has been written on the founder of the Maha Bodhi Society, Anagarika Dharmapala, but little has been written on the Sinhalese monks at Bodh Gaya who followed in his footsteps. As the personal assistant and chief disciple of Dharmapala, Devapriya Valisinha (1904–1968) played a pivotal role in advancing the Buddhist revivalist movement in India.[30] As a young boy, Devapriya was inspired by the missionary activities of Dharmapala during his lecture tours in Ceylon from 1911 to 1914, and moved to India in 1917, where he rendered his service to the Maha Bodhi Society while completing his education at the Presidency College in Calcutta. He was also the first Sri Lankan to be enrolled at Rabindranath Tagore's Shantiniketan School, but left after a year to assist Dharmapala in his work.

Following Dharmapala's *upasampada* ordination and his passing in 1933, Devapriya Valisinha was elected general secretary and treasurer of the Maha Bodhi Society, a post he held for thirty-five years, until his death in 1968. Like his predecessor, Devapriya Valisinha traveled extensively throughout his life, attending conferences and establishing new branches and partnerships throughout the Buddhist world. He also spent two years at the London Buddhist Mission and undertook higher studies in Pali and Buddhist philosophy at the School of Oriental Studies (now School of Oriental and African Studies), University of London. Devapriya Valisinha was also involved in advancing the Bodh Gaya Temple Act in 1949. Under this new legislation, he also served on the first management committee for the temple and was instrumental in establishing the Bodh Gaya Temple Advisory Board, recovering the sacred relics of Sariputta and Moggallana from the Victoria and Albert Museum and campaigning for the 2,500th Buddha Jayanti celebrations, all of which significantly contributed to the reawakening of Buddhism in India. Valisinha also maintained close ties with B. R. Ambedkar and was present, along with U Chandramani, for his historic conversion to Buddhism in Nagpur in 1956. Valisinha passed away in Colombo on August 3, 1968.

Another important Sinhalese figure in the development of Buddhism at Bodh Gaya was the soft-spoken and benevolent monk Bhante Pannarama (1926–1995). With the help of his assistant, Dediyawala Wimala Thero, Pannarama first visited Bodh Gaya in 1968 and managed the Buddha Gaya Centre from 1970 to 1994. Over the course of his tenure, Pannarama helped to promote the Maha Bodhi Society as a center of learning and culture through the propagation of Buddhist activities, seminars, symposiums, and literature. During this period, he worked closely with the local population and encouraged numerous philanthropic projects, especially among the large numbers of *dalit*s in the area. Even today some local residents recall his warm presence in the surrounding villages, where he would attend family functions and provide financial support to those in need.

Reflecting on his early years in Bodh Gaya, Pannarama was surprised that not a single Indian in Bodh Gaya could recite the three refuges and five precepts:

> More than two decades have passed since I had come to this place in 1970. That time only with a sense of veneration to this holiest Buddhist spot I started living here, worrying very little about other things. In course of time I felt that besides chanting Sutras, bowing to the Bo-tree, etc. individual religious routine [*sic*] something must be done for Buddhist reawakening in the surrounding area. Ven. Dharmapala's vow reminded me that the place of which every inch seems to have been sanctified by the Lord Buddha's feet, must have Buddhistic air in and around. (Maha Bodhi Society of India 1994)

Inspired by Dharmapala's mission as a *dharmaduta*, for nearly twenty-five years Pannarama and his assistant worked tirelessly to share the basic tenets of Buddhism with Hindu and Muslim residents in Bodh Gaya. As a result of these efforts, for the first time in the history of modern Bodh Gaya, three young postgraduate students from Magadh University—R. B. Prasad, Ram Swarup Singh (past Temple Management Commitee member), and Hari Manji (former senior officer of the Archaeological Survey of India)— were initiated into Buddhism by taking the five precepts on the memorable occasion of Buddha *purnima* day in 1971 (Maha Bodhi Society 1972). This was followed by several other Buddhist initiations from 1972 onward, including a nearby village of *dalits* that is known as Siddartha Nagar today.

In line with the missionary and philanthropic aims of the Maha Bodhi Society were the visits of Sri Lankan president Ranasinghe Premadasa (1924–1993). Although Sri Lanka was in the throes of civil war, the president made several trips to Bodh Gaya and other Buddhist pilgrimage sites in India between 1992 and 1993. On each of these occasions, his pilgrimage to the seat of enlightenment led to various religious and social developments that can still be observed today. These include two offerings to the Bodh

Gaya Temple Management Committee: the golden railings (*ran veta*) that surround the Bodhi tree and the gold-plated canopy (*ran viyana*) that now rests above the *vajrasana*, or diamond throne. He also initiated plans for the construction of one hundred brick-and-concrete houses and a community hall for *dalit* families living in nearby Mastipur village. After four months of work, commissioned by the Ministry of Housing and Construction in Sri Lanka, the president himself arrived in Bodh Gaya on April 13, 1993, and handed over the keys to each of the villagers. Inscribed on the foundation stone in front of the community hall is a plaque that reads "BuddhaGayagama—the village of Reawakened people" in Sinhalese, Hindi, and English. This reawakened village project proved to be his last meritorious act at the place of Buddha's enlightenment. Barely fifteen days after the inauguration ceremony, Premadasa returned to Sri Lanka and was assassinated by a suicide bomber as part of the May Day *padayatra* at Armour Street in Colombo in 1993.

Pannarama's health suffered the same year, and in 1994 he went to Sri Lanka for six weeks of medical treatment. In recognition of his twenty-five years of service at Bodh Gaya, a group of local residents held a public ceremony on May 15, 1994, where he was given a "scroll of honor." The function brought together a large number of Bodh Gaya's residents, university scholars, and international monks, who came forward to thank and register their reverence for Bhante Pannarama. As noted in the "news section" of the journal *Sambodhi* (1994, 48): "The one common point which emerged from the speeches was that nobility and simplicity reigns supreme in Bhante's personality. He is the best propagator of harmony, peace and goodwill." Pannarama replied in his laconic speech, "Though I was born in Sri Lanka, Buddha Gaya is the dearest to me, I would love to be reborn here if I get rebirth." A year after his departure from Bodh Gaya, Pannarama died in Colombo on May 18, 1995.

Bhante Pannarama, and by extension, the Maha Bodhi Society, did much to spread Buddhist teachings among the local Indian population—in fact, much more than other international groups in Bodh Gaya (for many, this is not a goal). Most Indians who have embraced Buddhism are in fact "self-converted" and follow the teachings and example of Dr. Bhimrao Ambedkar, who, as we will see, has had a significant impact on Bodh Gaya. A number of other prominent Indian Buddhists have also played a pivotal role in the revival movement throughout the twentieth century, some of whom worked in close collaboration with Anagarika Dharmapala and the Maha

Bodhi Society, spending several formative years in Burma, and especially Sri Lanka, at the Vidyalankara Pirivena undertaking Buddhist studies. These include Mahavir Singh (1833–1919), Kripasaran (1865–1926) (founder of the Bengal Buddhist Association in 1892), Dharmananda Kosambi (1876–1947), Bodhananda (1874–1952), Rahul Sankrityayan (1893–1963), Anand Kausalyayan (1905–1988), and Jagdish Kashyap (1908–1976).

In Bodh Gaya itself, the Indian Buddhist monk-scholar Jagdish Kashyap, with the support of the head *bhikkhu* of the Royal Wat Thai, Phra Debvisuddhimoli, helped establish the All India Bhikkhu Sangha in 1971.[31] Although the main headquarters and training center for Indian *bhikkus* were at the Royal Wat Thai, by the late 1970s, members of the *sangha* had acquired land from the state government to construct their own Buddhist center. However, due to a lack of donors and limited membership fees, it was not until 2003 that the main building was completed, including several commemorative structures in honor of prominent Indian Buddhist leaders, such as the Ananda Mitra Guest House, the Ananda Kausalayan Bhikkhu Training Institute, the Bhikkhu Jagadish Kashyap Library, and the Rahul Sankrityayan Seminar Hall. More recently, as a symbol of the longstanding Thai-Indian connections, a large statue of the Buddha was gifted by Thai Buddhist donors under chief monk Somdej Phramaharatchamangkhlachan, the lord abbot of Wat Paknam, in Bangkok, Thailand, on March 6, 2006.

When the All India Bhikkhu Sangha was first established in the 1970s, most of the members derived from the ethno-Buddhist background of the Barua and Chakma Buddhists of Bengal and Assam (Ahir 1989). This is no longer the case today. Within the last few decades, branches of the All India Bhikkhu Sangha have been established throughout the country, and the membership demographic now reflects the growing presence of *dalit* Maharashtran Buddhists, or neo-Buddhists, following the example of Ambedkar. Ambedkar used the prefix "neo" to suggest a new interpretation of Buddhism, one that contained a strong element of social and political protest (Singh 2010, 196). This element of social and political protest was certainly evident throughout the 1990s, with the campaign to "liberate" the Mahabodhi Temple from Hindu control. These demands for "complete control" of the Mahabodhi Temple first took concrete shape on April 20, 1992, when the All India Bhikku Sangha passed a resolution at its session in Bodh Gaya demanding transfer of the management and control of the Mahabodhi Temple to an "All Member Buddhist Committee" (Ahir 1994, 157). This resolution was followed by a mass demonstration during the Buddha Jayanti celebrations on May 16, 1992, when over eight hundred Indian Buddhists (other sources say the number was closer to two hundred) stationed themselves in front of the controversial *panchpandav mandir* adjacent to the temple and even assaulted the Brahmin priest on duty (Ahir 1994, Doyle 2003, Dhammika 1996). Following this altercation, the *dalit* Buddhists were ordered to leave town by the local police, but before their departure they circulated a memorandum outlining their grievances and vowed to return with more supporters (Doyle 2003).

The 1992 Buddha Jayanti demonstration was the first of a series of agitations that occurred in Bodh Gaya under the banner of the "Buddha Gaya Mahabodhi Mahavihar All India Action Committee" (henceforth, the Mahabodhi Action Committee) (Doyle 1997). All of these protests drew upon a discourse concerning the "liberation" of the Mahabodhi Temple from a Hindu "Other" and a concomitant desire to amend the 1949 act and place the temple in the hands of an all-Indian Buddhist committee. These demands for Buddhist reclamation of a sacred site have also mirrored the assertion of Hindu nationalism in the early 1990s, which culminated in the razing of the Babri Masjid Mosque. Like Ayodhya, Doyle (1997, 400–401) writes, the Mahabodhi Temple served as a "powerful symbol for regaining *dalit* Buddhists' rightful religious and cultural patrimony, forging a sense of group identity, and establishing their socio-political rights all of which they assert have been stolen from them by upper-caste Hindus." Despite these authoritative claims in the name of Indian Buddhism, one of the main leaders of the agitation was a Japanese monk (and naturalized Indian citizen) with a Nichiren background known as Bhadant Nagarjuna Arya Surai Sasai.[32]

Under the leadership of Surai Sasai, the agitation grew in size and became more aggressive and militant with each passing year. For example, coinciding with the Buddha Jayanti in 1992, Surai Sasai organized the Dhamma Mukti Yatra (Buddhist Liberation Process), modeled on the highly politicized Rath Yatra undertaken by Bharatiya Janata Party leader L. K. Advani in 1990. As a means of mobilizing popular support for the Hindu nationalist party, L. K. Advani drove a symbolic Bharatiya Janata Party chariot that traversed the northern part of India with the goal of liberating the birthplace of Lord Rama in Ayodhya. Although the Dhamma Mukti Yatra was not nearly as controversial as the Bharatiya Janata Party political pilgrimage, it certainly helped to raise public awareness for the New Buddhists. Another turning point was the *dharna*, or fast-until-death, that was held in April 1995. This event prompted the chief minister of Bihar, Lalu Prasad Yadav, to make changes to the composition of the temple

Procession of Indian monks from Maharashtra protesting the "Hindu" management of the Mahabodhi Temple on the Buddha *purnima* day, May 2006

management committee, assigning three of the four Buddhist positions to leaders of the movement: Surai Sasai, Bhadant Anand, and Professor P. C. Roy (a local Buddhist convert and Magadha University scholar).

Although these changes in the management structure afforded new opportunities to members of the Mahabodhi Action Committee, committee members also vowed to continue their campaign until they accomplished their ultimate goal of changing the 1949 Bodh Gaya Temple Act. During this time, a number of high-level meetings were held in Delhi between Surai Sasai and other leaders of the Buddhist liberation movement with the national minorities commissioner and the prime minister, P. V. Narasimha Rao. The national minorities commissioner suggested an amendment to the controversial act and proposed that the *dalit* Buddhist community be granted full rights, but these recommendations were never implemented. At this time, a delegation of Vishwa Hindu Prashad members visited Gaya and met with several Indian officials, including the district magistrate, vowing to undertake their own agitation if recommendations for complete Buddhist control were implemented (Banerjee 2000, 154). To appease the Indian Buddhists and generate votes among the large *dalit* population in Bihar, Lalu Prasad Yadav did initiate several changes to the structure of the temple management committee, including the removal of longtime "Hindu" general secretary Dwarko Sundrani and the appointment of Bhante Prajnasheel, a close associate of Surai Sansai, as secretary. The Ambedkarite Buddhist leaders were now securely in power, largely in control of the finances and oversight of the daily affairs of the temple.

During their three-year term on the temple management committee, there was considerable tension between the Ambedkarites, international Buddhist organizations like the Maha Bodhi Society, and the local business community in Bodh Gaya (Geary 2012). By and large the residents of Bodh Gaya and several foreign Buddhist monasteries wanted nothing to do with the Ambedkarite movement, fearing that "'another Ayodhya-type' situation would keep pilgrims away, disrupt business, and make a mess of their community" (Doyle 1997, 393). Instead of giving voice to anti-Hindu rhetoric and their ideology of separation, most of the foreign Buddhists distanced themselves from the campaign, viewing the recent upheaval as an internal domestic issue. It is for these reasons that their hold on the Mahabodhi Temple in Bodh Gaya was short-lived, and both Bhante Prajnasheel and Bhadant Anand were removed from the management committee in 2001 under growing scrutiny. During this period of heightened religious antagonism, there was considerable fragmentation among Indian Buddhist groups themselves, including the splintering of the All India Bhikkhu Sangha into two separate groups, the All India Bhikkhu Maha Sangha and the Bodh Gaya Mahabodhi Vihar All India Action Committee, which represents the more militant wing of the Mahabodhi Action Committee. One could argue that the Ambedkarites have not had a lasting influence in Bodh Gaya partly because of the pan-Asian Buddhist identity that I have described in this chapter. Unlike the prominent place of New Buddhism in Ambedkar's state of Maharashtra, in Bodh Gaya the proliferation of international monasteries and the lack of local support have been key factors in undermining exclusive "Indian-Buddhist" demands over sacred space. Although Nagpur-based organizations such as Samaj Kranti continue their agitation, usually on the Buddha *purnima* day each year, these demonstrations have become more muted in recent years and are just one among many public ritual events tied to the annual cycle in Bodh Gaya.

Further, Ambedkar Buddhists from Maharashtra do not represent the wider Indian Buddhist expansion that is currently under way at the navel of

Kids selling postcard packages of foreign Buddhist temples
in Bodh Gaya

the earth. In addition to the All India Bhikkhu Sangha, a growing number
of South Asian Buddhist centers are being built in Bodh Gaya. These include
the Bangladesh Buddhist Monastery, the Vajra Bodhi Society, the Three
Jewels Centre, the Dharmouday Buddha Vihara, the Chakma Buddhist
Temple, the Chandramani Buddha Vihar and Dhamma Chakra Mission,
the Ananda Vihar–Sanga Nayaka Ananda Mitra Memorial and Cultural
Centre, the Tai-Bodhi Kham, the Khuva Boonchum Buddhagaya Tai Temple, the Buddhagaya Banavihara and Meditation Centre, the Bodhidruma–
International Buddhist Sangha Trust, the Bodhi Raja, and the Sukkhita
Bhumi Buddha Vihara–Bihar Buddhist Society. I have included the Three
Jewels Centre because of its ties with Sangharakshita (b. 1925), the founder
of Friends of the Western Buddhist Order and Trailokya Baudhha Maha-
sangha Sahayaka Gana (TBMSG)—the Indian wing of the Western Buddhist
order that was established by Sangharakshita and Dhammachari Lokamitra
in 1979. However, unlike other foreign monasteries at Bodh Gaya, which
have financial support from a pious transnational network of devotees, by
and large, the Indian Buddhist groups face significant economic hardship,
and there is also considerable ambivalence toward the ideology of the
Ambedkar Buddhists and their social and politically motivated cause. The

future role of Indian Buddhism at Bodh Gaya is also limited by the growing economic benefits of heritage and tourism development for the state government. Since Bodh Gaya's designation as a UNESCO World Heritage Site in 2002, Indian Buddhists have certainly been outnumbered by the growing throngs of domestic tourists and Hindu pilgrims who now frequent the land of enlightenment to see the Great Buddha Statue and tour the colorful global landscape of foreign temples and monasteries.

CONCLUSION

> India was the home of the Buddha though in a sense his message embraced the whole world. We do not wish to deny the others their share but why must we not claim our own especially when he was one of the greatest sons of India? (Nehru 1956, 20)

Throughout the twentieth century, and especially following the 1956 Buddha Jayanti, Buddhist pilgrimage activities grew exponentially, activating the collective memory of Bodh Gaya as the navel of the earth and the center of a sacred topography of world Buddhism. Through monastic building, commemorative events, and ritual performances, these rites bridge the historical and narrative forms of social memory with embodied forms of religious practice that inscribe space with sanctity and physically affirm their claim to the new locality (Connerton 1989, Werbner 1996). The spatial appropriation of land by monasteries and temples is perhaps the most visible symbol of the transnational transformation of Bodh Gaya. Through their monastic architecture, these monumental structures provide the "bulwark" of "religious and cultural traditions" that seek to represent both national-cultural essences and contemporary claims of authenticity (Moran 2004, 86).

Ever since the Buddha Jayanti celebrations in 1956, the Indian state and the government of Bihar have been instrumental in encouraging these monastic developments at the place of Buddha's enlightenment. Many of these monasteries were established through foreign government sponsorship in order to serve the laity and cater to visitors at a time when there was little in the way of facilities for those undertaking pilgrimage to Bodh Gaya. Following India's independence, the growth and expansion of transnational networks from the religious diaspora came to reflect the aspirations of Prime Minister Jawaharlal Nehru, who viewed India's Buddhist heritage as a critical site for the ideological production of the nation-state and central to constructing and legitimizing its leading role as a cultural power in the region. With the support of the state government and an international advisory board comprised of Asian Buddhist elites, the religious diaspora helped to create a living taxonomy of national Buddhisms, as envisioned by Dharmapala. Although the number of Tibetan refugees and Himalayan Buddhists on pilgrimage to Bodh Gaya grew substantially following the 1959 Chinese occupation of Tibet, to a large extent, the pattern of Buddhist development following independence continued along Theravada Buddhist lines that mirrored the larger political geography of the dissolving British Empire.[33] However, by the late 1970s and 1980s, Theravada influence at Bodh Gaya had been eclipsed by the growing institutional presence of Mahayana Buddhism and the expanding Vajrayana networks within the Tibetan refugee community.

In view of the proliferation of monastic institutions, the Bodh Gaya Temple Advisory Board met on April 4, 1986, and decided that all Buddhist countries should be directed to maintain a representative "national" character and that land should not be allotted indiscriminately (Banerjee 2000, 143). However, in the historical and descriptive account of the different regional expressions of Buddhism from the late 1980s onward, national articulations of Buddhism proved to be a difficult receptacle for the complex transnational networks of the religious diaspora. This was partly due to a breakdown in the state government's land allocation policy under the Notified Area, but is also indicative of the extra-national reach of Buddhism and the popular appeal of charismatic leaders who now live their lives across borders. Modern transportation and the rapid growth of monasteries in recent decades have to some extent inspired a race for representation among various Buddhist leaders and lineages who compete for recognition by building ever more elaborate and opulent temples and images. At the same time, there is considerable support and cooperation between the Buddhist monasteries, as evidenced by the establishment of the Bodh Gaya Temple Advisory Board, and more importantly, the International Buddhist Council, which aims to look after the collective needs of the growing Buddhist community.

An important issue that is often raised in relation to diasporic religious communities is that of their political loyalty to the nation-state and the extent to which these transnational linkages influence crucial economic and political issues. Although Buddhism is often described as an other-wordly religion, it was essentially a social movement, and the fate of the *sangha* in

India and abroad was closely related to state politics and the fortunes of Asian empires and patrons (Ling 1968, Morris 2006). This long and intricate relationship between Buddhism and state politics remains just as important in Bodh Gaya today. While some of the monastic centers clearly fall under the supervision of national governments and rely on the generosity of the Indian state for land, Buddhist monks and nuns have different axes of affiliation that transcend national boundaries and are part of a growing network of disciples and monastic centers throughout the world.

While national, sectarian, and cultural-linguistic differences undercut a universal conception of Buddhism, the commitment to the symbolic and sacred primacy of place is undeniable in Bodh Gaya today. Through the renewal of pilgrimage activities and collective aspirations toward an enduring symbol of faith, Buddhism takes on the aspect of "world" religion at Bodh Gaya and place identity becomes central to the reconstruction of an international Buddhist ethnoscape. Significantly, the recent Ambedkar movement to liberate the Mahabodhi Temple had limited success largely because it was not representative of the "world religioning" of Bodh Gaya that had been under way throughout the twentieth century (Kemper 2015). As "one of the greatest sons of India," to use Nehru's words, the Buddha is India's gift to the world. And as the Buddhist world now looks to reclaim its holy land, there is an underlying tension between Buddhist cultural heritage anchored in the national polity and the deepening forces of religious globalization that look to transcend it.

3 The Afterlife of *Zamindari*

> In the hot, dusty countryside on the outskirts of Bodh Gaya, India, not much has changed since a wandering ascetic named Siddhartha Guatama first passed through 2,500 years ago. Men in white dhotis still guide plows drawn by water buffalo through a patchwork of brown and green fields. Golden haystacks shaped like stupas shimmer next to acres of mustard and lentils. Women in saris carry baskets of grain on their heads down crooked dirt alleys roamed by chickens, pigs, and hump-backed Brahman bulls. (Cushman cited in Aitken 1995, 78)

WHEN I ARRIVED IN INDIA IN THE WINTER OF 2002–2003, LIKE many visitors to the area, I was captivated by the pastoral rhythm that envelopes the surrounding agricultural landscape. In the authenticity of the village, as Anne Cushman poetically describes, very little has changed since the time of the Buddha over twenty-five hundred years ago. This yearning for a "timeless" and "unchanging" India immune from the destructive forces of modernity has long captivated both the Western and Indian imagination.

This reification of the idyllic, timeless Indian village and countryside masks the complex socioeconomic and political changes that have taken place in the Gaya District. We have seen how the modern rebirth of Bodh Gaya as the place of Buddha's enlightenment is mediated by pilgrimage and the sacralization of space through the built environment of Buddhist monasteries and temples. Although this surge of Buddhist ritual activities owes a great deal to modern developments in transportation and new transnational networks of Buddhist practice, the feudal structure that these monasteries supplant is politically significant both to the region and to wider social changes currently taking place.

Mirroring these changing configurations of religious influence is the Bodh Gaya Math. Located along the riverside road a short distance from the Mahabodhi Temple is the main headquarters of the Shaivite *mahant*—the main abbot, or head, of the Hindu religious order. The Shaivite Dasanami order in Bodh Gaya lays claim to a four-hundred-year history and was one of the largest *zamindars* in Bihar. But today, this Shaivite monastic complex that unfolds

Interior courtyard of the Bodh Gaya Math, with Mahabodhi Temple on the horizon

along a north-south axis next to the Niranjana River is a mere shadow of its former self. Inside the castle-like fortress there are few *sannyasins*, or disciples, to be found, and parts of the building are fast falling into ruins.

In this era of insurgent cultural politics and religious nationalism, exemplified by Rashtriya Swayamsevak Sangh and the Vishwa Hindu Parishad, how does one explain the vertical expansion of international Buddhism and the deterioration of this base of Hindu orthodoxy in south Bihar? To explore these changing social configurations, I examine the nexus of religious and economic power that gave rise to the Bodh Gaya Math's position of dominance as a *zamindar* during the British colonial period and how this was affected by *zamindari* abolition bills, land-gift movements, and land struggles in the aftermath of India's independence. Through my analysis of these changing local and regional power equations I show how the afterlife of *zamindari* has significantly undermined the Math's former suzerainty and given rise to new forms of communal and religious antagonisms.

THE BODH GAYA MATH

The rise of the Bodh Gaya Math builds on a long tradition of patronage of religious endowments in the Magadha region. From the early medieval period (ca. 600–1200 CE), several Buddhist monasteries and education centers rose to prominence, such as Nalanda and Vikramashila, as a result of generous grants of revenue-free land. The solidification of Mughal power by the sixteenth century further consolidated the systematic collection of land revenue and pushed migration further south of the Ganges plains. Emerging out of the old districts of Behar and Ramgarh in 1865, the Gaya District formed a transitional zone between the flat agricultural settlements under Mughal control to the north and the forested highlands of the Chota Nagpur plateau to the south, broken by low hills and isolated peaks. Unlike the northern part of Bihar, which has a long history of continued civilizational growth giving rise to political centralization and urban development, the hills and jungle to the south of Gaya presented a difficult terrain for cultivation and remained thinly populated by non-Hindu aboriginal, or *adivasi*, tribes. However, with the expansion of paddy-based agriculture in the seventeenth century, there was an increase in land revenue measurement under the Mughal *jagir* system, which gave rise to "palatial towns" based on garrisons, trade, and religious activity that emerged at the seats of established landed chiefs, or *zamindars* (Prakash 1990, 70–71).

A *zamindar* can be defined as an aristocrat, typically hereditary, who held vast tracts of land and ruled over and taxed the peasants who lived on the land. The word *zamindar* derives from the Persian term *zamin* (earth/land) and the common suffix *-dar* (holder)—meaning "landholder." In the Indian vernacular, these landholders can be further divided into *rais* (respectable persons), *rajas*, *taluqdars* (holders of an estate, or *taluqa*), and *maliks* (petty proprietors) who received the patronage of ruling elites and enjoyed favorable agrarian and commercial policies (Yang 1989). During the Mughal and British colonial period, for example, the *zamindars* constituted an important layer of the ruling class and were granted various rights and responsibilities in terms of collecting taxes and retaining revenue from land and production. With these entitlements and social privileges, many *zamindars* also acted as key public functionaries imparting judicial and military services at the local level. These informal networks of power contributed to a "limited raj" whereby the colonial administration could control vast territories and populations with only a handful of administrators and troops (Yang 1989). At the same time, the lack of formal state institutions at the local level also meant that much of the rural hinterland was in the grip of powerful and oppressive *zamindari* networks.

As historian Gyan Prakash illustrates in his seminal book *Bonded Histories*, the colonization of agricultural land in this rugged and forested area

to the south of Bodh Gaya would not have been possible without the extension of irrigation. Unlike the north of Bihar, where land had been monopo-
lized by a large number of dominant-caste owners who rose from the ranks
of peasant populations, in the south, relations of labor production were
characterized by an "extreme social hierarchy" whereby a few landlords
imposed themselves upon the existing population by means of immigra-
tion, conquest, taxes, and tribute (Prakash 1990). The need for irrigation
and a servile labor pool formed the social basis for the emergence of several
regional *zamindars* who conquered most of southern Gaya by the early
eighteenth century. Prior to the Battle of Buxar, when Gaya came under
British rule, this area was described as a "disturbed state" as a number of
rival *zamindars* began to expand their local influence in the area (Sinha
1921). Some of the more prominent landed elites that declared their independence following the invasion of Nadir Shah and the dismemberment of
the Mughal government were Kamgar Khan and his brother Mandar Khan,
in Narhat and Samai, to the east; Vishnu Singh, the *zamindar* of Siris and
Kutumba, to the west; Raja Ghulam Hussain Khan, in Pargana Sherghatti;
and the raja of Ramgarh, to the south (O'Malley 2007 [1906]).

This also appears to have been the case for the Bodh Gaya *mahant* from
the Shaiva Dasanami Order. The Dasanami Order (*dasa-nami* means "ten
names") was a federation of Hindu *sannyasins*, or religious mendicants, that
were divided into ten ascetic lineages, each lineage with its own distinctive
name and all of them tracing their spiritual descent from the seventh-
century philosopher of Advaita Vedanta, Sankara (Dazey 1992, Doyle 1997).
Established by Sankara in the four cardinal directions of the Indian subcontinent, these Shaivite Hindu ascetics, also referred to as Gosains, had
come to play an important part in the eighteenth- and nineteenth-century
economy in northern India. Through their annual cycle of pilgrimages
and their "spiritual jurisdiction" over a particular geographic area, they
formed a kind of "religious corporation" structured on a spiritual lineage
of *chelas*, or disciples, and achieved a striking degree of immunity and self-
governance (Bayly 1983, Dazey 1992). They also gained a reputation for
being important traders and soldier monks who controlled the flow of silk
and cotton across North India (Cohn 1964). During the upheaval of the
eighteenth and nineteenth centuries, for example, many of them were in a
strong position to take advantage of the social and political disintegration
of the Mughal Empire through their "ready-made trade networks" as a
result of pilgrimage routes and *maths* scattered throughout northern India
(Cohn 1964, 180–181). However, by the latter part of the nineteenth century,

it was primarily the Punjab commercial classes who rose to prominence along the indigenous trade routes in northern India, and many of the Gosains, like the Giri sect in Bodh Gaya, became settled religious communities who derived wealth not from trade but through their extensive landholdings as *zamindars* (Cohn 1964, 181).

The religio-political order of Bodh Gaya Math was structured on privileged landholdings mostly held free of taxation (see Dirks [1993] for a similar analysis of a South Indian kingdom). Starting from very humble beginnings, Mahadeva Giri (1642–1682) was first credited with building the Hindu monastery and formally was recognized as the chief *mahant*.[1] He was followed by Lal Giri (1682–1720) and Keshava Giri (1720–1748), the latter of whom obtained a *firman* (deed of agreement) in 1727 from the Mughal emperor, Muhammad Shah Alum, to hold the temple and its environs under his possession, including two nearby revenue villages, Mastipur and Taradih. The attribution of royal land grants and villages under Mughal authority continued, with each succeeding *mahant* helping to expand agricultural operations and contributing greatly to the increase of wealth and prosperity of the Math.[2] When a disciple of the Math dies, all his properties, movable or immovable, revert to the monastery.[3]

This growth was not confined to the Mughal period alone. In fact, the acquisition of land and the concession of rent-free villages to the Math appear to have accelerated during the eighteenth and nineteenth centuries, largely because of significant changes to the agrarian economy. Following the extensive documentation of land relations and property rights by the British as part of the Permanent Settlement in 1793, land control became the principal means of determining the social relations of production (Prakash 1990, 83). As a means of extracting profit and strengthening the administrative hold over land tenure, the territorializing legacy of the Permanent Settlement had far-reaching consequences for the British Empire and the social transformation of the Indian rural landscape.[4] Through the objectification and partitioning of land built on a hierarchy of land relations, several *zamindars* were declared "owners" of land and were now in charge of collecting tribute for the British government.

As British Settlement officer E. L. Tanner (1919) points out in the *Final Report on the Survey and Settlement Operations in the District of Gaya*, which covers the time period between 1911 and 1918, the greatest obstacle to the ascertainment of legal rents was the keeping of false records by the landlords themselves, a "habit so ancient, constant and notorious that it might be almost held a custom" (53). As soon as the partition of land commenced, "most of the proprietors began giving their shares out on *mukarrari* leases, some undoubtedly collusive, with the idea of still retaining a hold in the villages even though they lost all proprietary right in them as a result of the partition" (57). Producing false records and reshuffling holdings allowed for undetected illegal enhancements of rent, and a number of co-sharers, most notably the Bodh Gaya *mahant*, took advantage of the situation and became principal proprietors. Due to the benevolent standing of the Shaivite monks, prominent *zamindars* such as Raja Miarajit Singh of Tekari provided revenue-free grants to "religious persons" as a means of diffusing their power and dispersing their landholdings to circumvent the new provincial authorities. Although the land revenue records do not document the Shaivite monks as *maliks*, necessarily, Prakash (1990) asserts that they took on the dual role of recipients of revenue-free villages from *zamindars* to protect themselves from new colonial policies over land.

Thus the Bodh Gaya Math enjoyed the tax privileges of a revenue-free establishment on the basis of its "performance of noble works" and, as a religious endowment, it was also in a position to expand its estate by acquiring new "intermediary tenures" from nearby villages (Singh Bahadur 1893, 3).[5] This is evidenced by the growing list of villages documented in *A Brief History of Bodh Gaya Math*, which shows the consolidation of vast tracts of land under cultivation primarily to the south of Bodh Gaya in the administrative blocks of Mohanpur, Barachatti, and Dobhi. The monastery was in a strategic position to expand its agricultural operations mainly because of the presence of monks in every village. Under the *mahant* Shiva Giri (1820–1846), for example, the religious head had no fewer than fourteen hundred disciples that helped to bring the Math into a "most flourishing condition" (Singh Bahadur 1893, 2). Due to the difficult and labor-intensive demands of cultivation, harvesting, and maintaining the irrigation system in south Bihar, several *kutcheries* (landlord's farmhouses turned office/court) were dispersed and overseen by the religious intermediaries of the Math. These *kutcheries* not only performed a centralizing mechanism over vast tracts of agricultural land but also placed the monks in a strategic position to exploit and supervise a large number of *kamia* (scheduled caste/tribe laborers), who tilled the land through a system of debt servitude known as *kamiauti*.

Kamiauti refers to a social transaction based on an advance of grain, money, and/or a plot of land that would have been given to the *kamia* by the landlord at a specific time of need—usually at a time of marriage for the laborer's son or daughter. In receipt of this transaction, the *kamia* was required to undertake grueling work in order to maintain survival subsistence until the advance was eventually paid back (Herbert 2010, Kunnath 2009). The reality of this coercive relationship was that the laborer became an object of possession and was indebted to the *malik* (or landlord). And, if the debt was not repaid over the course of his life, and it appears that they rarely were, this form of subjugation was transferred to his son and grandsons, forming a generational chain of indebtedness (Prakash 1990). In other words, the *zamindari* not only reterritorialized the physical landscape but also the bodies of the workers and families who tilled the land, especially the Bhuiya—a semi-Hinduized aboriginal caste—who were the most prominent of the agricultural laboring groups in the area.

Under these conditions, as Gyan Prakash describes in *Bonded Histories,* the wealth of the Bodh Gaya Math was greatly enhanced throughout the nineteenth century—from an estimated Rs. 30,000–40,000 in the 1830s to over Rs. 100,000 in 1892 (Prakash 1990, 117–118). The Bodh Gaya Math emerged as one of the largest and most powerful *zamindars* in the region partly because its agricultural practices were wedded to its religious jurisdiction. During the period of Krishna Dayal Giri (1891–1932), for example, there were considerable renovations to the monastic complex and it gained a wide reputation, even among the British, as a place of great learning and ascetic power. These religious and economic entanglements are evident not only in the wide distribution of *sannyasins* who managed the vast agricultural estate but also in the symbolism of the Math's origin story, which explains how the monastery's suzerainty was divinely sanctioned.

Based on the Math's *itihasa* (history), recorded by Singh Bahadur in the late nineteenth century, Mahadeva Giri (1642–1682), the third *mahant,* was a strong devotee of Annapurna, the Hindu Goddess of nourishment, and built a small shrine in front of the Mahabodhi Temple that was dedicated to her.[6] Pleased by this devotion, Annapurna presented Mahadeva with a *katora* (cup) for the purpose of distributing grain, with the added blessing that if the *mahants* would continue to freely distribute alms from the *katora,* "they would never be in want" (Singh Bahadur 1893, 1). Furthermore, this talismanic cup is said to hold exactly enough to satisfy the appetite of whoever receives its contents—man or woman, child or adult.

When Lal Giri (1682–1720) took over as successor to Mahadeva in 1682, he established an almshouse next to the monastery where rice and pulse were distributed daily to "three to five hundred persons up to the present time," writes Singh Bahadur (1893, 3). During times of festival, such as Dussehra, *tilk sankranti,* or regular gatherings of the Gosains (members of

Throne of the Shaiva mahant with *sannyasin* caretaker

the fraternity of all the subordinate Maths), the display of generosity was also said to be of a "grand scale." For example, as part of the *bhandara* (grand feast) that accompanies the death of a *mahant*, a special spiced cake called *mal pua* was allegedly disseminated at the cost of lakhs of rupees, and all the sweets were made of pure ghee.[7]

Several residents of Bodh Gaya that work in the nearby bazaar recalled these stories of benevolent wealth and virtuous power during my fieldwork. Amarnath Gupta, a former driver of the *mahant* who runs a small petrol stand next to the front entrance gates of the Math, narrated a story to me that had been passed on by his father, who was also a former employee of the Math. With his course gray beard and red-beetle-stained teeth, he explained that in the early days, large numbers of Nagas (Shaivite religious ascetics) would come to visit and stay at the Math complex. "Some of these Naga *sadhus* would arrive through the jungle on elephants and with guns," he said. During these visits, the *mahant* was always cordial and ensured they were warmly welcomed with an abundance of food. "However, on one occasion a Naga *sadhu* decided to test the *mahant*, having heard the story of the *katora* cup and its magical powers to distribute food." On the day of his departure, Gupta recalled, "the Naga was provided with a gift basket of food but complained to the servants that it was not full. When the news reached Krishna Dayal Giri, he came down to the courtyard with the *katora* and with his left hand embracing the cup, filled the Naga's basket with four hundred kilos of rice. In disbelief, the Naga apologized for his actions, and the *mahant* replied, 'Why are you coming here to test me? Your stomach must be full in my place. No where else will you find this.'"

The magical properties bestowed upon the Math by the Hindu goddess Annapurna thus strengthened the spiritual authority of the Shaivite monastery, but this was not the only source of sacred validation. The Bodh Gaya *mahant* also claimed to be the principal guardian of the Bodhi tree and the Mahabodhi Temple. In *A Brief History of Bodh Gaya Math*, Singh Bahadur (1893) writes that a significant part of the *mahant*'s income derived from "presents" offered to the Mahabodhi Temple, personal gifts made by his disciples, and from the holy shrines in the Math itself. As noted in chapter 2, throughout the nineteenth century a number of Burmese missions were sent to Bodh Gaya during the reign of the Kon-baung kings with the goal of merit-making and restoring the ancient temple. During this time, several sources indicate that the king's envoys resided with the *mahant* in a nearby guesthouse, and copious offerings were made to the throne of enlightenment (Doyle 1997). Although the religious traffic in "gifts" provided by these royal Buddhist ambassadors must have carried significant prestige and value, this wealth was nothing compared to the reverence and devotion bestowed upon the sacred grounds by Hindu pilgrims.

During the eighteenth and nineteenth centuries, as the Mughal powers declined, Hindu devotion and temple construction surged (Bayly 1983). The patronage of *melas*, the sponsoring of rituals and the participation in pilgrimages, was all part of a "heightened religious sensibility in an age of expanding markets and trade" (Yang 1998, 120). This shift toward popular religious practices played a key role in maintaining the preeminence of many old pilgrimage centers, such as Banares and Gaya. Linked to the ritual traffic in ancestor worship at Gaya was the Bodhi tree—a minor *vedis*, or shrine, within Gaya's extended *sraddha*-performing network. Although the Gayawal priests and the British, through their administration of the pilgrim tax up until 1839, reaped the greatest source of income from the Vaishnava pilgrims, the Bodh Gaya Math also collected donations from pilgrims of all sects who came to offer *pindadana* at the Bodhi tree and other nearby sites. Worshiping at all forty-five *vedis* was seen as a mark of considerable social prestige and cultural capital among the Indian elite during the eighteenth and nineteenth centuries (Doyle 1997, Bayly 1983, Yang 1998). Those who could afford the most extensive (and thus, expensive) of Gaya-*sraddha*

Gaya-*sraddha* pilgrimage network, with Mahabodhi Temple and the Buddha far left

pilgrimages, according to Doyle (1997, 145), consisted primarily of "older princely families; powerful low-caste Mahratta, Jat, Bhumihar, and Rajput rulers; and Bengali nouveaux-riches merchants and government servants— all of whom were invested in demonstrating their power, wealth, and/or social status by visiting and performing elaborate *sraddha* rituals at the largest possible number of holy sites." As an example of "ritual town-building" (Bayly 1983), this upsurge in Hindu pilgrimage activity during the eighteenth and nineteenth centuries likely contributed to much of the commercial foundations of the Bodh Gaya marketplace today.

With the Bodhi tree emerging as an important site of pilgrimage within the network of *sraddha*, the Math was in an ideal position to bring its other-worldly religious providence in line with this worldly expansion of agricultural operations. Given the Math's status as one of the wealthiest and most powerful religious endowments in the state of Bihar, it comes as no surprise that the British authorities were reluctant to antagonize members of the Dasanami order during their reign. Unlike the Gayawal Brahmans, who had a notorious reputation as sly priests who used the pretext of religious benevolence to appropriate benefits from pilgrims, the Dasanami order was viewed in a favorable light—as worthy of honor and respect throughout the country. The Math had a reputation for providing food to the poor and needy, especially during times of famine, and the *mahant* claimed to have rendered assistance to the British during the Mutiny.[8] Partly due to this glowing reputation, the Bodh Gaya Math was exempted from attendance in courts of law on several occasions and was also presented with a "Certificate of Honor" by Queen Victoria when she was proclaimed Empress of India at the extravagant Delhi Imperial Assemblage held on January 1, 1877.

Thus, prior to India's independence, the "objectification of land" by the British Raj had a profound effect on the agrarian political economy of the south Bihar region that was defined by its high agricultural seasonality and the intensive labor needed for irrigation. Land settlement documentation and new legal arrangements initiated by the British government helped the *zamindars* to secure more land and to bind certain social relations to the land itself. It is in this context that the Bodh Gaya Math consolidated its power as a *zamindar* and a religious endowment with the resources to ensure that the landless laborers remained subordinate tenants. The Shaivite *mahant*, as I have also suggested, was by no means a mere rent-receiving landlord; the Math gained divine legitimacy through the ritual distribution of alms and as the principal caretaker of Bodh Gaya's sacred property. Thus the political, religious, and socioeconomic power of the monastery rested in its administration of land and through the received income provided by pilgrims to the sacred Bodhi tree and its surrounding properties. However, this position of hegemonic influence in the Bodh Gaya region was not secure, especially in light of the growing nationalist movement and the challenges to the *zamindari* in the postcolonial period.

AGRARIAN REFORM AND THE BODH GAYA LAND STRUGGLE

In the aftermath of British colonial rule and the violent Telangana uprising in Andhra Pradesh, land reform was central to the legitimacy of the state and the nation-building project.[9] During this period of strong Congress leadership, a number of wide-ranging agrarian reforms were enacted by Jawaharlal Nehru with the goal of transforming the colonial system, or "unsettling the permanent settlement," and improving the socioeconomic conditions of the peasant classes. India's new socialist-leaning leaders believed that the abolishment of *zamindari* and the equitable distribution of land were critical to the success of the nation.

These agrarian reforms took place in two broad phases within new modern democratic structures (Chandra et al. 2000). The first phase involved "institutional reforms" that started soon after independence and focused on the abolition of *zamindars* and other intermediaries, tenancy reforms to provide greater security to tenants, ceilings on major landholdings, and lastly, the launching of a number of cooperative and community development programs. The second phase involved "technological reforms" and took place in the mid- to late 1960s during the Green Revolution and the industrialization of the agricultural economy. It was hoped that the redistribution of land and the reduction of social inequalities would give farmers an incentive to produce more and help establish India as a developed, self-sufficient nation.

As part of the institutional reforms, *zamindari* abolition bills were introduced in several states within two years of independence, and by the late 1950s, they were firmly established in the legislature. Despite the broad consensus among Congress leaders regarding the abolishment of *zamindari*, with agriculture deemed a "state subject," all the central leaders could do was set certain guidelines with the expectation that state leaders would implement the reforms (Brass 1990). This process proved to be more complicated than expected, as the means of enacting these structural policies within the various state assemblies provoked some criticism and opposition from state leaders concerned about antagonizing the rural elites and land-controlling castes. As a result of the prolonged debates and amendments surrounding the legislation, several years passed between the introduction of the draft bills and their actual enactment. Moreover, even after the laws were passed at the state level, some landlords turned to the judicial system to challenge the bills and defer implementation. The result of these delays meant the land reform policies were co-opted by vested interests, poor landless laborers were forcefully evicted in anticipation of the new laws, and to a large extent the inequalities of the social order were preserved. As Chandra et al. (2000, 376) point out, the resulting evictions were tied to the inherent weaknesses in the abolition act and tenancy reforms, which ensured that many *zamindars* could obtain large tracts of land through the loose and ambiguous language of "personal cultivation."[10]

Similarly, the establishment of land ceilings with the goal of making land distribution more equitable was fraught with legal obstacles. In the early years of independence, the All India Kisan Sabha and the Congress Party established an economic program to ensure that a ceiling was placed on landownership whereby all remaining surplus land could be acquired and redistributed among village cooperatives under the *panchayat* system. Although these land ceilings were integrated into the First Plan (1951–1956), the exact limit, as with the implementation of the tenancy reforms, had to be resolved

by each provincial government, given the country's diverse agrarian histories and regional land issues. These efforts to establish firm land ceilings
through the various provincial nodes were also hindered by the absence of
clear land documentation records and the collusion between lower-level
revenue officials and the *zamindars*, who were unwilling to release information. It was not until 1961, following a wave of criticism at the Nagpur Convention of the Indian Congress in 1959, that the Land Ceiling Legislation
was finally introduced and formulated through the various state governments. As a result of these delays, as well as the nature of the legislation, land
ceiling reform had a muted impact on the *zamindars*, who devised various
strategies to retain excess land under false transactions (*benami*) in the
names of relatives or fictitious persons (Chandra et al. 2000, 387).

Although Bihar was the first state in independent India to legislate on
land reforms, it was also here that landlords put up the most resistance given
the high proportion of land under the control of a few powerful *zamindars*.
In this respect, the Bodh Gaya Math stands as a paradigmatic case in point.
When the *zamindari* abolition bills were first announced, the *mahant*
claimed personal rights over a vast territory of villages in the Gaya District.
All of this land had been vested in a trust that was originally formed in 1932
as a means of safeguarding and managing the rent-free estate under the
British Raj. When the Bihar Religious Trust Board (an autonomous board
established by government to oversee the affairs of the state's numerous
religious trusts) challenged the excess land under the trust name, its position was upheld by the revenue court and again by the Patna High Court.
The *mahant* than proceeded to appeal to the Supreme Court, and at this
stage, the parties involved, which included the Bihar government, the Bihar
Religious Trust Board, and the *mahant*, came forward with a compromise
under which the court decreed 2,300 acres to be the property of the Math
(under the Bodh Gaya Trust)—out of which the *mahant* was entitled to
rights over 240 acres and a monthly sum of Rs. 1,000 for "personal
expenses." The remaining lands, including some four thousand villages
(amounting to an estimated 9,577 acres) were decreed the "personal property" of the *mahant*, and neither the government nor the Bihar Religious
Trust Board could interfere with property management. The settlement was
dated September 9, 1957 (Kelkar and Gala 1990).

This unusual settlement between the Bodh Gaya *mahant* and the government was probably due to the ceiling legislation that was to be implemented
within a few years. Once the Bihar Land Ceiling Act was firmly established,
these laws would effectively nullify the earlier settlement and require the

Math to relinquish all of its excess land under "personal property" and in the name of the trust.[11] In reality, however, after the court decree of September 1957 the *mahant* gifted, sold, or settled all his "personal" lands in the names of 680 *chelas*, or disciples, many of whom, in turn, sold or transferred their land to others. Such transactions continued throughout the 1960s and 1970s, and even after all these transfers, the *mahant* still allegedly held over 1,712 acres of land in his personal name (Kelkar and Gala 1990). In terms of the Trust of Math lands, a formal notice was eventually issued under the Bihar Land Ceiling Act (1961) to surrender the surplus land, but it was not enforced for several years. During this impasse, the *mahant* further divided the Math land into seventeen separate trusts formed by the Deed of Arrangement of 1970 in the names of deities traditionally associated with the Math. As a result of the subdivision of the Math into small parcels of land below the legal ceilings and incorporated as "religious trusts," the estate was now arguably within the limits set by law.

Although the breakup of the Bodh Gaya Trust was contested and the government declared a substantial amount of the trust lands as surplus, it remained tied up in court for several years. There is little doubt that the chief manager of the Math—Jairam Giri-was a key figure in enabling the Math to manipulate the courts and maneuver through these legal obstacles. Jairam Giri was second in command to the elected *mahant*, Dhansukh Giri, and throughout the late 1960s and 1970s he also served as a cabinet minister in the state government and maintained close political ties with the ruling Congress Party.

The efforts to undermine the polarization of wealthy landlords and the exploited peasantry were not confined to the government. Running parallel with the institutional reforms under the Nehruvian government was the *bhoodan andolan*, or land-gift movement, led by Maharashtran-born, Acharya Vinoba Bhave (1895–1982). Frequently cited as the spiritual successor of Gandhi, Vinoba Bhave organized an all-India federation of social workers under the banner Sarvodaya Samaj, with the singular goal of obtaining fifty million acres of land through peaceful and nonviolent means. Walking on foot from village to village, the saintly Vinoba Bhave and his followers marched across the Indian countryside as part of their *padayatra* and looked to persuade large landowners to give one seventh of their land as *bhoodan* for distribution among the landless. Given the influence of the Champaran District of northern Bihar, which propelled Gandhi's civil disobedience movement, along with the entrenched social divisions between landowners and the landless, it is not surprising that

Vinoba Bhave invested a significant amount of time in the region. Accord-ing to Ramagundam (2006, 82), the state of Bihar was Vinoba's land of experiment, and it was the Gaya District that became his "laboratory for a non-violent revolution of land redistribution." Beginning in September 1952 and for the next eighteen months, Vinoba Bhave walked across Bihar and persuaded powerful landlords such as the Bodh Gaya *mahant* to vol-untarily gift their lands.

Under the Gaya District Bhoodan Collection Committee, the goal of obtaining land was met with some success in the area, and several large pledges were offered by prominent *zamindars*, including the Bodh Gaya *mahant*. Although Vinoba did not reach the three-lakh acres he had origi-nally hoped for, the number of "gift-deeds" offered by the landlords far exceeded the quota. As Ramagundam (2006) points out, it was also here that a number of problems with the *bhoodan* movement began to creep in. First, many of the "gift-deeds" that had been pledged by the wealthy land-lords consisted of lands that were not viable agricultural units; they were poorly irrigated and deemed unfit for cultivation. This included forest areas, barren wastelands, and riverbeds, which had historically come under the control of *zamindars* during the Permanent Settlement. Second, there were a number of anomalies and discrepancies when it came to the process of land confirmation and distribution by the government and the *bhoodan* collection committee. There were many false declarations of donations, and some of the land had also been sold, which effectively invalidated the trans-action. As a result of the myriad conspiracies over land allocation and innovative schemes to dispossess those who tilled the land, the task of redistribution became prey to all sorts of maneuverings.[12]

People in Bodh Gaya echo these views today. For example, Dr. Tulku, a retired professor in Buddhist studies at Magadh University, explained that when he first arrived in the early 1960s the *mahant* was still ruling the area. During that time, "there was no need for a court or District Magistrate. Even they would come and bow to the feet of the *mahant*. The area was completely dominated by the *mahant* . . . he was the *sarkar* [the functional equivalent of a ruling government or overlord for the region]. And, when his car rode through town, two people would sit next to the driver who were very strong and everyone would stand up to show respect."

Thus, despite Nehru's efforts to implement agrarian reform and elimi-nate *zamindari*, to a large extent the dominant classes seized the apparatus of the colonial state and remained socially and politically isolated from the popular masses. However, by the late 1960s and early 1970s, increasing political repression, violent peasant uprisings, and strong movements for democratic rights had emerged. Under these changing social and political circumstances the Bodh Gaya Math would come under increasing pressure and scrutiny. It was in this social milieu that the poular socialist leader in Bihar Jayaprakash Narayan (better known as JP) called for the dissolution of the state assembly and launched a student-led campaign for a total revolution.[13]

To aid in his purification of government and politics, JP formed the Chatra (student) and Jan (people's) struggle committee, or Samitis, which would serve to implement these revolutionary reforms. One particular wing of these Samitis was the Chatra-Yuva Sangharsh Vahini (CYSV)—an organization of students and youth workers committed to breaking up the power structure in rural areas, improving the lives of the landless laborers, and raising the consciousness of the people. His dictum for the CYSV was that the struggle on behalf of any particular area had to be led by persons drawn from within that community, and the struggle had to remain nonviolent (Chandra 2003, 252–253). The membership was restricted to those under thirty years of age, and included women in every tier of the organization.

Two prominent Sarvodaya leaders from South India, Sankaralingam Jagannathan and his wife Krishnammal, responded to Jayaprakash Narayan's call for "total revolution."[14] The two Sarvodaya leaders had participated in the earlier student demonstrations in Patna and stayed at the Samanvay Ashram for some time. It was during their time in Bodh Gaya that Jagannathan and Krishnammal became aware of the brutal conditions of the landless laborers and their connections with the Bodh Gaya monastery, especially the vast network of *kutcheries*, from a twenty-two-year-old son of a Math employee named Pradeep. After appealing to the district magistrate of Gaya and the *mahant* directly, Jagannathan and Krishnammal became convinced that pressure needed to be applied by the masses themselves.

In order to mobilize support for the Bodh Gaya land struggle, Jagannathan asked Pradeep to take a leading role in the agitation. When I interviewed Pradeep about his encounter with Jagannathan forty-plus years ago, he noted that at first he was reluctant to be involved, especially given his close ties with the monastery and the family benefits derived from these arrangements over a long period. Retelling his meeting with Jagannathan at his family home one afternoon, he explained how Jagannathan was surprised to see over a hundred landless laborers of the Bodh Gaya Math *kutcheries* leaving the fields of the Math to take lunch. "All the male members were half naked, barely wearing clothes, and the women were covered in mud," he recalled. "Then Jagannthan asked me: 'Who are they?' And I replied, 'They are the landless laborers working for the Math.' 'But the *mahant* . . . is this not a religious place?' he asked. At that point Jagannathan convinced me that the Bodh Gaya Math is for development of the Hindu religion and these workers should not be hungry and half-naked."

After deciding to fight against the *mahant*, the group began to collect information from the surrounding villages and describe the means of agitation against the Math. These efforts to mobilize the laborers and raise the consciousness of the oppressed culminated in a thee-day hunger strike outside the Math building in April 1975. On this occasion JP visited Bodh Gaya in support of the movement and addressed the crowds, telling them not to fear the tyranny of the *mahant* and his henchmen. Lending weight to the cause, especially among the *dalits*, was also Pradeep, whose family members were employed by the Bodh Gaya Math. Despite these initial efforts and inroads into the surrounding villages, the movement faltered as a result of the state of emergency that was called by Prime Minister Indira Gandhi on June 25, 1975. Several leading activists and laborers were placed in jail, and the movement quickly dissipated.

Following the elections of 1977, which led to the removal from office and arrest of Indira Gandhi, the land struggle once again revived, this time with the full backing of the Chatra-Yuva Sangharsh Vahini. Given the earlier groundwork of Sarvodaya activists and Pradeep, members of the CYSV now chose Bodh Gaya as the *saghan kshetra*—the "intensive area of struggle"—because of the disproportionate concentration of agricultural land in the control of the Math (Sinha 1991, Kelkar and Gala 1990).

The first demonstration took place outside the gates of the Shaiva Monastery on April 8, 1978. Several hundred student volunteers and landless laborers sat in protest against the ceiling surplus and *benami* lands, chanting, "Jo zameen ko boye jote, voh zameen ka malik hai" (Those who sow and plough the land are the owners of the land) (Kelkar and Gala 1990). Following the demonstration, CYSV leaders announced that there would be full-time advocacy work and mobilization activities by a team of volunteers to increase pressure on the Math through a noncooperation movement on the four main blocks tied to the monastery: Sherghatti, Barchatti, Mohanpur, and Bodh Gaya proper. Drawing on the groundwork of Jagannathan and utilizing strategies employed by Naxalite groups, a handful of volunteers, or "movement officers," traversed the countryside over the next few years organizing *mazdoor-kisan samitis* and meeting, eating, and working with the *dalits* in no fewer than forty villages in the Gaya District (Kunnath 2009, Louis 2002). As one student activist, Priyadarshi, recalled during an interview in Patna, "We were committed to peaceful means, not like the Naxalite groups who carry arms. There was to be no means of violence; this was our conviction. But for mixing with the people we followed the Naxalite way, by living with the untouchables in their houses and eating with them. Those days the food among the families was inhuman," he recalled. "I was also living with them, but it was very difficult."

After months of networking and mobilizing laborers across the four main blocks in the Gaya District, the CYSV activists began to concentrate their efforts in Gosain Pesra, a village that had been a key site of resistance during Jagannathan's time. This village had a spacious old *kutcherie* that was used by the monks and staff of the Math who lived there and supervised the cultivation done by eighty *kamias*, nearly all of them from the Bhuiya caste (Sinha 1991). From Gosain Pesra, many of the *dalits* began to implement a series of noncooperation tactics that included boycotting the winter harvest crops and interfering with contract laborers that had been hired by the Bodh Gaya Math to carry out seasonal work. With the village used as an example, the noncooperation tactics helped to inspire wider agitation in the surrounding areas, including Mastipur, located directly west of the Mahabodhi Temple, near the Indo Nipponji Temple. It was on the outskirts of this village, where the Shakyamuni College is located today, that the land struggle reached a new level of intensity. On August 8, 1979, a violent clash erupted between the *mahant*'s henchmen and the *dalits*, resulting in the death of two laborers and an employer of the Math (Pradeep's uncle).[15]

Although the attack on the Math employee threatened to derail the reputation of the Bodh Gaya land movement as a nonviolent struggle, the confrontation led to the arrest of several Shaiva monks, including the powerful manager of the estate, Jairam Giri. Among the landless laborers, this was seen as a major achievement and the beginning of the downfall of the Bodh Gaya Math.

In the face of mounting pressure and persistent agitation by the CYSV activists and landless laborers, the Bodh Gaya *mahant* once again turned to the Indian judicial system to protect his vested interests. He filed an appeal to both the State High Court and eventually the Supreme Court as a means of blocking the demands for redistribution and challenging the findings of the commission that had been investigating the Math's land since 1978. In August 1987, after years of deliberation, the Supreme Court reached the conclusion that the Math could only have a maximum of seventy-five acres of land in the names of deities and twenty-five acres in the name of the *mahant*. In other words, the movement led by the former landless laborers and youthful CYSV activists had succeeded in liberating some 3,000 acres of ceiling surplus land (as declared by the government in 1979–1980) and another 3,679 acres of surplus land that was to be distributed to the rural poor (Kelkar and Gala 1990). For many, this order by the Supreme Court seemed to be the final deathblow to the Bodh Gaya Math and its longstanding system of labor servitude, and it strengthened the determination of the rural poor to continue their struggle for rights to land and livelihood.

BUDDHISM AND JUNGLE RAJ

The decline of the Bodh Gaya Math has been one of the more significant events in Bodh Gaya's recent history yet is often overlooked or downplayed by contemporary scholars, who emphasize the recent global Buddhist resurgence at the site. The Math's decline, however, is important because the historical trajectory of heritage legislation in Bodh Gaya has to be read alongside over three centuries of agricultural reform and struggle in the surrounding landscape. These historical conditions, which predate the arrival of World Heritage, deeply inform the ways in which current residents come to make claims over space and place. The 1987 court decision stripping the Math of its illegal landholdings also overlapped with a particularly volatile period in Bihar involving a near collapse of law and order, and a dramatic restructuring of power relations that became synonymous with "Jungle Raj" (Das 1992, Yadav 2001; Thakur 2000, 2006). Arvind Das, in his *Republic of Bihar* (1992), characterized Jungle Raj as the law of the jungle, where the uncivility of civil society becomes the norm. Jungle Raj, arguably, finds its ultimate embodiment in Lalu Yadav, the controversial and unapologetic politician with criminal links who ruled the state for fifteen years between 1990 and 2005.[16]

During this period of rapid decentralization and the violent dismantling of traditional feudal power structures and caste hierarchies in Bihar, a number of charismatic leaders from "backward castes" rose to prominence, modeling themselves after the success of Lalu. In Bodh Gaya, for example, one politician who rose to fame was the tough-talking leader of the Paswan caste—Rajesh Kumar. Although Kumar is not originally from Bodh Gaya, he settled there in the mid-1970s at the peak of the land struggle movement and slowly began his political ascent as the Bodh Gaya Math was declining.[17]

Arjun, a shopkeeper in the Bodh Gaya bazaar, mentioned that "when Rajesh Kumar first arrived in Bodh Gaya, he was not that proud. He was not wearing white kurta pajamas yet." But with support from the community and the decline of the *mahant*'s power, Rajesh Kumar began to "walk more proudly."

With the high concentration of scheduled castes in the Gaya District and Bodh Gaya Block, the emergence of leaders like Kumar helped to raise the political consciousness of low-caste groups and some of India's poorest and most marginalized. As a reserved constituency for scheduled castes in the Magadh division, political parties can only put candidates forward that belong to groups such as Musahara, Paswan, Dusadh, and Manjhi. Thus, rather than aspiring to move up the social ladder in what is commonly referred to as "Sanskritization," low-caste individuals in Bodh Gaya claim lower status in order to access the benefits allotted to disadvantaged communities; such self-identification is also part of the heightened political consciousness of these groups. Nevertheless, social power in Bihar still inheres largely in controlling the land, and this has consequences for foreign Buddhist groups who look to establish a monastery or temple in Bodh Gaya.

As noted in the previous chapter, several Asian Buddhist communities were provided land on long-term lease agreements from the government of Bihar under the Notified Area Committee. This policy of land distribution was established in the decade following India's independence and continued until the mid-1980s, when it was largely supplanted by alternative land acquisition methods and strategies deployed by an expanding Buddhist population. Laws such as the Land Acquisition Act (1894) and the Transfer of Property Act (1884) prevent the direct purchase of land by foreign nationals, but Buddhist groups can acquire freehold land and register their monastery as a charitable trust or religious society, a process akin to establishing a nongovernmental organization under the Societies Registration Act (1860).[18] The Societies Registration Act was first enacted by the British colonial government to provide a legal context for voluntary organizations that had become widespread and were perceived as a potential threat to British rule (Bornstein 2009). Under this act, foreigners can acquire land for the purpose of building religious structures, but they cannot be involved in commercial activities. Furthermore, in order to receive tax exemptions from the Indian government under Section 80G, an Indian majority is required in the overall structure of the registered governing body, which also must demonstrate that foreign contributions are being utilized for charitable aims and public welfare objectives.[19]

The legal context for charity in India, as anthropologist Erica Bornstein (2012) shows in her book *Disquieting Gifts*, is an incredibly complicated landscape and there are currently nine laws regulating giving practices. Built on the architecture of colonial legislation and more current attempts to transform these laws at both national and state levels, these laws have created ample room for "extensive bureaucratic tangles" and "potential government corruption" (Bornstein 2009, 641). Numbers provided by the Ministry of Home Affairs indicate that foreign contributions to religious societies in India amounted to Rs. 10,803 crore (one crore is equal to Rs. 10 million) through over twenty thousand registered associations and nongovernmental organizations in 2008–2009 (Vij-Aurora 2011). According to Vij-Aurora, this number is likely an underestimate because "more than 15,000 organizations failed to submit their account books to the government as is legally mandated" (50). Although the Indian government has recently clamped down on foreign contributions to NGOs under the Narendra Modi government, many religious organizations did not disclose their source of funds in the past, and there were few measures in place to document the extent of funding they were receiving locally and/or from abroad. These challenges are compounded by the structural limitations of the Foreigners Division of the Ministry of Home Affairs, which is chiefly responsible for these regulations rather than the provincial state governments.

In other words, as powerful vectors of charitable giving, religious societies and trusts can "form a large undocumented economy" in which donors and recipients can exist outside account books and taxation (Bornstein 2009, 640). This lack of documentation, "combined with the prevalence of 'paper charities'—false charities set up in name only to shelter funds and provide tax advantages—[can] perpetuate an environment of growing suspicion and distrust surrounding the work of the nonprofit sector" (641). These suspicions are particularly heightened in a pilgrimage site like Bodh Gaya, where deep social inequalities are entrenched and where some wealthy transnational Buddhist networks—in the eyes of some local residents—have simply replaced the *zamindars* of earlier times.

Linked to these suspicions is the virtuous practice of *dana*, which refers to the religiously sanctioned practice of "generosity" or "giving" and is universally recognized as one of the most basic human virtues and a source of great merit in the Indian context (Parry 1986, Bornstein 2012, Copeman 2011). Of the various expressions that *dana* can take in a Buddhist context, the most valued form is directed toward the Buddha and the *sangha*, who represent the highest moral cultivation and physical embodiment of religious ideals. As institutional receptors of generosity, the monks and nuns who reside at the various monasteries are benefactors of this ritual exchange and sacred reciprocity, where virtuous deeds at a holy place translate into a field of merit. Among the large number of Buddhist pilgrims who visit Bodh Gaya during the winter season and stay at the pilgrim lodges run by the various monasteries, *dana* is often presented as a concrete transaction, usually in the form of money (often foreign currency), food, and clothing such as robes. In exchange, the laity are the recipients of teachings, counseling, ritual performances, and above all merit—all of which can affect their present and future lives. Thus as a crucial source of economic sustenance, the spiritual economy of *dana* circulates widely through the monasteries in Bodh Gaya and is especially prevalent during auspicious ritual occasions such as the full-moon days and robe ceremonies (*kathina dana*) that mark the end of the monsoon season.

Given the importance of these merit-filled practices in Bodh Gaya, some intense rivalries have developed with Indian hoteliers, who also look to benefit economically from the international Buddhist pilgrimage traffic. Several hoteliers I spoke with during my fieldwork referred to these Buddhist monasteries as "five-star religious centers" or "spiritual resorts" that provide premium lodging and hospitality to international pilgrims on preplanned tours.[20] One hotelier, Ajay, claimed that these monasteries are *not* running as centers of worship but as an industry exploiting government tax breaks, running shopping complexes, and conducting business for their own people as "mini-embassies." The hoteliers, he explained, must pay taxes and other levies required under domestic state laws. "There are five to seven busloads staying at the monasteries at any given time," he said. "Some say they provide *geisha* and air-conditioned rooms. The Buddha says we should leave behind the luxurious life, yet the Buddhists are providing all these services and it is creating a hurdle in the livelihood for many local people." For these reasons the Bodh Gaya Hotel Association has petitioned the Ministry of Tourism to investigate, demanding greater transparency and clearer guidelines for foreign donations. With a clear sense of frustration in his voice, he continued, "Monasteries should not do business or they should be charged with taxes. We have to pay luxury taxes on rooms, meals, commercial electricity bills, commercial gas bills, sales tax, and income tax on all transactions. There are also municipal taxes on the land we are running and this stands in sharp opposition to the monasteries."

One specific point of contention between the hoteliers and the growing Buddhist monastic community in Bodh Gaya are the fixed rates offered by some monasteries for pilgrim lodging. Although several monasteries suggest a recommended donation for accommodation based on the practice of *dana*, many centers offer fixed rates but strongly object to the idea that they should pay a holding tax to the Bihar state government that reflects their commercial (expensive) or residential (inexpensive) rates. For example, the former *bhikkhu*-in-charge of the Sri Lankan Maha Bodhi Society, Bhante Seewalee, noted that pilgrims and religious-based tourists have a different motivation when they come to the place of enlightenment. "Their purpose is different from visiting the Taj Mahal," Seewalee told me. "This is a religious and peaceful atmosphere. They meet with monks and do *puja* [acts of worship]. No one can demand of the tourists or pilgrims where they should stay." The problem, from his point of view, is that the Indian hoteliers are putting pressure on Sinhalese pilgrims to stay at their establishments. "But there are those people who are going to holy places and want to stay in a *dharamshala*. It is the same with Hindu pilgrims, Thai people . . . Thai temple, Burmese . . . Burmese temple. This is mainly for reasons of food, language, culture, and *puja*. Others think the monasteries run like hotels, offering air-conditioning . . . but we are not living in ancient times; we also need these facilities."

In line with Seewalee, a Vietnamese abbot countered that Buddhist monasteries do not advertise "cheaper rates," "better accommodation," or "compensation to the customer." "We never put forth that kind of advertising," he said. "If we are initiating this kind of thing, then we are in a position to be blamed. We have no advertisement like 'customer satisfaction guaranteed' or 'around the clock hospitality.' Monasteries believe in religious practice and pilgrims have respect and reverence. No one can stop them."[21] These ongoing disputes and growing commercial/religious antagonisms have recently prompted the Bihar state government to prepare a database of foreign monasteries, and they are considering implementing new regulatory provisions that will require monasteries with more than ten rooms to be designated as commercial ventures. The monasteries must also prove to the municipal authorities that the rooms are being used for religious purposes only.

A few Buddhist organizations, like the Daijokyo Buddhist Temple, are now having to renegotiate their thirty-year land lease. Previously, the land was leased to monasteries at roughly Rs. 20,000 to 30,000, but they are now being charged upward of eight to nine lakh (roughly Rs. 900,000) alongside other annual land fees and charges (Qadir 2016). As Tibetan monk Lama Kelsang explained from his monastery, "In the 1970s there were very few Buddhist pilgrims and tourists to Bodh Gaya. It was the development of

Buddhist monasteries that spurred the growth of tourism," he stated. "The problem," with respect to the Indian hoteliers, "is that they never realized this. [And] with the growth of visitors to Bodh Gaya many of the politicians started building hotels and became jealous of the monasteries." This was followed by a downturn in pilgrimage activity that left many of the hotels without any guests, he explained. "So they started accusing us and informing the government, writing in the newspapers . . . all bad information. The hotels even formed a committee attacking the monasteries accusing them because of their lack of customers." In response to these accusations and the escalating tariffs imposed on the foreign monasteries, several members of the expatriate Buddhist community refused to pay the taxes for several years.[22] Not only have these ongoing quarrels and disputes over hospitality services redefined the spatial environment in terms of growing commercial and religious antagonisms, but they have also heightened communal fault lines between Buddhist and Hindu communities in Bodh Gaya. As Bhante Seewalee from the Maha Bodhi Society explained, "No other monasteries in India are paying. This is a charitable project," he said with emphasis. "The local Indians are thinking we are receiving so much money from foreigners. Sometimes we feel very sad; this is Hindu territory and no one is supporting us. Instead we are attacked. They are always looking down upon us. This is creating a strong Hindu-Buddhist sectarian view. They forget that it is because of the monasteries that Bodh Gaya has developed."

While many of these Buddhist monasteries do create employment opportunities and also contribute through various charitable endeavors and social welfare projects, from the viewpoint of many hoteliers and tour operators, they are also in direct competition with Indian-run businesses and services. For these reasons, hotels have begun to diversify their economic portfolios, with some hoteliers looking to promote Bodh Gaya as a wedding destination to make up for the loss of Buddhist pilgrims, especially in the off-season. Given the surplus of hotels that offer a range of price-points, it is not uncommon to have droves of boisterous men from nearby towns using the streets of Bodh Gaya for their *baraat* (a groom's wedding procession) and the hotel grounds for lavish wedding celebrations and ceremonies that last late into the night. The fireworks, loud music, generators, and accumulated refuse associated with these occasions have certainly strained the already tenuous relationship with the Buddhist monastic community.

One example of a unique hotel resort that aims to capitalize on pious Buddhist pilgrims, wedding parties, and corporate clientele for conferences

"Goa in Bodh Gaya"—signage for the Sambodhi Retreat

and meetings is the luxurious Sambodhi Retreat. A novel experiment in religious tourism, the resort is located near the village of Hathiar and was launched in November 2008 by construction industry giant Vinay Tiwari, from the Chhapra District. With its advertising slogan "Goa in Bodh Gaya," the retreat offers "a heaven on this earth, a heaven which not only provides luxury accommodation and best of all facilities" but also "a unique natural experience for the self-realization of you and your family."

When I sat down with Manoj, one of the managers, in a pyramidal hut, he informed me that this was the first state-of-the-art luxury resort built in Bihar. With unobstructed views of the Mahabodhi Temple across the Niranjana River, Sambodhi offers a retreat center with a range of luxury services that include spa treatments and a beauty clinic, world-class dining, conference facilities and leadership programs, outdoor and indoor games such as billiards, hot yoga, meditation and gym space, a swimming pool, a garden area with manufactured waterfalls and fountains, a golf cart for guests, a "hookah" bar, and a nightclub. According to Manoj, "There are many hotels in Bodh Gaya but no resorts that are stretched over eight acres of land along the riverside where the Buddha walked." Although Sambodhi Retreat is certainly not Goa, the place is definitely psychedelic with its Green Cave Duplex rooms, Egyptian-modeled pyramidal cottage, Igloo-inspired

Eco-houses, and reconstructed Thai village. It is hard to imagine a remote place like Sambodhi Retreat surviving in this competitive market, but judging by the number of guests who were there to attend an Indian petroleum conference and business meeting, they may just pull it off.

Conflicts over a "virtuous economy" and the blurred distinctions between religious and economically motivated hospitality at Bodh Gaya are inextricably tied to the escalating land prices in the surrounding area. Increased competition over space in close proximity to the Mahabodhi Temple has brought a huge inflation of land prices, and most land is no longer affordable for Bodh Gaya residents. Many Buddhist groups and Indian entrepreneurs, like Tiwari of Sambodhi Retreat, are now looking to acquire property in the surrounding area, where agricultural land is still relatively inexpensive. When I spoke with Aadesh, a social worker in Bodh Gaya, he explained that in the 1980s, Rs. 6,000 (US$125) per *katha* (approximately 720 square feet) would have been considered a high price. Now it is four lakhs (Rs. 400,000, or US$7,000 to 8,000) per *katha*. For Bodh Gaya residents like Aadesh, these skyrocketing prices are directly related to the mushrooming of well-financed international Buddhist monasteries. The accelerated conversion of agricultural land into religious architecture over the past twenty to thirty years serves as a daily reminder of the purchasing power of these Buddhist transnationals and their networks of devotees. And it is precisely under these conditions that Buddhist groups have been susceptible to various forms of corruption, bribery, and extortion.

While most foreign nationals acquire freehold land and register their monastery as a charitable trust or society, some acquire land through a land broker, in contravention of the Land Acquisition Act, and also violate building construction laws. Determined to gain a clearer picture of these complicated exchanges and the moral calculus involved, I visited Dip Nath, a well-known lawyer in the nearby city of Gaya who specializes in land relations for foreign nationals. From his office, Dip Nath explained to me that court cases have multiplied since the early 1990s because of the fraudulent behavior of the land mafia working in collusion with corrupt revenue officials. He said, "If they [Buddhist groups] choose to follow the crooked path, there are numerous ways to exploit gullible foreigners and also take advantage of the poor uneducated people who own the land." These misdeeds, according to Dip Nath, include the sale of government land, multiple sale of the same plot, and the transfer or leasing of nonsalable land allotted by the government to *dalit* beneficiaries during the redistribution of Bodh Gaya Math surplus land. After the land is purchased and construction begins, conflicting reports over the land title begin to emerge, providing ample opportunities for extortion.

One well-known case of fraudulent behavior is that of the Nyingma Buddhist Institute, which had been embroiled in legal battles for nearly fifteen years. The popular Nyingma Monlam, or World Peace Ceremony, has become a regular feature of Bodh Gaya's annual ritual cycle, bringing thousands of Tibetan Buddhist monks, nuns, and lay practitioners to the sacred locality over the course of three weeks in the winter season. In light of the growing importance of the Nyingma Monlam, five acres of private land were acquired from different landowners in the early 1990s to provide the necessary lodging for upward of ten thousand devotees each year.

The manager of the Nyingma Institute in Bodh Gaya explained to me some of the challenges Tibetans have faced in the past due to the lack of accommodation during these major religious gatherings. For example, as part of the Kalachakra teachings in 1985, "tents were scattered all around the Kalachakra *maidan* and people were just sleeping on the ground," he said. "Due to the poor conditions, people were getting sick as a result of all the dust and dirt. There were also unnecessary local people entering into the tents and stealing things . . . There was absolutely no safety at all," he complained. "If storms were coming through, we were also washed out by rain and wind. There were all these problems, so Rinpoche decided to give us land for these safety reasons."

Two years after construction of the Nyingma Institute began on the five-acre plot of land, the manager was confronted by a well-known agitator with ties to the land mafia, claiming that this land had belonged to his ancestors. These accusations led to a district court case in 1996 between the rival camps and continued for another four years, all the while blocking the Nyingma Institute from further construction. Although this is not the place to examine the specifics of the land dispute, in the end, the Gaya District judge (some say he was bribed) rejected the land title of the Tibetan Buddhist organization and required them to pay a hefty fee. This response prompted the Nyingma Institute to take further legal action and raise the case before the Patna High Court, and after several years of legal deliberations, the High Court decided to revoke the lower court decision, declaring a "stay order."

Matters appeared to be settled, but after two years, the same judge from the earlier decision returned as the criminal judge magistrate of the Gaya District. Shortly thereafter, the manager of the Nyingma Institute was once again confronted by the same provocateur, this time complaining that all his money had been drained through earlier court expenses. The manager was then kidnapped and roughed up, and some rupees were taken from his wallet. When the case reached the criminal judge magistrate, the accusations of *dacoity* were reversed and the manager of the Nyingma Institute was promptly thrown in jail, where he stayed for a month. In light of these escalations, the Nyingma Institute eventually chose to reach an agreement. "My Guruji and followers come here to Bodh Gaya for good things," the manager said. "We did not want to continue quarreling, so we eventually decided to compromise with a payment of forty lakhs [est. US$90,000]. This was in February 2006. They said that the court case could take another thirty years to resolve. So we decided to settle. We made peace."

Promoting world peace through the Nyingma Tibetan Monlam and other Tibetan festivals has certainly come at a cost for many Buddhist organizations in south Bihar. Reflecting on his recent trip to Amaravati in the South Indian state of Andhra Pradesh for the 2006 Kalachakra festival, the manager concluded, "The state was so supportive and everything was done so well . . . Here the block officers, they take so many bribes. Their view of foreigners is that they have lots of money so let's rob them . . . It can be so difficult here." Although the difficulties encountered by Tibetans may be more acute because of their precarious exile status in India, they are not the only Buddhist community implicated in these moral and ethical quandaries over questionable land transactions, which have multiplied in recent years.[23] Many of these institutions have followed the path of the Nyingma Institute and "made peace" through some undisclosed financial agreement—but at the cost of perpetuating the corruption and bribery that has become institutionalized in Bodh Gaya and Bihar. The manipulation of records by the land mafia to create grounds for new land title has also led to a near collapse of the municipal waste treatment system around Bodh Gaya, with the blockage of former water bodies and channels due to the upsurge in construction.

These problems over land are certainly compounded by the fact that few Buddhist monks and nuns are familiar with the Indian legal system governing the process of land acquisition. One exception is the Indian Buddhist monk Priyapal Bhante. Priyapal is a student of political science and is part of the Chakma ethnic community, which comes from the Chittagong Hill tracts of northeastern India and Bangladesh. Ever since Bhikkhu Priyapal arrived in Bodh Gaya in the mid-1990s, he has been battling the corruption and bribery that underlie land disputes at Bodh Gaya. When I first met Priyapal nearly ten years ago, his temple was situated on the outskirts of town, far removed from the commercial hub of the bazaar. Ten years later, the modest, three-story Chakma Buddhist Temple is hemmed in by an explosion of hotels and guesthouses that encircle and tower over it. As we sat in the dim light with the hammering of construction work around us, he described some of the difficulties the international Buddhist community faces in Bodh Gaya. In particular, Priyapal noted that the sectarian growth of international Buddhism at Bodh Gaya, the subsequent language barriers, and the lack of political commitment have undermined the strength of their position as a collective group.

"It is in the best interest of the hoteliers that we remain divided," he said. But after years of tackling corruption and trying to mobilize the Buddhist monasteries into political action, he was acutely aware of the obstacles.

> Buddhism believes in clarity. I have had to read these books and advise on the basis of the law. Most of these people do not want to invest their time in legal intricacies and would rather build temples and get sponsorship. The International Buddhist Council has been involved in these court cases. There are so many of them embroiled in land knots. It is difficult to convince our colleagues otherwise. The system in Bihar is difficult. Foreigners also do not want to go through the details. They would rather keep the mentality of bribery. The Indian system is slow and corrupt . . . there is no doubt about that. So they would rather use the money to pay the government employee, then transfer. Then later, they are requested to pay more money . . . It is an endless cycle.

CONCLUSION

For many Buddhists, like the Indian monk Priyapal, undertaking pilgrimage to the place of Buddha's enlightenment helps to generate good merit, ensure a wholesome rebirth, and yield blessings from enlightened teachers. The production of merit in a holy place like Bodh Gaya is amplified by such moral and ethical practices as building monasteries and practicing *dana*, or generosity, actions that help to purify the intentions of the giver. Monks and nuns who have the financial means to travel between countries are well positioned to take advantage of an increasingly interconnected world. With the relatively inexpensive travel opportunities available to Asian and Western Buddhist pilgrims, many of Bodh Gaya's diasporic community are able to purchase land and labor (at relatively low costs—at least in the past) to build their dream monasteries and temples. Catering to the religious diaspora at the doorstep of transnational devotional flows can also be very lucrative, especially when the power of the sacred becomes intertwined with the virtuous economy of *dana* and both religious and modernist aspirations for world peace, social development, and aid.

This is not to deny that many of these Buddhist groups take enormous risks, especially financially and legally, in establishing monasteries at Bodh Gaya under complex legal and bureaucratic regimes. Their use of government tax benefits, though, has become a point of contention in recent years, giving rise to new commercial and religious fault lines. Among some Indian hoteliers, it is argued that pilgrimage activites generate significant capital that evaporates along transnational circuits and is not necessarily reinvested in the local economy. The 2011 discovery of more than $1.6 million in twenty-five foreign currencies at the Karmapa's monastery in Dharamsala is an example some use to confirm these suspicions.[24] Further, the growth of monasteries has drastically altered the cost of land in and around Bodh Gaya and for some has come to symbolize the *zamindars* of earlier times.

Bodh Gaya is an urban landscape that is undergoing rapid social change, and the expansion of Buddhist monasteries and temples at Bodh Gaya can be interpreted as a by-product of religious transnationalism from above; but this expansion is tempered by moral and social pressure from below, including land malpractice and various forms of extortion. In this part of North India, where the public perception of the state is linked to widespread corruption, many Bodh Gaya residents model their strategy for survival on the state and caste leaders who have accumulated wealth and power, using corruption to achieve social mobility and empowerment (Witsoe 2011). Land malpractice—as in the case of the Nyingma Institute—has become a common occurrence and a potential zone of advancement by drawing international Buddhist groups into a labyrinth of illicit bureaucratic knots.

One religious monastery that has remained quiet over the last few decades is the Bodh Gaya Math. Although the *mahant* retains a hereditary position on the Bodh Gaya Temple Management Committee and continues to generate some profit from his large estate, his current wealth pales in comparison to previous splendor. The huge monastic complex that stretches along the riverside no longer exhibits the affluence, educational opportunities, or religious superiority it once did. Inside the now ghostly complex a half-dozen or so *sannyasins* are scattered about. One of the *sannyasins* I met in 2011 was an eighty-year-old monk who first went to Bodh Gaya as a disciple of Harihar Giri (1932–1958). Today, the elderly monk in peach robes is immobilized on a *charpoy* in a shady corner of the forty-foot-long courtyard verandah. He explained to me one afternoon that he has been in Bodh Gaya for over sixty years and has witnessed the near collapse of the Shaivite monastery. In our conversation, the monk frequently referred to the decline of food quality and availability at the Math. He is still alive today, he said, because he ate such healthy food in the past. But these days, "Ab to ye halat hai ki chawal baahar se mangana padata hai" (Even many of the resident monks have to purchase rice from outside).

Similarly, many of the Math's properties and former *kutcheries* have been demolished by Maoist rebels and/or are fast deteriorating. One example is the Math's Samadhi burial ground, to the east of the Mahabodhi Temple entrance. Wandering through the graveyard filled with shiva lingums and miniature votive stupas one afternoon, I was struck by the colorful pastel images of various deities such as Shiva, Kali, and Ganesh that covered the walls of the large, impressive tombs of former *mahants*. Except for these ghostly images, there was no one to be found. The owner of a chai stall nearby explained to me that few people visit the Sanskrit College, Samadhi graveyard, or other Math properties, save the occasional wandering *sadhu*. Instead, they have become popular haunts for youth as place to consume alcohol and smoke *ganja* (marijuana) through the night without fear of public reprisal. These decrepit buildings, overrun with jungle, now stand in stark opposition to the opulence of the Mahabodhi Temple Complex, the foreign Buddhist monasteries, and many luxury hotels. As with other heritage places in India that have been converted into upscale resorts, one cannot help but speculate that the Bodh Gaya Math may have a future in the burgeoning hotel industry.

4   Tourism in the Global Bazaar

> In the summer months there is no business. For six months there
> is no business. This is difficult for the locals. We can survive off
> four months, but without tourists it is boring. (Virendar, Buddha
> handicraft shopkeeper)

FOLLOWING SIX YEARS OF EXTREME AUSTERITIES, PRINCE SID-
dhartha abandoned the path of asceticism and accepted milk-rice from a
young woman named Sujata on the outskirts of Uruvela. Prior to meeting
Siddhartha, Sujata had pledged that she would offer milk-rice daily to the
spirit of the tree if she gave birth to a son. Once this wish was fulfilled, she
asked her servant to visit the tree and prepare the place for offering. To the
servant's surprise, when she reached the site, Siddhartha was sitting beneath
the boughs and she mistook him for the tree-*deva*. She quickly hurried back
to the village and reported the event, whereupon Sujata joyfully prepared a
special dish of milk-rice. With great reverence, Sujata returned to the tree and
offered the food in a golden bowl to the emaciated young prince. The milk-
rice from the young mother helped to restore his strength and prepare his
mental concentration for enlightenment under the Bodhi tree.

The tale of Sujata is often evoked by Bodh Gaya's residents as a way of
demonstrating their historical and cultural ties with the ancient site. It also
refers to a tradition of respect for visitors that is captured by the phrase
atithi devo bhavah, or "guest is god."[1] Although many still work in agriculture, the rising influence of international Buddhist activities in Bodh Gaya
has opened opportunities in religious tourism.[2] Like agriculture, the pilgrimage and tourism industry is also marked by a high degree of seasonality. Between October and March there is a surge of pilgrimage-based
activities, which contributes to a range of entrepreneurial opportunities in
the growing hospitality and service sector. Just as changing weather patterns affect farmers' yields, so domestic and global market pressures affect
the number of visitors each year. There are droughts to be endured and
small fortunes to be reaped.

With the backdrop of the fragmentation of *zamindari* and the changing
local and regional power equations in the last few decades, religious tourism

has become an important vehicle through which many residents, as well as recent migrants to Bodh Gaya, have gained new forms of economic and social mobility, especially in the informal sector. In this transformation from an agricultural economy to service-oriented labor, the Buddhist memory of the site is also renegotiated by Hindu and Muslim residents who draw upon and transform these claims into local histories of belonging. This area has traditionally had high unemployment, but the boom in construction and tourism has created opportunities for social advancement and economic improvement, especially for those with limited education and vocational training. As a means of exploring these economic lifelines and diverse local experiences in relation to tourism development, I use the term *global bazaar* as both a guiding metaphor and a site of ethnographic analysis.

BODH GAYA'S GLOBAL BAZAAR

> Poverty is there, but those who are connected with tourism, they
> have done hard work. The rich people today, they have worked hard
> and were able to establish themselves in the tourist market. They
> were once very poor, and most of them are not literate. Some of them
> were living as agricultural laborers for the *mahant*. They were simply
> laborers and everything belonged to him. Then they saw the pilgrims,
> began working for them, guiding them. They were all coming from
> lower castes and a few upper castes, and a few from outside. (Ranjan,
> Bodh Gaya travel agent)

Located a short distance from the front entrance of the Mahabodhi Temple Complex is the Sharwa tea shop. With several benches surrounding a large, shady *peepal* tree, this popular chai stall provides an ideal vantage point for observing the sacral-commercial activities that constitute Bodh Gaya's colorful global bazaar. The Sharwa tea shop is one of fifty-eight semipermanent shops that line the pedestrianized footpath as part of the commercial business district. In this bustling market area a number of Bodh Gaya residents have built reputable businesses and devoted clienteles over the years, specializing in Buddhist crafts, trinkets, souvenirs, *mala* beads, jewelry, incense, candles, and other devotional materials, as well as general stores, travel agencies, bookshops, barbershops, restaurants, and internet cafés.[3]

During the winter months the popular footpath and nearby roadside areas bring a large number of seasonal Tibetan refugee traders and Himalayan merchants to Bodh Gaya. With open-air stalls and plastic sheets strewn along the pavement, they specialize in goods ranging from antique artifacts to liturgical objects, silver jewelry, and necklaces made of lapis lazuli, coral, and turquoise beads. Next to the Himalayan merchants are several hawkers and informal sellers who peddle their goods and souvenirs with a close eye on the local municipal authority. Usually at some point during the day, a hide-and-seek drama unfolds between the formal and informal economy, especially during VIP stopovers at the Mahabodhi Temple. And due to the frequency of high-profile guests, these illicit entrepreneurs have skillfully mastered the art of vanishing and can quickly pack up their goods and dissolve into the background of the marketplace in a moment's notice.

Rubbing shoulders with reverent pilgrims in the bazaar are also a number of young boys who flock to tourists with rosary *malas* draped around their neck, postcards of foreign monasteries, CDs of Buddhist chants, dried Bodhi leaves, and a keen eye for first-time visitors as potential prospects for student sponsorship initiatives. Modeling themselves after the street-savvy youth are a number of scruffy children from the surrounding villages who playfully dart and dodge through the pedestrianized traffic zone seeking *dana*, schoolbooks, shoes, biscuits, and other small offerings through their famous one-liner, "No father, no mother, please give me dollar." Beggars, especially older women from outlying villages or those suffering from polio or leprosy, are also a common site on the fringes of the crowded bazaar. With their begging bowls, they scuttle along the edge of the footpath or line up next to street performers and blind *dalit* musicians who sing Bhojpuri songs to the beat of drums throughout the day. There are also plenty of dogs bathing in the afternoon sun and the occasional goat and humpback bull that lumbers through the crowds hoping to score some flower garlands.

At each end of the footpath the spiritual economy of the temple expands to include the wider rural-urban marketplace that serves the commercial needs of the town and outlying areas. Near the post office at the base of the Gandhi statue are a number of fruit and vegetable sellers who stake claim to the public space next to mobile hawkers pushing trolleys with fresh orange juice, sweets, betel nut, roasted corn, peanuts, chickpeas, and puffed rice with salty spice mixtures. There are also a number of tailors, tea stalls, confectionaries, and clothing shops that have gained a popular reputation among Indian visitors from Gaya and surrounding villages, especially during the wedding season. In these high-congestion zones the chanting from the nearby temple is replaced by a cacophony of horns as cycle rickshaws, auto-rickshaws, motorbikes, and trucks compete for space along the narrow winding roads that encircle the Mahabodhi Temple Complex.

As an anthropologist with a weakness for sweet chai, I found the vernacular cultural dynamics of the bazaar and the multitude of stories and social ties that it affords a key locus of ethnographic investigation during my fieldwork. In the South Asian context, the bazaar has long been inscribed through Orientalist representations as a traditional and essential feature of the cultural landscape (Yang 1998, Bayly 1983). During the British colonial period, for example, it was primarily used as a technical descriptor for the "indigenous" sector that was characterized by its "informal" money markets and trading systems, which took place next to more "formal" market structures regulated by the colonial state (Jain 2007). However, several critical reevaluations by historians in the last few decades have shown that far from being a uniform and essentially "static indigenous arena," like the mythologized place of "caste" and "village" in the Orientalist imaginary, the bazaar is in fact a vital and dynamic arena of mercantile exchange and circulation with a long history of trade networks stretching far beyond the Indian subcontinent (Jain 2007).

As historian Anand Yang (1998) explains,

> Both as an analytical unit and at a metaphoric level, bazaars speak the language of exchange and negotiation, of movement and flow, of circulation and redistribution—in short, of extracommunity or supracommunity connections and institutions. The India of Bazaar is therefore not confined to a particular site at the expense of wider ties. Such linkages, after all, did exist, and the village never suffered from that rather artificial quality of isolation that had been constructed for it in the colonial imagination. (16–17)

Insisting on a more dynamic view of Indian agrarian society, Yang posits that the bazaar provides a key site of "historiographical rupture" and an important setting in which to reconstruct and narrate the lived experiences of people as played out against the backdrop of changing market relations.

Coupled with this historical and critical reevaluation of the bazaar is the empirical focus on the Indian marketplace as a space of convergence and a mediating idiom that brings economics together with other aspects of social life, such as religion and politics. Far from being a "secular" commercial arena divorced from public religious life, there has long been a blurring of boundaries between the sacred and the commercial in the Indian context (Jain 2007, Parry 1989). In her rich analysis of the economies of Indian religious calendar art, for example, Jain (2007) shows how sacred imagery figured as an integral element in the construction of a wider moral-commercial ethos. These mercantile networks and marketing institutions, according to Jain, helped give shape to a "sense of moral community" that was built on flexible and expansive networks of trust that crosscut caste and sectarian boundaries.

Building on these perspectives here, I examine the bazaar as a site of ethnographic analysis and use it as a heuristic tool for exploring how individuals shape their lives through spaces of cultural encounter and commercial exchange that are increasingly characterized by transnational ties and interactions between the local and the global. I view these interactions in the bazaar as "transnational social fields," which refers to those connections that extend beyond national boundaries even if movement is restricted or not available (Brennan 2004). Among these transnational social fields, the return of a Buddhist diaspora has certainly been a catalyst in forging networks and relationships that span two or more nation-states. While many of the monks, nuns, and managers tied to the establishment of Buddhist monasteries spend part of the year outside of India, many connections are forged in the marketplace by local intermediaries who do not necessarily have the means to cross national borders.

In exploring these transnational social fields, I argue that it is in the public life of the bazaar that place becomes a lived space and Buddhism is transformed and given meaning through people's social exchanges, memories, and daily interactions with foreigners. It is also a social arena where individuals, to different degrees, seek to reinvent or to improve the conditions of their lives through various means. These casual and intimate encounters with pilgrims and tourists in the bazaar stand in sharp contrast to the "once in a lifetime event" for many Buddhist pilgrims (Doyle 1997, 426). For these reasons, I draw here on a set of life histories and stories involving Tibetan merchants, restaurant workers, hoteliers, and friendly guides to show how these groups mediate larger global processes and illuminate the ways in which Buddhism and the public life of Mahabodhi Temple fuel the local economy and provide a creative space for empowerment and social change.

TIBETAN REFUGEES AND LEGACIES OF SERVITUDE

Through my interviews and conversations with various interlocutors in Bodh Gaya it became clear that a major turning point in the transformation of Bodh Gaya into a global destination was the 1985 Kalachakra festival. Prior to this large international gathering, there was only one morning and one evening government bus to Gaya city (and railway station) along the dusty riverside road, and the main form of local transportation was horse-cart or cycle rickshaw. Acquiring basic food provisions such as a loaf of bread sometimes took a full week, explained Kiran Lama, the caretaker of the Daijokyo Buddhist Temple. "It was also difficult acquiring building materials for the monastery," he said. "As for communication services, you had to book a phone to connect the number. It was just a sleepy village. There were no proper roads, and during the monsoon season it was muddy and full of snakes. But it was also lovely and peaceful." Tara Doyle also recalled that there was a clear division between "the season" and "the non-season" in the "old days." "There was not a great deal of merchandise being sold, and only a few families were employed by the Buddhist monasteries. With the shops across from the Burmese temple," for example, "it was like, 'The Antioch group is here, so let's order more biscuits.'"

Although there is a long history of contact among "hosts" and "guests" in Bodh Gaya, from the viewpoint of residents, it was the large influx of Tibetan refugees, sometimes referred to as Bhotia (a generic term for several groups of people inhabiting the Tibetan and Himalayan region) that really transformed the place. Bodh Gaya has become a popular meeting ground for the deterritorialized Tibetan refugee community and an important site for the revitalization of cultural and religious activities in exile. As part of their seasonal and shifting transmigration in search of economic opportunities, for roughly three to four months over the winter season, large numbers of Tibetan pilgrims, traders, and merchants settle in Bodh Gaya following the movement of lamas and spiritual leaders from each of the four major Tibetan schools.

According to Rajesh, a shopkeeper who has long maintained close ties with the Tibetan community, "They were the first big thing. It started with the Tibetans who were buying rosary *malas* and Bodhi leaves," he said.

The Tibetans were also very dirty, wandering here and there. But this was a new thing for the people of Bodh Gaya and it sparked the growth of tourism. Also, our minds developed with contact among foreigners, such

as the Tibetan, Western, and Japanese groups. This in turn made some
locals wise and eventually we came out of the clutches of the feudal lord
[reference to the *mahant*]. So during this time, there was a shift of population toward tourism business.

As one can imagine, the tremendous expenditure of funds required for
some of the large Tibetan ritual gatherings such as the Kalachakra and the
Nyingma Monlam created several business opportunities for residents of
Bodh Gaya and seasonal Tibetan merchants, who began to develop close
economic and social ties in the marketplace.

One early manifestation of these growing connections is the popular
Tibetan Refugee Market. This market began more than thirty years ago and
was originally situated in front of the Mahabodhi Temple, where the pedestrianized footpath and main bazaar are located today. Over the years, the
seasonal market has moved to various locations. It was near the Kalachakra
maidan on the edge of Pacchetti village for over ten years; now it is near the
recently built Bihar state tourism market complex and bus transit zone in
Node 1. The Tibetan Refugee Market operates during the winter season
between 8:00 a.m. and 8:00 p.m. daily and has roughly fifty shops.[4] Although
there are a few Indian families who operate stalls in the market complex,
most of the shopkeepers are Himalayan women who migrate to Bodh Gaya
from various locations such as Darjeeling, Haridwar, Mysore, Dharamsala,
Siliguri, Dehra Dun, and Nepal. While the merchandise varies slightly each
year, broadly speaking, most of the shops specialize in winter woolen goods
such as sweaters, jackets, socks, shawls, blankets, scarves, and sleeping bags,
to name a few. These items are in high demand during the cold months of
December and January, and many Indian patrons from the surrounding
districts of Gaya, Patna, and Sherghatti frequent these shops each year. Tashi,
a Tibetan merchant who operates a booth in the refugee market, told me
that "each season the business varies . . . sometimes good, and sometimes
not so good. But for pilgrimage and *puja*, coming here is very important."

Also catering to the seasonal influx of Tibetan Buddhist pilgrims is an
entire street of tent restaurants built with plastic tarps, bamboo poles, rope,
and dried mud and brick. Each restaurant has a dozen or so plastic tables
and benches, an illuminated shrine dedicated to the 14th Dalai Lama or
other prominent Rinpoches, small descending light fixtures, and a stockpile
of candles in case the electricity or generator fails, which is not uncommon.
The rustic menus are also fairly standardized, offering popular Himalayan
dishes such as *momos*, *thukpa*, and *thenthuk*, chow mein, chop suey,

nonvegetarian items, and both Indian and English breakfasts. Relatively quiet during the day, in the evenings the tent restaurants tend to be packed with Tibetan and Himalayan pilgrims who come to relax and watch popular Asian music videos and Bollywood films after a long day of prostrations at the temple.

As one would expect in a popular pilgrimage town like Bodh Gaya, a number of restaurants have a longstanding reputation among repeat patrons and clientele. A Tibetan woman named Amala, who set up a small food stall next to the Mahabodhi Temple in the early 1970s, is widely viewed as the first seasonal Tibetan restaurant owner. Another famous Tibetan tent restaurant is Loyag, which opened in 1983 prior to the Kalachakra festival. Annie Loyag, the founder of this restaurant, is now a Tibetan nun who previously worked in a restaurant on the outskirts of Lhasa. After moving to Gangtok and Darjeeling in the 1970s, she decided to set up a small restaurant near the Mahabodhi Temple, where she benefited from regular contact with Tibetan pilgrims and repeat Western patrons such as the Antioch Buddhist Studies group. There are also several rustic Indian-run establishments that gained a popular reputation among pilgrims and tourists during this time. These include the Kalayan Restaurant, the Madras Café, the Fujiya Green, the Ram Seevak, and the popular hangout Shivanath—now rebranded the Shiva Hotel Restaurant.

While cordial relations are common among Indian and Tibetan restaurant owners in Bodh Gaya today, some underlying tensions have developed because of the growing number of restaurants each year. Take the popular Tibet Om Café as an example. Today, this restaurant and clothing shop is located inside the Mahayana Tibetan Guest House, and like many of the Tibetan restaurants, was launched in the aftermath of the 1985 Kalachakra. The owner of the café is Tsering Bhutti, a soft-spoken Tibetan woman from Dharamsala who manages the restaurant with the help of her adopted sister's children, Dasang and Yangtse. Like other seasonal Tibetan merchants, Tsering Bhutti operates a satellite restaurant and garment store back in Dharamsala, where they reside during the summer months.

The Tibet Om Café is famous for its wide selection of specialty foods, breads, and desserts, which include the coveted choco-balls, brownies, and chocolate-banana cakes. The restaurant boasts that all of its food is fresh, clean, and prepared in a hygienic manner. The Tibet Om Café received a warm review in the 1987 *Lonely Planet Guidebook*, which increased its success and reputation among a growing number of travelers. But as in other popular tourist towns, a successful business in Bodh Gaya is often prey to deceptive imitations. As with other longstanding Bodh Gaya restaurants, such as the Old Pole Pole and the Original Pole Pole, the "Om" name was hijacked by an Indian entrepreneur when the new entry road was built. When I spoke with Tsering about these developments, she complained, "People now think that *they* are the original Om Café, and we have lost some of our very special customers. When our patrons ask them, 'Where is Om Café?' they reply, 'It has been closed.' Sometimes they also commission local guides to bring visitors to their establishment, but we do not offer commission here. So the customers will have to find the restaurant on their own."

In addition to these ongoing rivalries over popular restaurant names, the Tibetan refugee community must also negotiate dietary differences in a multi-religious environment where food sensibilities can be a contentious topic. One particular point of cultural interchange that has led to strains between Hindus and Tibetan Buddhists is the consumption of nonvegetarian meals in Bodh Gaya. According to Tsering, prior to their new location at the Mahayana Tibetan Guest House, the Tibet Om Café was situated on the roadside and was often frequented by young Indian boys who would pester customers. On one particular occasion, she recalled, three young men entered the restaurant and demanded to see if we were cooking meat or not. "Where is your authority? Show me your license!" she shouted. In response, the boys flashed some papers and then proceeded to enter the kitchen, where they threatened her and the restaurant staff, searching for meat. "Fortunately," she added, "there were some official people outside who were visiting the Tibetan refugee market and overheard me shouting. It was just a coincidence. So they came in and confronted them." Although the three boys left the restaurant and nothing happened on this particular occasion, the café has, like other Tibetan restaurants, been targeted with threats by concerned Hindus in the past.

For these reasons, since 2000, the Tibet Om Café has offered a strictly vegetarian menu, but this is not the case for all the Tibetan tent restaurants in Bodh Gaya. While it is widely assumed that Buddhists promote a vegetarian diet, among many Tibetan and Himalayan Buddhists the act of eating meat is not prohibited, and this has led to inevitable cultural conflicts. As Toni Huber (2008, 317) has noted, "Dietary differences have long been used to construct indigenous ethnic classifications upon which attitudes to outsiders are based," and many Tibetans have faced modern religious intolerance toward their customary meat-based diet, especially in India. These conflicts are not only between Tibetans and Hindus but also among different Buddhist sects and groups, such as the Maha Bodhi Society, which views

Tibetans for a Vegetarian
Society poster calling for
a vegetarian zone

nonviolence and vegetarianism as central pillars of its modern Buddhist
social ethics (Huber 2008). Anagarika Dharmapala campaigned against the
ritual sacrifice of animals within the precincts of the Mahabodhi Temple
and also publicly berated "beef-eating Tibetans" for offering meat at the
throne of enlightenment (Huber 2008).

Although the consumption and offering of meat by Tibetans is far less
frequent today, it still remains a potential source of deep cultural conflict
at the navel of the earth. In recent years several campaigns by various grass-
roots organizations have declared Bodh Gaya a 100% vegetarian zone.[5] With
support from the 14th Dalai Lama, the 17th Karmapa, and Hollywood
Buddhist icon Richard Gere, several signs in the marketplace during the
winter season call for dietary reform and abstaining from eating, buying,
and selling meat in the holy land. However, the stigma of beef-eating
Tibetan Buddhists continues, and many local Hindu residents shun the tent
restaurants, fearing that the chow mein or *momos* contains traces of meat.
On the flip side, a few Hindu-run restaurants, such as the Shiva Hotel,
Madras Café, Kalayan Restaurant, and Fuji Green, have gained a popular
reputation among Indian clientele for serving *pure* vegetarian food.

Several local Hindu residents indicated that there are many moderate
Hindus who are willing to turn a blind eye during the winter season to

ensure the continuing economic benefits of tourism and pilgrimage that the Tibetans provide. This temporary social distance from religious taboos has also, to some extent, fueled a niche market for the scheduled castes in the area, especially the Bhuiya and Chamar, who are known to handle meat and raise pigs. Although the majority of beef, goat, buffalo, and pork is slaughtered in the Muslim quarters in nearby Gaya city and delivered to Bodh Gaya in the early morning, it is largely handled by young male Bhuiya staff, who occupy the concealed kitchen spaces and cleaning area of the tent restaurants. When I was conducting a survey of the different restaurants in Bodh Gaya in 2006–2007, many of these young boys were from scheduled castes and had developed some proficiency in the Tibetan language. Thus as an inversion of their ethno-historical status as a ritually polluted group confined to debt servitude as *kamias*, in the restaurant industry their polluting status provides a market niche that ensures some seasonal employment among the Tibetans through the winter months.

In order to shed further light on these religious and cultural interchanges between the Bhuiya, Muslim, and Tibetan refugee communities in Bodh Gaya, let me turn to the case of Mohammad's Restaurant. Mohammad's Restaurant, like the Om Café, is one of the most popular hangouts during the winter season, with a strong following of repeat Western and Asian Buddhist pilgrims and tourists. Inside the restaurant, Mohammad and his staff provide a diverse culinary experience that combines Tibetan, Chinese, Western, Mexican, and North Indian cuisine. On most nights during the winter season the restaurant is packed with travelers sipping on ginger-lemon tea to relieve their sore throats, discussing the latest Buddhist teachings and Rinpoche gossip, and using the free wifi. Mohammad's entrepreneurial success, like that of many of the locals I describe in this section, is a function of both his hard work and the transnational pool of opportunities that increasingly defines Bodh Gaya's global bazaar.

Born in the area known as the Harijan Colony today, Mohammad has eight siblings and comes from a poor Muslim background. Both of his parents are illiterate, and his father worked as a builder helping to construct the Gelug Tibetan Temple and the Mahayana Rest House. "Back then," he recalls, "my father was making 75 *paisa* a day [equivalent to fifteen cents] and through this work he became very close with the Tibetans." Like many of the young Bhuiya you see in the back quarters of the restaurants today, Mohammad worked at his brother's restaurant, called Dorjee, starting when he was twelve years old. Dorjee had emerged from the family's close ties with the Gelug Tibetan Temple and Monastery. This seasonal work afforded him the opportunity to meet many travelers and nurtured his dream of running his own tent restaurant one day. One year later, this dream came to fruition when Mohammad's Restaurant was formally opened during the winter season in 1996. At the age of thirteen, Mohammad was running a staff of four that included two for cooking (including himself), one for service, and one for cleaning.

At the beginning, he admits, the restaurant was not very successful and mostly catered to a few Tibetan pilgrims. But after a while, many Western friends and repeat customers from the Dorjee Restaurant began to take notice. As a result, each successive year the restaurant grew in popularity and eventually outperformed Dorjee. With loyal customers and a friendly supportive staff, Mohammad's Restaurant has become a major hub for travelers on the *dharma* circuit and a highly profitable venture. The restaurant earnings were recently invested in a three-story guest house located in the nearby village of Siddhartha Nagar, where Mohammad currently resides.

When I met with Mohammad outside his new guesthouse one afternoon, he expressed, in his usual humble and gentle way,

> I am very proud of my fate. All together things are going well. It has been my dream to save money and put aside a separate amount for my brother and me when we are old. But for forty years I will have to do hard work. I also want to buy a little plot of land and keep some goats. My other dream is to visit Europe and also use some money for charity. This is also good karma and for the next life; and also for my son if he should require any. But before, my family was very, very poor. Everyone has blessed me. The customers have always supported me and given me much energy. On one occasion, friends from the United Kingdom also gave my father blood when he was sick. This was in 2004–2005. Once I was also given Rs. 400 from my dear American friends to use toward my English and spoken classes, and I have always remembered their kindness.

Mohammad is also the first to acknowledge that the continuing success of the restaurant is tied to honest and dedicated support staff like Prem and Ramesh. Prem is a soft-spoken Bhuiya from the village of Jagdispur, located at the base of Dungheswari Mountain. This remote village, like many in the surrounding region, was directly under the control of the Math and its extensive system of bonded labor before the Bodh Gaya land struggle. "Previously, my father and the generation before him worked as *kamias*," Prem explained. "They were all working for the Math, especially the Bhuiya. We had no land, just this mud hut. I remember some days we had dinner and some days we had none. There was no *nasta* [breakfast]. During difficult times, our family would share one single *chapati* [unleavened flatbread]." Like many former agricultural laborers, his family had few opportunities with the decline of the Math, so he sought informal work among the Tibetan monks who resided at the nearby *gompa* at the base of Malakala cave. At that time, he recalls, they were paying him around Rs. 4 per day. Although Prem could not speak English, he did learn some Tibetan vernacular, and he eventually shifted to Bodh Gaya in search of seasonal work at one of the tent restaurants. At that time, he was eight years old.

Prem started working at Mohammad's Restaurant when it first opened in 1996, which is when his father died. Because he was the oldest son, there was considerable pressure to support his family, and he spent the entire winter season in Bodh Gaya, eating and sleeping at the restaurant and saving all his monthly earnings. These pressures were compounded by his early marriage at the age of fourteen to a Bhuiya girl who was a bit younger than he was. Despite these challenges, after four years of hard work, Prem was able to purchase a small plot of land in his home village and to help support his family, which now includes four sons and one adopted girl who lost her mother. Thus for over fifteen years, Prem has been working with Mohammad, first at the restaurant and now at the guesthouse, which has enabled him to earn a living, learn English through regular contact with foreigners, and become a great chef. "It is my dream to have a small restaurant in Dungeshwari," he told me, "but my mother's health is not good because she was recently diagnosed with polio." Neither Prem nor his wife has any formal education, but one of their sons, Ranjeet, has shown some promising academic potential and they support his education. Today, Ranjeet attends the highly coveted Magadha Cambridge Residential School in Gaya; his parents hope that their investment in an elite private school will prove fruitful in the long run. The rest of his children are attending the nearby Sujata Academy—a Korean charitable organization and school run by the Join Together Society.

Prem is just one example of the many young Bhuiya who regularly migrate to Bodh Gaya and other tourist towns during the winter season in search of employment in the informal sector. Although the pollution taboos surrounding the consumption of nonvegetarian food is certainly a contributing factor in their employment niche at the seat of enlightenment, it is important not to overlook the poverty-stricken position and underlying ethos of untouchability that continues to be exploited in the first place. Behind the walls of many monasteries, Indian hotels, and restaurants are young boys from scheduled castes whose family once served as bonded laborers and *kamias* under the tyranny of the Bodh Gaya Math and other *zamindars*. Whereas previously the Bhuiya relied heavily on a form of agricultural reciprocity tied to the Bodh Gaya Math and its cycle of economic and psychological indebtedness, today, many of these young boys are part of a new regime of wage-based labor servitude in the informal service sector, where cheap labor is exploited to meet the demands of seasonal restaurant work at the navel of the earth.

The fate of many young Bhuiya boys is not as positive as Prem's. In the past, Tibetan and Indian merchants were known to buy child labor from a *sadar* (middle man) in the poor villages surrounding Bodh Gaya and recruit them as servants for a menial wage in distant cities, towns, and mobile markets along the Tibetan transmigration routes, such as Dharamsala and Ladakh (Qadir 2007b). There are virtually no regulations covering their seasonal employment. This is not the same form of bonded labor that characterized agrarian relations under the Bodh Gaya Math, but they have inherited a legacy of servitude nonetheless, and their situation is a seriously underrepresented and invisible aspect of the thriving tourism and hospitality sector in many parts of India today.

HOTELIERS, GEOGRAPHICAL DOWRY, AND JAPANESE WIVES

The booming hotel and guesthouse industry that is visible throughout Bodh Gaya today, like the popular Tibetan tent restaurants, also flourished in the aftermath of the 1985 Kalachakra festival.[6] During the Dalai Lama's teachings, it became apparent to the state government and many residents that Bodh Gaya lacked adequate accommodation facilities to meet the demands of this growing international destination, especially in the winter season, during popular festivals and ritual events. Further, few local residents had the financial resources to purchase land and invest in hotel construction during the twilight years of the Bodh Gaya land struggle. Helping to resolve the fiscal limitations was the upsurge in Japanese pilgrimage throughout the 1980s, which left a significant economic footprint on the social landscape that continues to reverberate today.

Following World War II, leisure and extended travel were discouraged in Japan as the government embarked on a program of rapid modernization that emphasized devotion to work and home (Chambers 2010, Morean

2004). This commitment to domestic growth continued until 1964—the year of the Tokyo Olympics—when the government began lifting its restrictions on foreign currency allowances and many Japanese people began to see international travel as a desirable activity (Morean 2004). This, coupled with the rapid growth of the Japanese "miracle" economy beginning in the late 1960s, helped spur new leisure and travel incentives for Japanese groups, especially middle-aged Japanese Buddhist pilgrims, who looked to India as a travel destination that included spiritual purpose. By 1979, more than four million Japanese people were traveling overseas on either business or pleasure, and expenditure on international travel in 1979 alone was US$4.8 billion (Morean 2004, 111). This made Japan the third largest country in terms of scale of travel after the United States and West Germany, and these numbers only increased in the 1980s and 1990s, following Prime Minister Tanaka's push for "internationalization" (111).

As Virendar, owner of a Buddhist handicraft shop in Bodh Gaya, explained to me, "The Japanese began arriving in the late 1960s and by the mid-1980s things really took off! During that time the Japanese developed an interest in Bodh Gaya and other Indian Buddhist sites and were providing very good business." He continued, "The Japanese were also very simple or ignorant you can say . . . and locals were charging very high prices. They were heavy buyers and were also blind. Some people also started having good relations with the Japanese. Some were even going to Japan. The owner of the Sujata Hotel, he was the beginning."

The story of the Sujata Hotel and the legend of Kedar Prasad are well known to local residents. Coming from an "Other Backward Caste" (a collective term used by the government to classify socially and educationally disadvantaged castes), Kedar Prasad settled near the government-sponsored Harijan Colony, not far from the Japanese temples. From a young age he was well known as as a horse-cart driver in Bodh Gaya, providing pilgrims and tourists with this rustic form of transportation before the arrival of motor vehicles. He also opened a small roadside handicraft shop, where he catered to early Japanese patrons, including a Buddhist priest who later sponsored members of his family to acquire permanent settlement visas in Kyoto. With eight children, including five sons, Kedar's family has since cultivated strong business ties with the Japanese market as owners of the popular Sujata Hotel (a branch of Hotel Niranjana), which opened in 1995. With its air-conditioned rooms, marble flooring, and exclusive *ofuro*-styled Japanese steam baths, the hotel advertises quality service and traditional Indian hospitality. Helping to showcase their hotel and travel agency is their family-run Sujata Restaurant, located in Kyoto. Rahul, one of the young family members who frequently moves between Japan and India for business, noted that "due to the connections with Buddhists in Kyoto, they all know we are from Bodh Gaya and through them we receive much support. So in Kyoto, we give thanks to Lord Buddha and serve typical Indian food."

An entire generation of enterprising young people benefited from the growing Japanese ties in Bodh Gaya. Most of them began as mobile hawkers selling rosary *malas*, photos, precious stones, dried *peepal* leaves, and other sacred souvenirs. With their footloose business acumen, these hawkers would chase the Japanese pilgrims and sell gifts on bed sheets near the Mahabodhi Temple or at the front gates of the Indo Nipponji Temple. Some gained a sly reputation for selling rare Buddhist statuary and images found in the surrounding areas, including the Mahabodhi Temple grounds (before the boundary wall was erected), fetching a significant profit among Japanese and other international buyers. Other youth gained leverage by learning to speak Japanese, a linguistic asset that helped strengthen cultural intimacy with these early Japanese pilgrims.

From the viewpoint of two shopkeepers in the bazaar:

> In Bodh Gaya the Japanese were coming in large groups. There were also Thai pilgrims but their economy was not good. So we only bothered with the Japanese. They were not foolish people but would pay much more than the actual price. If something would cost Rs. 10, the Japanese would pay US$10. Some of us were getting US$50 in one day, and back then Rs. 200 (equivalent of US$4) would have been big money. So the Japanese had lots of money and there is some complex among them . . . they want to bring home unique things.

> During that time the Japanese used to have trust. There were very few travel agents back then. The Japanese would come to Bodh Gaya and also visit other tourist sites like Agra. But the Buddhist places were of central interest. They were very much here for the shopping. It is a custom among Japanese people, wherever they go, they buy something.

The tendency for group travel accompanied by a guide and the obligation to purchase gifts for those who remain back home are integral to the modern Japanese culture of travel (Guichard-Anguis and Moon 2008). It was for these reasons that the Mala Photo Association was established in Bodh Gaya by a loose membership of young entrepreneurs who began to claim exclusive rights to the Japanese.[7] The Mala Photo Association flourished, and some in the group chose to reinvest their earnings in land, with the dream of building a hotel and running their own handicraft empire. Although better off than many of the scheduled castes from the surrounding villages described in the previous section, most of the early hoteliers rose from the ranks of "Other Backward Castes" (OBCs) such as Kahar and Yadavs, as well as a few Muslims and upper-caste Hindus. There were few underlying religious or caste divisions among the Mala Photo Association members, and almost all of them came from agricultural backgrounds with little or no formal education. As one shopkeeper, Nitin explained to me, "They were not literate, so you can say they were educationally backward but economically forward."

Rumors of the Japanese Buddhist bonanza and the growing power of this emerging business class also spread among the criminal mafia networks in nearby Gaya city, and they began to target the Mala Photo Association with bribery demands. During the height of Lalu Prasad Yadav's Jungle Raj, these threats prompted many of the aspiring hoteliers to hire their own *goondas*, and it was in this context that Rajesh Kumar gained notoriety as a powerful political leader and broker who sought to protect emerging business interests. A number of hotels, guesthouses, travel agencies, and handicraft emporiums were built during this period of heightened economic prosperity and Japanese expenditure in particular. The first wave of hotels was constructed opposite the Buddhist monasteries when the new access road was built in the early 1990s—the Shanti Buddha Guest House, the Sujata Hotel, and the Hotel Embassy. Exploiting loopholes in the town development plan (see chapter 5), all the hotels had a shrine room on the first floor in order to entice pilgrims, as this land was originally earmarked for Buddhist temples.

The first wave of hotels began in the early 1990s; after 1995, there was an explosion of multi-storied buildings along the central spine of the new entrance road, with developers hoping to capitalize on the lucrative traffic of Buddhist pilgrims from the Far East. The mushrooming of hotels also coincided with a number of changes to the urban landscape, including a modern water system, an electricity substation, a telephone exchange, and the construction of the footpath in the main bazaar. Most of these improvements were financed by oversees Japanese loans under the Organization for Economic Co-operation and Development (OECD). Unfortunately for these hoteliers, the number of Japanese pilgrims began to decline following the bursting of the Japanese asset price bubble in 1991. The impact of this economic recession left many of the hoteliers and guesthouse operators in a vulnerable position, and this frustration became directed toward several foreign Buddhist monasteries described in the previous chapter. As Shiva, a shopkeeper from the bazaar, explained, "Today the hoteliers are all wearing white *kurta* pajamas, but underneath they are black due to corruption. Many of the hoteliers also have no credit in the market because their hotels were built on bank loans that they have not been able to pay. So now they are accusing foreign Buddhists."

One of the more surprising ethnographic findings in relation to the development of tourism entrepreneurship in Bodh Gaya is the extent to which many of these hoteliers have (or have had) Japanese wives and girlfriends. As in other popular tourist destinations, transnational courting at the place of enlightenment is increasingly common. It is believed there are upward of thirty to forty local men who have foreign wives; most are Japanese. Such success stories circulate widely in the bazaar as symbols of increased social and economic mobility. Within the local taxonomy of preferred guests, the Japanese are still widely seen as the "ideal type" for their enthusiastic spending habits and as a potential stepping-stone for marriage-based migration. Many imagine that their dreams of a better life will be attained through migration outside of India.

To explore the flights of imagination and fantasy that flourish between Bihari men and Japanese women, including the cultural constraints and disappointments they experience, let me introduce one of the more famous married couples in Bodh Gaya today: Yuki Inoue and Sudama Prasad, the owners of Hotel Mahamaya. Like many youth in Bodh Gaya today, Sudama aspired to work in the tourism industry and eventually moved to Delhi, where he was employed as an interpreter for Coxs & Kings, one of the most established travel agencies in the world. In Delhi, Sudama met his future wife, Yuki, who was visiting India on a sightseeing trip with her father, a fine arts professor in Kyoto. During the guided tour, the two fell in love and thereafter a flurry of romantic letters and phone calls were exchanged.

When I spoke with Sudama in the lobby of the Hotel Mahamaya one afternoon, he told me that after his initial meeting with Yuki he was invited to Japan, where he met with her parents and they agreed to the marriage. Sudama lived and worked in Japan for some time, but he found the Japanese work culture very difficult, and there were few opportunities available to him at that time. So, in 1998, the same year Sudama and Yuki were married, he quit his work as a guide, took out a bank loan, and began constructing the Hotel Mahamaya, where they currently reside. As Sudama explains,

"We got married in 1998 and have been living a very happy life. But in the beginning it was difficult, not so much for me, but for my wife. Many local people were abusing her when she first arrived. She did not understand Hindi so well at that time. But now she has become Bihari. She has even adopted many Hindu practices and has become a traditional Indian woman, you can say."

As Sudama suggests, Yuki's transformation into a "traditional Indian woman" has not been easy, and she was surprised at just how different Bodh Gaya was from New Delhi. Yuki told me, "When I arrived [in Bodh Gaya] for the first time, there was no electricity for ten days and I had to live with an extended family of twenty-five people."

> Although I have enjoyed living here, it has been very difficult at times. Because my husband was a tourist guide I thought I would travel a lot, but after marriage he quit the guide work and began constructing a hotel. At that time I was very alone and the entire family spoke Hindi. Only the youngest sister could speak some English. After one year I also found that the Hindi was different from the book I was using to practice with. Later, I discovered that they were speaking Maghi [regional dialect]. So slowly I began to learn both Maghi and standard Hindi. It has also been difficult to meet other Japanese here. The home is very conservative. It is very traditional here, although my husband is not. Only after marriage would the family allow me to open the windows and speak with others. I have had to adjust by following the local customs and learning local cooking.

One local custom that was not afforded to Yuki on her wedding day was entrance to the Vishnupad Temple in nearby Gaya. Although their marriage took place just outside the temple, when they tried to enter the shrine, Yuki was refused entry because non-Hindus are barred from entering the popular Hindu shrine. "Even though I am married to a Hindu and have followed Hindu custom I am still not allowed to enter Vishnupad," she said with disappointment. "The police even arrived on the occasion and blocked us from entering."

Another challenge that comes with transnational courting in south Bihar is the jealousy and suspicion that surrounds interracial romance in this rural area. According to Yuki, for many local people in Bodh Gaya today, it is believed that "if you marry a foreigner you will get rich. The people are just thinking about status and money, not family. There are many cases of divorce here. They also chase after Japanese girls because they think they are easy." She continued, "In our case, Sudama had pulled together the funds for building the hotel before our marriage, but the perception among local people is that he became rich *because* of our marriage. The truth is, after construction of the hotel began, we got married. Sudama has had success through his own hard work." Despite Yuki and Sudama's efforts to counter these assumptions and put an end to the flow of gossip in the bazaar, their recent construction of Mahayana Palace on the banks of the Niranjana River, a prime real estate area, has only fueled the suspicion that foreign women translate into material prosperity.

As Indian journalist Sanjay Jha (2003, 68) reports in an *India Today* article entitled "Knot Uncommon," the practice of transnational courting is becoming widespread in Bodh Gaya. "East is increasingly meeting East in this temple town," he writes. "Call it happenstance, call it heaven's blessing, but youths in the land of Buddha's nirvana now court Japanese girls with rustic aplomb." While many Japanese women, like Yuki, live in Bodh Gaya year round, a growing number of young men reside in Japanese cities such as Sapporo and Kyoto, and have started hotel businesses, restaurants, and travel agencies that cater to the Indo-Japanese traffic in Buddhist tourism. Many of these success stories perpetuate the myth of a "geographical dowry" and the role of marriage as a means of obtaining financial security in a "developed" country (Jha 2003, 69). These few instances of locals migrating to Japan as the husbands of Japanese women only propel the fantasy of the "opportunity myth" where "anything could happen" (Brennan 2004).

For some of these Indian men, the "performance of love"—the idea of pretending to be in love with someone—is deployed strategically as a form of transnationalism from below (Smith and Guarnizo 1998) that "emerges as an economic strategy as well as a legal route to securing the papers necessary to migrate" out of India (Brennan 2004, 30). The transactional use of marriage as a form of social mobility and a means of crossing national borders has become more common in a globalizing world. For many of these young Indian men, coming from poor agricultural backgrounds with limited education and resources, it is one of few viable options available to secure the papers necessary for legal migration. By laying claim to a geographical dowry, it is widely believed that one's material comforts will be improved and the possibilities to remit money back to families will be expanded. While salaries are much higher in Japan than in Bodh Gaya, the working conditions in Japan often fall short of expectations, and the economic fantasies of an easier life are often not fulfilled. There are considerable legal constraints against migrating outside of India; further, living in

Japan can be hard work, especially for those isolated from family and community. In fact, most stories I have heard are not very successful, and the spousal visa does not meet expectations. Few relationships last, and there is often little improvement to the Indians' economic status over the long run; most eventually return home.

Despite these difficulties a considerable amount of social capital is harnessed by living in a "developed" country, regardless of the brevity, and upon return these migrants act out wealth and perpetuate the image of Japan and other foreign countries as places of abundant riches and possibility. One also wonders if this transactional form of marriage through a geographical dowry challenges some of the culture-bound assumptions and ideals about what constitutes good marriage in rural south Bihar, where caste and community are seen as an integral part of maintaining social status. At the same time, it is well known that economic imperatives have long underlined the dowry exchange and usually outweigh romantic variables in arranged marriage proposals between families and endogamous caste communities.

Although it is commonly held that transnational courting has become a strategic means of improving economic standing and social mobility for local men, finding out why the Japanese women are attracted to the home-grown Bodh Gaya type is not an easy question to answer. It is well known that a large percentage of Japanese tourists abroad are women (Ivy 1995, Morean 2004). In *Discourses of the Vanishing*, Marilyn Ivy (1995) describes how much of the promotional efforts by the Japanese tourist industry in the 1960s focused on Japanese women, assuming "that young, unmarried women were the appropriate pacesetters in encouraging greater societal acceptance of leisure travel" (cited in Chambers 2010, 63). Men, on the other hand, viewed leisure travel as superfluous and were constrained by work and social expectations around family honor. Thus, in a reversal of the tendency to view Western tourism as having developed through a "masculine gaze," Ivy argues that women were less bound to social conventions and helped to broaden the travel market because "where women go, men follow" (63). Morean (2004, 122) also suggests that many of these Japanese women aimed to postpone marriage until their thirties and viewed travel as an international opportunity to rebel against a masculine Japanese work ethic and to escape the drudgery of an employment system that failed to make the most of their skills.

As Deepak, a local guesthouse owner with long ties to Japan, explained to me one afternoon, only a few residents in Bodh Gaya have *any* knowledge of Japan. "What they have heard," according to Deepak, "was from the elders who were making money." The image of Japan from the 1980s was that they were very rich and foolish, he told me. "They just give money." Also, it was believed that Japanese women were not satisfied with Japanese men. "When the women come to India, they see our culture where the women do not work in formal jobs. Instead, they stay at home and take care of the children. They also receive respect from the society. So they likely felt that the Indian men are good to marry, giving time to their wife and children."

Another reason, according to Deepak, is that Japanese men simply do not have time for their wives. "In one week, maybe they have only one day. The Japanese men are work machines. A close friend of mine calls them 'economic animals' because they just work, work, work. There is no care for family and society. They have money and brains, but no heart. So the Japanese women come to Bodh Gaya and get heart, respect, and sexual relations." Deepak acknowledged, however, that the reality often did not live up to the dream.

> You can call it emotional blackmail. Locals requesting marriage when they are only staying here for eight to ten days and during this time there is lots of talk. This is followed by proposals from the men and women's side . . . So you can say there are two reasons: one, the Japanese women are marrying Indian men for culture, not for money; even though they do not know the status of the man, his caste, or how much money he has. And second, among the Bodh Gaya men, they just want to marry so they can go to Japan and stay there. It is a spousal visa. They can work there on a spousal visa and as a result they can earn much more money. After they get married, maybe after two or three years, they separate, but the men still manage to obtain a visa. So there is no harm to marry for six months.

Although it is difficult from an ethnographic point of view to distinguish between relationships based on love versus those geared toward obtaining work visas, the idea of Indian culture—if not the reality of it—appears to be one of the underlying factors that contributes to Japanese women's motivation to marry Indian men.

These findings stand in contrast to Karen Kelsky's (2001) ethnography *Women on the Verge: Japanese Women, Western Dreams* and her analysis of Japanese women's lives and careers. In this book, Kelsky explores the complicated and contradictory role of transnational desire among young

Japanese "internationalists" who seek romance with Western men as a means of circumventing their country's oppressive corporate and patriarchal family structures. She argues that the feminine allegiance to the West and the "occidental longings" among Japanese women are seen as a "potentially transgressive and transformative force" (Kelsky 2001, 4). In contrast, Japanese women in Bodh Gaya do not emulate the global West as the model of unfettered freedom but rather see Indian culture as a potential step toward new opportunities. In leaving behind the excesses of patriarchy and oppression in Japan, though, they must learn to adapt and adhere to various social expectations in terms of gender, family, and household responsibilities in the Indian context. Thus, instead of escaping oppression, they trade one form of oppression for new asymmetries of domination—at least in the case of Yuki, who has had to adopt many Hindu practices and reconfigure her status as a "traditional Indian woman."

The circulation of images, fantasies, and desires in Bodh Gaya reflects changes in the global economy, which is a major force in forming new inter-Asian transnational ties and connections in the early twenty-first century. Unlike sex tourism destinations, where racial differences are eroticized and commodified, in Bodh Gaya, religion and culture appear to arouse marital desires, which plays into the flights of imagination and fantasy among Indian men and Japanese women. For many of these young Japanese women, the dream of visiting the place of Buddha's enlightenment—the sacred center of Buddhism—prefigures these transnational encounters and opens up romantic prospects in the holy land. As Sanjay Jha (2003, 69) notes, it is "the spiritual significance of Bodh Gaya among the Japanese . . . that contributes to cross-cultural matches between the East and East. When Yuki's father was asked about his daughter's marriage to Sudama, he said, 'Like Lord Buddha, my daughter came here to get ultimate enlightenment. . . . It was her fate that she got married at Bodh Gaya to Sudama.'"[8]

Many hoteliers and guesthouse operators who transcend religious and caste boundaries have gained a prominent social standing as "big men" in relation to tourism development in Bodh Gaya. With their intimate sojourns with foreign women and business acumen in the hospitality and service sector, they have developed growing political influence as a new entrepreneurial class, especially as the traditional feudal base of power deteriorates. At the same time, the tourism industry, like agriculture, is not a secure growth industry and is particularly vulnerable to shifts in supply and demand, including economic recessions from sending countries. Like the fluctuating weather patterns that puncture seasonal crops with devastating droughts, the swift exodus of Japanese Buddhist pilgrims in light of the "Lost Decade" left many of those aspiring hoteliers in debt, holding loans they could not pay back. One of the ways in which some young men have sought to secure a foothold in the Japanese market is to build transnational bridges with foreign women, with the prospect of marriage and a spousal visa, thus escaping economic uncertainty and hardship. These strategy-driven performances of love are intimately tied with the goal of obtaining a geographical dowry in order to leverage greater financial security.

While the Japanese still remain the "ideal type" for many of Bodh Gaya's residents today, new networks of transnational Buddhism have become more prominent in recent years that are helping to reverse the economic downturn. These days, it is the East and Southeast Asian pilgrims from Thailand, Taiwan, mainland China, and Singapore that are showing the most promise, especially since the introduction of the new Gaya International Airport in 2002. Many of these pilgrim groups demand a high degree of quality control that only Buddhist monasteries and luxurious hotels can provide. It is well known that there is a high level of vertical integration in the tourism industry, and many large chain hotels are better positioned to weather such temporary setbacks, such as the Hotel Lotus Nikko (formerly the Hotel Bodh Gaya Ashok) and the Royal Residency. These well-financed establishments claim to offer the most modern and luxurious accommodations and have even captured some of the elusive Japanese package groups who are starting to return. Part of the continuing success of these luxury brand hotels, like the Royal Residency, is that they also operate at other prominent Buddhist sites, such as Kushinagar and the Centaur properties in Rajgir and Lumbini in Nepal. Through their vertical integration along the Buddhist circuit, hotel chains are able to cater to a large number of air-conditioned tourist buses on highly structured packages that transport pilgrim groups through the holy land.

TOUTS, FRIENDLY GUIDES,
AND THE INFORMAL ECONOMY OF EDUCATION

As in other popular pilgrim and tourist destinations in contemporary India, commission work and guiding (*dalali*) are integral parts of the commercial landscape and contribute to both the formal and informal economy.[9] For most of the hoteliers described in the previous section, their rite of passage in the service and hospitality sector began as a young street tout or guide, often in pursuit of the lucrative Japanese pilgrim groups.[10] Following in the footsteps of these hoteliers are several young men who self-identify as "friendly guides" today, and who can be found just outside the Mahabodhi Temple seeking amusement and opportunities in the local-global counter-flows. As cultural ambassadors between India and the foreign world, they are what Hannerz (1998) describes as the "other transnationals," those "who are seldom the focus of anthropological research but who nonetheless constitute small rings in the global chain of exchanges across national borders" (cited in Favero 2003, 556).

Tolerated but not officially sanctioned by the Indian government, unlicensed guides, street hawkers, and commission brokers can be viewed as a social ill and a potential impediment to host/guest relations in the modern tourism industry. Although they are part of the economy that spurs consumption, they move in circuits seen as illegal in relation to the formal economy and defy distinctions between private and public realms (Anjaria 2011, Rajagopal 2001). These footloose, enterprising young men are not usually dependent on wages, either. Instead, they rely on varying degress of emotional labor and impart a form of "strategic hospitality" designed to cultivate personal connections and render tourists' experience of Bodh Gaya "intimate and compelling" (Huberman 2012, 142).

Two related questions frame the analysis of tourism entrepreneurship that follows. First, in view of ethnographic research in the field of urban youth, development, and globalization, how do spatial practices that involve hanging out in the bazaar near the Mahabodhi Temple become a form of public education and line of work for these Bodh Gaya youth? Second, how does informal guiding provide opportunities and new life chances to escape the extensive poverty in south Bihar? As anthropologist Akhil Gupta (1998) has shown in his analysis of postcolonial development in India, poverty and underdevelopment can inform a key part of the subjectivities of people in the "developing world." This is especially pertinent in Bodh Gaya, where international charity and religious philanthropy directed toward the poor can provide urban youth with multiple earning incentives.

In recent years there has been a growing literature on the myriad ways youth engage and mediate processes of globalization, especially under dire and rapidly deteriorating conditions of social and economic uncertainty (see Halperin and Scheld 2007, Jeffrey 2010, Cole and Durham 2008, Comaroff and Comaroff 2000). Craig Jeffrey's (2010) study of young men in the neighboring state of Uttar Pradesh, for example, describes how Indian youth engage in *timepass*—which refers to both the passing of time through

Hanging out in the bazaar: young men selling *malas*, Bodhi leaves, and Buddhist chanting CDs

long periods of hanging out in the street and to their sense of detachment from formal education and/or the feeling of being left behind. As a distinctive mark of modern society, formal schooling and university degrees are often correlated with opportunities for increased social mobility. However, in the case of Bihar and Uttar Pradesh, the public education system during the 1990s and early 2000s greatly deteriorated as a result of underfunding, corruption, and poorly run colleges and universities (Jeffrey 2010). This has contributed, according to Jeffrey, to "multiple spatiotemporal insecurities" among Indian youth, such as the "disappointment of being unable to acquire secure salaried work despite having spent a long time in formal education, the frustration of being unable to travel and start a family in the manner of a 'successful man,' and the sense of loss that accompanies being removed from spaces associated with modernity and development" (477).

Thus as a social occupation and crucial site of identity formation for these unemployed youth, hanging out in the bazaar provides an important cultural arena where young men can participate in the informal economy, build networks, and express their temporal anxieties. The notion of timepass also has much in common with *adda*—the practice of "hanging out," drinking tea, watching, commenting, and debating—that reflects a particular way of dwelling among men in northern India (Chakrabarty 1999, 113). In this context, *adda* can also refer to a "workplace," and these leisured activities in the public sphere provide an important setting for fashioning a masculine identity and exploring economic opportunities, including the prospects of transnational courting. Thus, as a culturally meaningful space where young men reflect on the changes taking place in contemporary urban India, Bodh Gaya's global bazaar provides a resource for young men to imagine "new lives and desires" through their everyday encounters with various kinds of "others" (Favero 2003, 554). Through observation and direct interaction with visitors, these tourist encounters provide an informal education through their accumulation of knowledge about foreigners—learning and practicing languages, having sexual relations, and cultivating useful social contacts that may prove relevant to their quest for employment. As a form of cosmopolitanism from below, what is remarkable about their cultural toolkit is their ability to shift linguistic and national address depending on the visitor's country and gender, deploying a number of verbal techniques to activate conversation.

Hanging out in the bazaar also becomes an important resource for these urban youth because it provides a degree of distance from the village and the social expectations surrounding kinship and family honor. As with Paolo Favero's (2003) young informants in Janpath Market in New Delhi, "Their choice of careers and free-time activities are, in fact, consciously planned to avoid being absorbed into the lifestyle represented by their families. Hence, they refuse arranged marriage; they aim to live on their own; and they spend money for leisure in a manner that their parents look on as outrageous" (2003, 556–557).

It is no surprise that for many of the friendly guides in Bodh Gaya today, the hotel owners and tout legends who have scripted "rags-to-riches" tales as a result of prosperous transnational ties with foreign nationals provide their source of inspiration. For example, Ravi, a seventeen-year-old tout from the Yadav caste, told me that he wanted to be a "big man" like Sudama at the Hotel Mahamaya or Rahul from the Sujata Hotel. "You can say these are my role models," he said. "I am also looking for a European or Japanese girl to marry and get citizenship and work abroad. And then I plan to open one big school for children. I do not want a sitting job. I also want to do something for my society. Perhaps I will have two wives like Alok, both a Japanese and a local girl." Here, Ravi is referring to a well-known Japanese guide in Bodh Gaya. "But if I get married to a local girl it will be too much tension. Having a child, I will also be tied down. All of sudden I will have to support my wife and child. There will be many things to think about. With a Japanese wife I can get a visa."

Like the hoteliers, the self-employed friendly guides were not necessarily divided along religious or caste lines. According to one guide, Ashok, "This business is not dependent on caste, anyone can do it. Tourism is not caste or religious based. Caste only matters with marriage." Although there is some underlying competition between guides in their quest to secure sponsorship, what tends to unite these disparate castes, as Jeffrey points out in his study on Uttar Pradesh, is a "shared anxiety about the possibility of downward mobility and a determination to exploit available resources to shore up their positions" (Jeffrey 2010, 466). It is for these reasons that youth turn to unlicensed guiding as a form of entrepreneurial activity in Bodh Gaya.

Ashok, twenty-two years old at the time of my fieldwork, is a good example of how friendly guides acquire "commission" and other forms of social capital through their skillful mediations with visitors. Over a cup of chai, Ashok, who was born in the market area of Bodh Gaya, explained that the main motivation for guiding is to earn money for himself and his family. In the winter season he works as an independent friendly guide in Bodh Gaya, and for the remainder of the year he moves to other popular tourist destinations like Delhi, Dharamsala, and Manila, where he works as a tourist escort, earning commissions from hotels and a Punjabi travel agent.

When asked about his guiding activities in Bodh Gaya, he explained,

> I take people walking around and show them good places. You can say I am a friendly guide. Since two years ago I started doing this. It all depends on the traffic. Some days I can make Rs. 200, and other days Rs. 500—on a trip to Malakala caves let's say. I primarily show people the Buddhist sites, like where Sujata offered the milk-rice to the Buddha, and I never give the impression of working for money. I never ask for money in advance. I like to think of them as guests. Money is not important . . . it is their choice . . . My first ambition is to make friendship, second, cooperation, and third, to think about money for myself.

Ashoka's self-identification as a friendly guide exemplifies his skillful orientation toward the "other." As an unofficial tourist guide who offers local knowledge and emotional companionship, he not only upholds a tradition of hospitality but also shores up opportunities for significant earnings due to the multiple social and economic outcomes that can emerge out of sustained interaction with a visitor.

There is an interesting parallel here with the infamous Kuta cowboys of Bali. The 2009 documentary film *Cowboys in Paradise*, directed by Amit Virmani, documents the lives of young men from poor fishing families who "work the beaches" of Bali seeking customers (primarily women) through informal talk because it's fun, profitable, and easier than manual labor or fishing. The young men have long hair and beach shorts, have a few catchphrases in various foreign languages, and approach women on the beach with their big smiles and playful charm. As the film illustrates, the Kuta cowboys utilize a three-pronged approach when it comes to cruising the beach: (1) Make them laugh. (2) Shower them with attention. (3) Show them a good time. In order to "climb a mountain," explains one of the beach boys in the film, you have to pace yourself with a guest. It is more than just sex. The Kuta cowboys, like the friendly guide, never charge for sex or guiding. Rather, every woman is seen as a potential asset, and the longer he holds on, the greater his returns. Their success hinges on providing these foreign women with a "day-long orgasm," showering them with attention and affection. And, if the young men are successful in managing their assets over the tourist season, these intimate interludes can translate into "exceptional gains," ranging from rent payments, new clothes, motorcycles, cars, land, and opportunities abroad.

As with the Kuta cowboys of Bali, the key for many Bodh Gaya friendly guides is to "work" the main target areas and arrival points to establish first contact. From this initial point of social interaction and greeting, a chain of possible commission exchanges can unfold in the marketplace by directing visitors to restaurants, hotels and guesthouses, internet cafés, and handicraft emporiums. The brokering of these commercial transactions between tourists and vendors is an integral part of the fluid exchange opportunities within the informal economy of Bodh Gaya's global bazaar. And, as subtle experts in anticipating pilgrim and tourists' needs and desires, they play a significant role in terms of mediating and directing the flow of tourist traffic that supports wider consumption practices.

One of the main services provided by these touts, as Ashok indicates, is to organize day trips to some less familiar Buddhist sites in the surrounding landscape. Although some travelers are uncomfortable with this informal arrangement and may request a set price in advance, almost all the guides I met, like Ashok, refuse to set a price and forgo a guiding fee. Instead, they prefer to take their chances cultivating a deeper and more meaningful friendship with the guest in the course of the excursion. As part of the day's itinerary, visitors will also encounter numerous rustic schools, orphanages, and charitable trusts located at nearby Buddhist sites such as the Sujata stupa in the village of Bakroar—a major hub for NGOs and charitable initiatives. Many of these derelict educational centers are the product of foreign sponsorship, and, like the hotel and restaurant industry, some of them are seasonal and run during the winter season when tourist visibility is at its peak. Akin to a religious society or NGO, these charitable trusts can be propped up quite easily, and their recent flourishing has earned Bodh Gaya the dubious status of "NGO capital" based on a rough estimate of two to four hundred NGOs in an area of a few square kilometers (Sinha 2006). Not surprisingly, many of these charitable trusts and educational schools are managed by former street touts who have turned to social work among the destitute as a means of ensuring long-term financial sponsorship and economic security.

According to Jitendra, a former tout who is familiar with the process, "There are different ways to get *janpakra* [to catch people for business]." He continues, "The main motivation is a friendly guide. Most of these boys are coming from the local villages and are very poor. They want to become modern and dream of moving to a foreign country. You can say they have an interest in Western culture and activity."

> These people are seen as examples so they model themselves after Western culture. Whereas for those who are educated, they have the goal of being a doctor where full-time work is given. But most have not passed their tenth year or have no education. Still they want to leave Bodh Gaya so they try to earn easy money. It is also connected to sponsorship. Trying to get sponsors for schools and then the money disappears. These schools should be clear on how many sponsors they have. We have all seen in the community how people with schools get rich quickly. Although educated people are working hard for one month and maybe get a salary of Rs. 10,000, if you open a school you can get Rs. 50,000 very quickly . . . in one shot.

As Jitendra explains, for many of these urban youth, one of the quickest ways to earn "easy money" is to run a school for the destitute and capitalize on the benevolent and charitable aspirations of visiting pilgrims and tourists. Through social work under the rubric of NGOs, these activities can transform poverty into profit by offering student sponsorship at a relatively low monthly cost to foreigners.

Internet cafés have also provided an effective tool for social networking and ensuring financial aid and sponsorship throughout the year. As one shopkeeper explained to me, "We say in Bodh Gaya, 'Different seasons, different kinds of beggars.' There are email beggars who send emails during the winter season to potential donors, saying, 'It is really cold here, and the children require sweaters and blankets. Can you please contribute in this way.' During the rainy season they write, 'We need money because the water is leaking in our homes.'" It is not surprising that many of these internet cafés also provide commission to local boys and allow them free access to the internet in exchange for customer patronage. Through the strategic use of technology and new communicative mediums, urban youth are able to keep transnational ties open by cultivating social networks and foreign donors online that can prove advantageous, especially during heightened periods of economic insecurity (Brennan 2004). With the arrival of Western Union and other digital money transfer services, these technologies have also greatly improved the ease of fund transfers at a relatively low exchange rate with limited government regulation.

What is perhaps most troubling about these arrangements between friendly guides and the recent upsurge in NGOs and charitable trusts is that one cannot help but be disturbed by the cosmetic use of education that destitute children receive as seasonal props in the pursuit of foreign sponsorship.[11] According to Ahmed, a travel agent who openly expressed his disapproval of these activities in the surrounding area, "I do not like the nature of people here as beggars. Even though there is so much labor work available in Bodh Gaya, still they prefer to beg." He continued, "People are getting easy money very quickly by starting a society [charitable trust]. Local people do not want to do labor or service work, especially when rice, clothing, and money come free. The local children are becoming habituated. Small children are now chasing after people. They are saying, 'I am very poor, I need a book'; then it is resold back to the shop for commission. They are only five or six years old, and these things are beginning to happen on a large scale."

Although the boundaries between begging and entrepreneurship, like the blurring of love marriages and spousal visas, are difficult to discern in this context, I would argue that most of the urban youth in Bodh Gaya are acutely aware of the calculus of morality that confronts these informal exchanges. Similarly, both transnational courting and charitable operations provide an important zone of advancement to help escape poverty and strategize for the future. Growing up on the outskirts of a world-famous religious site makes timepass possible and also offers a public arena for learning and reflecting upon their own limitations in the "global south" as well as the gross inequalities within India and abroad. Moreover, these sharp global economic disparities provide the stimulus for many grass-roots initiatives in Bodh Gaya, and there are enough success stories circulating in the bazaar to inspire people. While there are those like Ahmed and Tsering from the Tibet Om Café, who openly show their disproval of these commissioning activities, far more locals tolerate and support these informal patronage networks because they are well aware of the difficulties facing the poor and the lack of employment opportunities available.

CONCLUSION

A variety of economic lifelines and transnational social fields support the growing hospitality and service sector in Bodh Gaya today. The life histories and stories involving Tibetan merchants, hoteliers, shopkeepers, and friendly guides describe some of the possibilities of globalization and the challenges that arise in a place increasingly defined by transnational encounters. Many Bodh Gaya residents imagine Buddhism differently from those pilgrims and visitors who come to the land of enlightenment seeking spiritual nourishment at the navel of the earth. Residents have a different spatial relationship with the Mahabodhi Temple and equate Buddhism primarily with new forms of wealth and income. With limited access to quality education and professional jobs, both the formal and informal economy of tourism offers an important source of employment for Bodh Gaya's residents outside the agricultural sector, which has been in sharp decline for several decades.

In this rapidly growing hospitality and service sector, contact with pilgrims and tourists offers an array of economic, social, and romantic opportunities that are not generally available to other Biharis and Indians in other parts of the country. Although tourism wages are comparable to agricultural and construction wages, contact with foreign travelers can lead to new opportunities (Brennan 2004). For these reasons, a large number of male youth in Bodh Gaya seek jobs with a "high degree of interaction" (Brennan 2004). The payoff might be marriage and migration out of India. Or, the payoff might be ongoing financial sponsorship through NGOs and charitable programs, bringing a reliable source of income and livelihood throughout the year. This is certainly apparent among the friendly guides who spend their days in the bazaar seeking interactions and opportunities with tourists because the resulting contact offers a wider set of possibile lives to imagine and enact (Appadurai 1991, 197).

Although Buddhism has given rise to new forms of employment in tourism, these opportunities are still limited; numerous constraints exclude locals from these transnational social fields. With a growing population and a lack of diversification in job opportunities, urban poverty and social ills such as begging have become a growing concern. This, along with the threat of *dacoity* and sexual violence, such as the 2014 attack on a young Japanese woman en route to Bodh Gaya, can rapidly undermine the prospects of tourism in south Bihar. It is for these reasons that a tradition of respect for visitors is widely upheld in the marketplace and a moral-commercial ethos that transcends caste and sectarian difference remains at the core of guest relations.

Tourism as a source of livelihood can generate divergent experiences that involve new relationships of economic empowerment and powerlessness. The lived environment of the global bazaar as a nexus of social relations captures some of the complexity of these emerging transnational processes and the ways in which some residents creatively respond to the high seasonality of tourism and pilgrimage in order to move beyond everyday survival.

5 A Master Plan
for World Heritage

A range of low forested hills silhouette the small hamlets flanking
the glistening, sandy banks of the river. Monks and nuns rub
shoulders with tourists and believers from all over the world. An
all-pervading calm envelops the town, giving visitors a sense of
peace. (Bihar state tourism pamphlet 2006)

FOLLOWING THE TWENTY-EIGHTH SESSION OF THE WORLD HERI-
tage Committee Meeting in 2005, a joint mission was scheduled by members of the International Council on Monuments and Sites (ICOMOS) and
the World Heritage Centre to review and assess the current conservation
measures in Bodh Gaya—three years after the Mahabodhi Temple Complex was formally inscribed on the UNESCO World Heritage List. The
team of heritage advisors consisted of UNESCO member Junko Okahashi,
ICOMOS technical expert Herb Stovel, and several senior Indian officials
from the Archaeological Survey of India, the Housing and Urban Development Corporation (HUDCO), the Bihar state tourism department, and
both local and regional municipal authorities.

Upon their arrival in Bodh Gaya, the visiting delegation was surprised
to find all shops in the commercial business district closed and the bazaar
at a complete standstill. In response to the high-profile meeting, a two-day
silent protest had been organized by shopkeepers, landowners, and concerned citizens under the banner Nagrik Vikas Manch (Citizens Development Forum). Mainly, they objected to the provisions of a proposed "master
plan" that would impose restrictions on all construction activities within a
kilometer of the Mahabodhi Temple Complex, which, they feared, would
result in their eviction and displacement.

When Junko Okahashi was confronted by an Indian reporter on this
matter, she replied, "The people of Bodh Gaya must develop a sense of
belonging to the rich cultural heritage of the place and cooperate in the
preservation and maintenance of the World Heritage site" (Kalam 2005).
However, many Bodh Gaya residents held a different view of cultural

heritage and conservation management, one that was premised on a history of displacement and resettlement. Dwarko Sundrani, who took part in the two-day protest, said, "They say they want this area for public space . . . but there was no decision on the master plan and then the government proceeds to give land to foreigners. What about the people of Bodh Gaya? . . . There are earlier issues over land, but no one is listening."

These antagonistic views toward World Heritage and the aligned discourse of conservation and urban redevelopment were widespread during my fieldwork from 2005 to 2007. At first I was quite surprised by these responses, especially given the growing importance of tourism as a source of livelihood for many residents in the area. How could the recent international spotlight on the Mahabodhi Temple be detrimental to local socioeconomic aspirations?

In this chapter I show how World Heritage designation has brought new demands and pressures to Bodh Gaya's spatial environment to ensure its world-making status as both an object of global patrimony and a model of enlightened stewardship for the state government. While the 2005 protest represents a key flashpoint in the deepening effects of the neoliberal state and market forces over claims to cultural heritage and sacred space, this is not an isolated case (Breglia 2006; Collins 2008, 2011; Herzfeld 2006, 2010). For these reasons, it is important to excavate the history of town planning and government land acquisition that gave rise to current struggles and shaped the horizons of political consciousness in Bodh Gaya today. Central to this task is a genealogical analysis of the "master plan."

A master plan can be interpreted as an iconic form of modern urbanism that is central to political power and techniques of governmentality (Foucault 1991). Since the end of the nineteenth century, the rise of urbanism as a discipline has combined the planning of space with political control based on scientific and rational modes of understanding (Rabinow 1982). Through its functional efficiency and detailed mapping of the urban landscape, it represents a "spatial syntax" that aims to achieve uniformity by ordering spatial elements and encoding the syntax with information about actions that can take place in those environments (Hancock 2008, 78). At the core of the master plan is a progressive reformulation of space, including the provision of infrastructure, tourism development, the maintenance of housing and livelihood spaces, the importance of public community resources, and the phasing in of various development schemes in coordination with the release of public funds. Through the implementation of zoning laws and subdivision regulations, the master plan can also generate conflict among restive populations as both public and private agencies seek to advance their interests with ambitious proposals under circumstances of great uncertainty.

THE NOBLE STRIVING OF A MASTER PLAN

> I suggest that we should undertake the task of improving in every way the places in India connected with the Buddha. . . . Bodh Gaya which is the most important of all these places, is at present in a bad condition. The whole place is dirty and all kinds of odd structures are being put up. Nobody is responsible because it does not come within the sphere of the Gaya municipality. . . . I suggest that we might send an engineer and an architect to visit these places and to make recommendations as to what should be done. (Nehru 1955b, 452.)

> Obviously, at this holy land of rich and noble memories, technology must subserve higher ends, and, imbiding the spirit of its renaissance, re-create the old glory in its new setting. (Draft Master Plan 1966, preamble)

Shortly after India's independence, the central government looked to impose a town development strategy that involved cataloging and displaying the pasts of its holdings while also prescribing a liberal discourse that equated urban planning with societal well-being (Hancock 2008). During this period of strong Congress leadership, "futurity was the central trope of the national narrative," and various traditions were also evaluated "according to their contributions to national development and integration" (48). As an important cultural asset with wider foreign policy ramifications, Bodh Gaya provided a key resource for the state government in line with its goals of economic development and tourism promotion.

In anticipation of thousands of Buddhist pilgrims and foreign dignitaries visiting India during the 2,500th Buddha Jayanti in 1956–1957, the state and central governments launched a coordinated national development scheme designed to improve regional communications, transportation, and tourist facilities at all the major sites. Some of the prominent changes in Bodh Gaya during this time were repairs to roads linking Bodh Gaya with Gaya city and Rajgir, the construction of a rural water and sewage system, the electrification of the entire temple compound, the building of a central government rest house and tourist dormitory, the construction of a small archaeological museum, the building of a state government inspection bungalow, and the cultivation of several garden spaces. With the goal of turning the immediate area around the Mahabodhi Temple into parkland, a small *basti* (village of huts) was relocated to a nearby government settlement called the Harijan Colony today.

Following the resettlement, the Mahabodhi Temple Complex received a significant facelift, including restoration that was carried out between 1953 and 1956. During this time, the state and central governments repaired parts of the temple as well as votive stupas and broken images, put on a fresh coat of color wash, constructed the compound railings around the temple and *vajrasana*, cleaned and gilded the main Buddha image in the temple, and opened an inner and outer circumambulating path, or *parikrama* (Sundrani 1986). To reinforce the temple's Buddhist authenticity under the new temple management committee, archaeological excavations and repair work were done at the nearby lotus tank, and an Ashokan pillar was installed to the south of the Mahabodhi Temple.[1]

Following the 2,500th Buddha Jayanti celebrations, urban planning and development discourse revolved around a proposed master plan. As Ron Inden (1995, 268) has noted: "Planning was the utopian principle through which Nehru and his government hoped to embody the foundational Reason of democratic socialism and hence bring about economic development." Under India's third five-year plan, between 1961 and 1966, several metropolitan master plans were mandated throughout the country (Hancock 2008) with the explicit goal of creating a "well structured landscape" that would improve "imageability" to attract tourist visitation. The first Draft Master Plan for Bodh Gaya was formulated by the Bodh-Gaya Town Planning Authority in 1964 and formally published through the Superintendent Secretariat Press of Patna, Bihar, in 1966. This fifty-page comprehensive review of Bodh Gaya's town infrastructure involved a fifteen-person project team with both central and provincial state support by the prime minister, Indira Gandhi; the chief minister of Bihar, K. B. Sahay; the minister of L.S.G. (town planning), S. N. Sinha; and the Patna division commissioner, H. N. Thakur.

As an expression of the Nehruvian legacy and the Indian government's wider socialist aspirations, the Draft Master Plan outlined a phased development program at Bodh Gaya that would extend over seventeen years (1964–1981) with a budget of Rs. 17 million for implementation within the suggested time frame. Within the 2,800-acre landscape proposed under the

Bodh Gaya master plan scheme, the majority of the land was conserved for agricultural uses, with the goal of sustaining its rural economy. However, 1,200 acres of land were earmarked for specific development initiatives, with 580 acres proposed for specific government land acquisition. In terms of executing the Draft Master Plan, the Town Planning Authority (TPA) was entrusted with the task in conjunction with the Notified Area Committee (NAC), which included members of the Local Self-Government Department and Housing Department. These changes would also take place in accordance with new state legislation under the Bihar Restriction of Uses of Land Act (1948) and the Bihar Town Planning and Improvement Trust Act (1951).

Based on the 1961 Indian census figures, the Town Planning Authority reported a population of sixty-three hundred residents in Bodh Gaya: 72% from scheduled and backward castes, 12% institutional, 8% Muslim, and 8% higher castes. The TPA also observed a slow rate of urbanization, with development largely confined to a rectangular area one and three-quarters of a mile long and half a mile across in which 80% of the population resided in 219 acres of land. These dwellings consisted of largely *kutcha*-style homes (thatched and mud walls) lacking basic amenities such as piped water and sanitary facilities. The relatively slow rate of urbanization up to this point, according to the town planners, provided an important "sociological asset" giving the authorities some "breathing time for action" (Draft Master Plan 1966, 11).

As cited in the document's preamble, two guiding principles or "imperatives" governed the master plan: "a) the preservation of its supremely important historical, cultural and archaeological background, and b) the necessity of channelling [*sic*] physical and economic development in a manner that highlights the dominance of nature and spirit and does not either compromise or obscure the basic character of the town." In terms of spatial management, the master plan divided the landscape of Bodh Gaya into seven major topographical sectors (eight including the nearby village of Bakroar), with each sector having various zoning ordinances to regulate land-use activity. Given the overall importance of the Mahabodhi Temple and the Bodhi tree, the main focus of the plan is the rehabilitation of the temple sector—which included a total non-institutional population of 1,791 people, mainly in the former "revenue" villages of Taradih and Mastipur. The physical landscape of the temple sector correlated with a raised mound surrounded by two floodwater catchments that principally drained off along a channel running south to north, skirting around the Mahabodhi Temple to the west.

By far the greatest concern associated with the temple sector was the archaeological mound, which had become, in the eyes of the town planners, overrun by "unrealistic exploitation" by both public and private agencies that were "adversely affecting . . . the serenity and aesthetic beauty of the sector" (Draft Master Plan 1966, 46). Following the extensive archaeological work initiated by Alexander Cunningham and J. D. Beglar in the 1880s, land use now highlighted "an almost tragic exploitation of the archaeological area for far less significant uses" (Draft Master Plan 1966, 14). Not only did this give rise to a "confusion of multifarious land uses," but due to the acute paucity of roads within the town, "unrelated pedestrian and vehicular traffic" now concentrated in the area (14). Some of the building structures contributing to this "confusion" included the Maha Bodhi Society Rest House, a Muslim cemetery, Jagannath Temple, the Bodh Gaya Temple Management Committee building, the Samanvay Ashram, a police station, hospital buildings, and the expanding number of shops in the bazaar, which ran between the Bodh Gaya Math and the main temple precinct in a "grossly insufficient ribbon of roadside land" (8).

In other words, from this early point in the formulation of a master plan for Bodh Gaya, an image of disorder was conjured in the temple sector posing a direct threat to its positive imageability. For these reasons, the town planning authority wanted to prioritize the archaeological sensitivity of the site and to remove all institutional development and residential dwellings around the temple sector. In their own words, "Ideally no structures apart from the Maha Bodhi Temple and quadrangle should exist within this area, but in practical terms, we envisage that, while residential, business and commercial uses could be expeditiously removed, the hard core formed by the shrines, monasteries, museum, central government rest-house and the water tower would remain within it" (Draft Master Plan 1966, 20).

With the removal of these "multifarious structures" in the temple sector, the master plan envisioned a site of productive nostalgia consistent with the "natural" virtues of a hermitage where Shakyamuni Buddha obtained enlightenment.

> To our concept, the treatment should reflect an honest and sensible utilisation primarily of the gifts of nature rather than the ostentations of man, and a simplicity and harmony of functions rather than an induction of new confusions to supplant the discarded old ones. Thus while velvety lawns and flower-beds fringed with shrubs; fountains, pools and rockery garden; pathways and avenues lined with coniferous and low-flowering

trees—as also subtly placed clumps of shady trees, lighting and park-furniture have their natural place in it, care has to be taken to avoid a multiplicity of ostentatious and pseudo-artistic structures or sculptures and functions. (Draft Master Plan 1966, 20)

The aesthetic vision of the Draft Master Plan echoes Hirsch and O'Hanlon's (1995, 1) definition of "landscape" as a socially constructed form that involves tensions between imaginative and/or idealized settings that form the "background" against which the "foreground" of everyday lives and experiences are embedded. Ironically, it is only through the "ostentations of man" that the gifts of nature can be realized. Restoring the Buddhist hermitage would require the acquisition of two villages from the foreground in order to bring about the "simplicity and harmony" of functions within the temple sector.

While the temple sector was certainly the focal point of the Draft Master Plan, other topographical areas are relevant to this spatial genealogy of Bodh Gaya's landscape. One of these was the southern sector—due south of the Mahabodhi Temple. Based on the Indian census figures, this area had a total population of 462 people in the hamlets of Tikabigha and Urel—which some regard as the original location of the ancient Uruvela. To revive the ancient memories of Bodh Gaya as a place of "mental concentration," the town planners emphasized the vital importance of establishing a ninety-acre park in this area in order to provide an "ideal environment for sheltered and secluded meditation" (Draft Master Plan 1966, 25). This included a series of small meditational groves informally distributed around pools and approached by winding tracks sheltered by a fringe of tall and spreading trees around three to four rows deep (26). As with the temple sector, the goal of creating a forest environment conducive to mental concentration required the acquisition of residential land from the two villages. To "elevate the mind to a higher plane and prepare it for meditation" would require the "dislodging" of Tikabigha village, creating green spaces that could be linked with the existing mango grove and vacant land that lay at the bend of the water channel (25–26). Failure to realize this green space would run counter to the desired effect: "Neither the sight of a herd of deer, nor that of a newly planted mango grove, would restore the mental concentration of a person (in this modern age) frequently disturbed by whiffs of spicy smell and sound of traffic" (24).

Other sectors were earmarked for residential and commercial growth. The northern sector, for example, was identified as a major residential hub and a significant "point of contact" between tourists and local people. At the time of publication, the northern sector had a population of 1,971 residents and was composed of several village hamlets—Dehariabigha, Upadhyaybigha, Rajapur, Sonubigha, and Pacchetti. This sector was also designated as the zone where several existing villages and commercial enterprises around the Mahabodhi Temple could be resettled at a future date. The Draft Master Plan did not make it entirely clear how and when these resettlement operations would take place, but it did stress the need to implement these changes in the near future.

> The present ribbon of shopping area, at the edge of the mound and to the east, (viz., the riverside) of the Maha Bodhi, is cramped for space and has already begun to objectionably creep up to the sacred precincts. Since the longer it occupies its present site, the greater would be the difficulties encountered in its relocation, an overall urgency attaches to the construction of a new shopping centre to accommodate the present as well as future needs of expansion. (Draft Master Plan 1966, 33)

The TPA also proposed significant changes for the rehabilitation of the northwestern and southwestern sectors. Comprised largely of agricultural land, the northwestern sector had a total population of 775 residents and included a government high school, a state seed farm, the hamlet of Miyabigha (Siddhartha Nagar), and other remote village hamlets such as Janpur, Bhagwanpur, Baijubigha, and Bhum toli. For the most part, the TPA proposed maintaining the large agricultural base in this sector, which sustained many in Bodh Gaya. However, a new approach road to Bodh Gaya was planned to cut through the land, linking the old riverside road with the new entry road just east of the Royal Wat Thai and tourist dormitory (see Bihar State Tourism Complex). The construction of this new entry point and the development of a "rational road grid" system would help to ensure that the bulk of traffic remained on the perimeter, so Bodh Gaya would retain a "pedestrian character" (Draft Master Plan 1966, 38). Finally, the plan envisioned that a "symbolic deer park" would be erected in this sector to complement the Buddha's ancient links with the deer at Isipitana (Sarnath).

For the southwestern sector, the TPA envisioned a space for more Buddhist monasteries and government buildings. When the Draft Master Plan was completed in 1966, 514 people were living in this sector, which included the small hamlets of Pipalpati and Mastipur, along with the recently constructed Royal Wat Thai, a tourist dormitory, the block development office and staff quarters, the resettlement Harijan colony, a small library, and the youth hostel. While the Draft Master Plan clearly outlined the importance of monastic growth in this area, it also suggested limiting foreign Buddhist countries to twelve and imposing strict architectural regulations upon them. For example, the existing Burmese monastery in the northern sector was described as "architecturally uninteresting" and not in conformance with the proposed zoning scheme. The plan also stressed the need to enforce architectural and planning measures on all future monasteries in order to "express their national personalities in an ensemble as pleasing, if not more, as the recently built Thai monastery" (Draft Master Plan 1966, 24). To complement the growth of pleasing Buddhist architecture in the southwestern sector, the town planning authorities also proposed the acquisition of land for a new inspection bungalow, a hospital, and several other public institutions, including an international research center, a language institute, and a Buddhist art gallery.

Clearly, Bodh Gaya's (and India's) Buddhist heritage was a key site of investment in the planned welfare state of the 1950s and 1960s. Underlying the master plan vision of Bodh Gaya is the nostalgic production of an ancient forest hermitage and a progressive model of city growth that could unite local needs with international pilgrimage. The Draft Master Plan for Bodh Gaya, like other city master plans during this time, invoked national heritage in alignment with the dominant development ideology of the postcolonial era. As Indira Gandhi wrote in the introduction to the plan,

> Bodh Gaya has special historical significance for us and for Buddhists the world over for whom it is a place of pilgrimage. It is, therefore, important to see that this city does not develop haphazardly but according to a well thought out plan with consideration to the needs and conveniences of the local population as well as of tourists and pilgrims. I hope the Master Plan for the development of Bodh Gaya will blend reverence with beauty and will indicate how greatly India values this ancient site of Buddha's enlightenment. (Draft Master Plan 1966, preamble)

Despite the optimism of India's leaders, the idyllic master plan and those that followed remained largely in draft format, and the government enacted few changes. As anthropologist Mary Hancock (2008, 48) has noted in relation to her study of cultural heritage in Chennai, part of the difficulty in implementing the economic and social goals prescribed by the five-year plans was that there was little coordination between the central and state commissioning authorities and the local town planning agencies. And as time passed, there were changes among ruling political parties, so amendments were often required. This was certainly the case in Bodh Gaya, where the master plan was revised in 1972 (and approved in 1973) to accommodate the changing needs of the site, especially the dramatic increase in land requests by Asian Buddhist groups and a growing desire to relocate the village of Taradih, which spread around the Mahabodhi Temple Complex.[2]

For these reasons, in early April 1980, with an armed police force and two bulldozers, 380 village dwellings were demolished under the direction of District Magistrate G. S. Khan and the new temple superintendent, Gyan Jagat.[3] According to Prashant, a former Taradih resident who recalled the chain of events, the state authorities began by dismantling the house of a prominent employee of the Bodh Gaya *mahant*, Guir Shankar Prasad Singh. "And once the villagers saw his home being crushed," he said, "the villagers began to run." He continued, "At that time, it was also the summer season and was very hot. There were no water facilities either. They arrived and began to demolish our homes with bulldozers. So people fled. Many did not receive adequate compensation. Some are still waiting. They should not have done it like this," he added. "We requested the government to construct the buildings first and then resettle with our compensation funds, but instead they removed us first."

Thus during the warm summer months of 1980, Taradih village was razed to the ground, and its residents were relocated to Bhagalpur (lit. translation, "to run away"), or New Taradih, as it is often referred as today. The only structures that were not demolished were a small Muslim mosque and the upscale Indian Tourism Development Corporation (ITDC) hotel, located to the west of the main temple. While many former Taradih residents that I spoke with during my fieldwork are content with their location in Bhagalpur today, they recall the enormous challenges of trying to rebuild their homes during the summer and monsoon season without adequate roads, electricity, or water provisions. Many residents suffered from heat stroke and were forced to live in tents for over three months before some basic housing structure could be erected. There were also many elders and children who became sick due to the lack of amenities.

When a map of the Revised Master Plan was once again updated in 1982 by the Town and Country Planning Organization, it identified the former Taradih village area as a tourist complex and the future site of Gautam Van (Buddha forest), reflecting the sylvan attributes of the hermitage environment, albeit one safeguarded for upscale tourism consumption. When I

Residue of the former Taradih Village archaeological excavations by the Bihar state government

interviewed a former Bihar state tourism official in Patna, he noted that the Gautam Van project was designed to include a number of self-contained tourist cottages surrounded by gardens and an artificial stream. Under contract with the ITDC in collaboration with the Temple Management Committee under Gyan Jagat, the first initiative by the state planning authorities was to erect a large boundary wall around the recently vacated seventeen-acre plot of land to secure the space for future landscaping and beautification.

Among the former Taradih residents I spoke with, the construction of the boundary wall was viewed as another exclusionary measure that privileged foreign interests and neglected the use value of Bodh Gaya's residents, especially the village roads, short cuts, and paths connecting to the main bazaar. In response to the concrete restrictions in the temple sector, several residents protested and even demolished a section of the boundary wall in opposition to the Revised Master Plan. During this time, the state archaeological department also raised the concern that the construction of tourist cottages would undermine the archaeological value of the site. With the land cleared of residential dwellings, they argued that priority should now be given to excavation, which had long been neglected. In support of this decision, archaeological excavations led by head officer Dr. Ajit Kumar Prasad took place in 1981–1982, but there has been no sustained effort to restore or protect the archaeological grounds of Taradih, which lie directly west of the Mahabodhi Temple and have become a popular waste dump. There were also those of left-leaning opinion who felt that a park should be built to commemorate Jayprakash Narayan, who stood for the emancipation of the poor, not their displacement.[4] Given these discordant views, the Revised Master Plan and Gautam Van tourist complex never came to fruition; once again, the plan was buried until a more opportune time.

BUDDHIST CIRCUITS AND SPIRITUAL TOURISM

In the last few decades, tourism has become an integral part of India's economic liberalization program and central to the image management of various levels of government.[5] As one of the first government-sponsored industries to be privatized, tourism is seen as a major driver for economic development through its contribution to foreign exchange earnings. These changes were reinforced by the government's declaration of the 1990s as the "Decade of Tourism," which viewed tourism as a "commercial and moral endeavor that advanced the goal of liberalization while still containing it within the integrationist message of cultural nationalism" (Hancock 2008, 129–133).

As part of a broader decentralization strategy to diffuse the economic and infrastructural benefits of tourism, broadening out from the popular "Golden Triangle" of Delhi-Agra-Jaipur, state governments were responsible for developing their tourism promotion strategy and identifying key historical and cultural sites for future infrastructural development. Following on the heels of the first comprehensive tourism policy in India, formulated in 1982, the promotion of selective "travel circuits" designed to maximize the benefits of tourism gained wide currency (Hannam and Diekmann 2011). In Bihar, not surprisingly, the promotion of spiritual tourism through the development of a Buddhist circuit was identified as a key investment priority.

In many ways, these efforts to promote religious and spiritually motivated travel in Bihar can be seen as part of broader trend in international tourism development in the modern era (Timothy and Olsen 2006). Emerging alongside other prominent markers of tourist imagery such as "sun, sex, sea and sand" (Crick 1989) is the "lure of the metaphysical" and the promise of enlightenment, renewal, and healing. Although the marriage of pilgrimage and commerce is by no means a new social phenomenon in the Indian cultural landscape, the outfitting of sacred sites and spaces of worship with explicit consumerist messages certainly is (Hancock 2008, 134–135). And, the integration of these sites into larger circuits of consumption helps to regulate tourist flows through a networked geography and to increase profit margins for the state government and other invested agencies. The emphasis on spirituality is also important. As Carrette and King (2005) have noted, the term *religious* generally has institutional connotations, prescribed rituals, and established ways of believing, while *spiritual* emphasizes personal experience and deep motivations to achieve life meaning and wholeness. As a vague and ambiguous signifier, the term *spiritual* functions well in the market space of tourism as an inflection of religious orthodoxy that can appeal to individual consumer tastes and preferences.

As part of these efforts to strengthen and promote the Buddhist circuit, from the mid-1980s onward, basic tourist infrastructure such as tourist bungalows, cafeterias, restaurants, and transportation facilities were established in several locations throughout Bihar. This is certainly the case in Bodh Gaya, where an entire tourist bungalow complex was built by the government, including three hotels—the Siddhartha Vihar, the Buddha Vihar, and the Sujata Vihar—along with the Siddhartha Restaurant, a bus booking counter (connecting two daily buses to Patna), a tourist information center opposite the railway reservation office, and a Bank of India branch. The ITDC tourist complex was also regionalized under the Bihar State Tourism Development Corporation (BSTDC) and was renamed Ashok's Travelers Lodge. In line with the country's liberalization goals, Buddhism was viewed as one of the country's greatest cultural exports, and a task development force was initiated by the central government to provide a detailed report on tourist locations associated with the life of the Buddha and bring them up to international standards.[6]

Looking to attract financial investment and improve connectivity along the Buddhist sector, the Ministry of Tourism and Culture established several new partnerships and technical collaborations between foreign governments, such as the United States and Japan, during this time. One organization that showed interest in jointly undertaking the task of uplifting the Buddhist sector was the United States National Park Service (NPS). Created in 1916, the NPS is a federal agency that manages all national parks along with several national monuments and other conservation and historical properties throughout the United States. In June 1987, the International Affairs Office of the National Park Service created a design assistance team that consisted of faculty and students from the Landscape Architecture Department at the University of Illinois, specialists from Japan, and architecture consultants from the NPS. As part of this preliminary survey, the design team surveyed nine sites in the state of Bihar and Uttar Pradesh, including Sankassa, Shravasti, Piprahwa, Kushinagar, Sarnath, Bodh Gaya, Rajgir, Nalanda, and Vaishali in order to determine which locations should be adopted for further site-specific conceptual master plans.

Sarnath was prioritized by the NPS design assistance team, whereas the state government selected the New Delhi–based School of Planning and Architecture (1991) to provide a draft plan for Bodh Gaya and Rajgir-Nalanda that could be synchronized with conservation and development aid provided by the Japanese through the Overseas Economic Cooperation Fund (OECF).

Under the OECF, a number of proposals initiated by the Task Development Force were taken up by the Japanese government, providing economic assistance in support of infrastructure projects that improved connectivity along the Buddhist circuit throughout the 1990s.[7] With the Bihar tourism department as the nodal agency for implementation of the OECF funds, basic infrastructure was provided at Vaishali, Rajgir, Nalanda, and Bodh Gaya in four main areas: electricity, water, landscape, and roads. In Bodh Gaya, for example, the OECF helped finance the bridge to Bakroar village, several connecting roads, the popular footpath in the bazaar, and several landscaping and beautification initiatives around the Mahabodhi Temple precincts. These loans by the Japanese government were not exclusive to Bihar, but were also taken up in other Indian States such as Uttar Pradesh and other prominent Buddhist-heritage sites such as the Ajanta-Ellora temple cave complex.

Building on the negotiations between the OECF loan agreement and the Ministry of Tourism, a joint venture was also coordinated between Pacific Consultants International in Tokyo and Consulting Engineering Services in New Delhi to produce a report on the development of the Buddhist sector for the Japanese market (Department of Tourism, Government of India 1992). This fascinating market survey explores the prospects of spiritual tourism, especially among the "postwar baby boomers" in Japan, who reached their retirement age at the beginning of the new century. These changing generational demographics and the subsequent rise of a Japanese leisure class, it is hypothesized, will have a favorable impact on the Buddhist circuit in India. To anticipate the future growth in the Japanese travel market, the survey compiles a wide range of information on people's views of India, derived from interviews with Japanese consumers, experienced tourists to India, travel groups, pilgrimage organizers, and Japanese tour wholesalers/ travel agents.

The survey findings indicate that there is great potential for the Buddhist sector in India, especially with important changes in life priorities in Japan. This change in attitude, it is suggested, might also trigger a change toward a "less workaholic" and "more leisure-oriented society in the near future" (Department of Tourism, Government of India 1992, 9). In line with Japan's growing GDP and the appreciation of the yen since 1986, OECF data indicate that Japanese travel expenditure amounts to US$2,187 on average per person, which is more than double that of other major countries, including France, the United States, and the United Kingdom. The survey report attributed the purchasing power of the Japanese tourist to three key factors: (1) a higher percentage of group tourists and fewer individual budget tourists than in other countries; (2) the social obligation to buy souvenirs for one's colleagues, friends, and sometimes neighbors; and (3) the relatively high price of imported goods in Japan, which encourages consumers to shop abroad (for many overseas destinations, including India, "shopping" is regarded as a principal motivation for travel [11]).

The survey also indicated that two-thirds of tourists travel to overseas destinations for fewer than eleven days, and tour itineraries tend to be relatively short. With 93% of Japanese overseas travelers using travel agencies and 58% of them participating in group tours, there is vast potential in states like Bihar for stimulating packaged tourism itineraries along the Buddhist circuit. While package tours along the "Golden Triangle"—Delhi, Agra, and Jaipur—remain very popular, the number of Japanese visitors to India doubled from 29,103 in 1982 to 58,707 in 1989, and this only strengthens the potential of the "Buddhist Sector" as an alternative. To compete with the Golden Triangle, however, the survey report indicated that "security" and "sanitary conditions" must be improved, as they are key factors determining travel destinations among Japanese consumers, showing that Japanese tourists "are very sensitive to travel environments" (23).

In terms of prevailing images among the Japanese public toward India and the Buddhist sector, the survey indicates that there is a strong association with the cultural and historical attributes of India, which "seems to be almost synonymous with seeing the Buddhist sector" (Department of Tourism, Government of India 1992, 25). Japanese respondents predominantly viewed India as a "religious" and "mysterious" place, accounting for 87% and 70% of responses, respectively. The travel motivations for the majority of these Japanese respondents are also linked with a desire "to see" or "to know" India, rather than to relax or to enjoy themselves (38). One female interviewee commented that if one goes to India, it is expected that he or she will "become like a philosopher."

Outside of these general-interest tourists, a significant amount of marketing data is collected from Japanese Buddhist pilgrims who are largely coordinated through specific group tours organized by Buddhist societies, sects, and priests. Three Buddhist societies interviewed by the Japan Travel Bureau Foundation in January 1991 were Nichiren-syu, Rissyo Kosei-kai, and Jodo syu. Among these sects, the principal motivation for visiting India and the Buddhist sector was "spiritual," including remarks such as "to reach a state of mind like . . . Buddha had attained" or "to feel as if one's soul was purified." At the same time, interviewees shared concerns about the poor sanitary conditions and the quality of transportation in areas like Bihar. A Japanese pilgrim who had recently returned from Bihar said that he would like to see more education for the Indian tour guides. Tour guides "seem to be uneven in their ability and morals" and their main concern and motivation "seems to be the commission they get at souvenir shops" (Department of Tourism, Government of India 1992, 40).

These collaborations and state-sponsored initiatives designed to lure international tourists and promote the Buddhist circuit exemplify a conscious shift toward a more outward-looking demonstration of tourism reflexivity built around a strategic investment in advertising and image promotion.[8] Although the Maha Bodhi Society can be seen as the vanguard in promoting the Buddhist circuit through its full-page journal advertisements (e.g., "Visit the Sacred Places Associated with the Master, Lord Buddha"), by the turn of the millennium, half of India's tourism expenditure budget was earmarked for overseas marketing (Hannam and Diekmann 2011, 19–20), which has become a cornerstone of India's own self-promotion on the world stage through the Incredible India campaign (Geary 2013b).

Ever since the popular tourist campaign was launched in 2002, the Ministry of Tourism has aggressively promoted the Incredible India brand in both domestic and overseas markets through a range of mediums: print advertisement in tourism literature, cultural presentations at trade fairs and exhibitions, TV/video, promotional films, and both electronic and internet media. Building on an earlier development strategy to create "brand equity," each state government was encouraged to develop its own regional image and logos, which could be encapsulated by the "mother" brand and help to promote both diversity and integration (Geary 2013b). In Bihar, the main cultural tourism asset continued to be the Buddhist circuit, now merging with glossy exotic and Orientalist images to elevate select destinations like Bodh Gaya as premier spiritual attractions. In support of the Incredible India image campaign, the government of Bihar has also launched its own brand campaign to attract visitors through its new logo, "Blissful Bihar," which includes an image of a *peepal* tree under which the Buddha attained enlightenment.

To capitalize on its greatest international export and cater to the financially lucrative religious diaspora, the launching of the new tagline was synchronized with several major tourist initiatives under the rubric "pilgrimage with pleasure" (Pandey 2006). Three are worth highlighting here. The first initiative was the revamping of the former Gaya aerodome, spread over 971 acres into the Gaya International Airport. When the Gaya International Airport was first opened in 2002, it was only accessible by foreign airliners from neighboring countries with Buddhist influence, such as Sri Lanka, Thailand, and Bhutan, as well as Singapore and Myanmar, which operate charter flights during the winter season.[9]

The second major tourism initiative was the launching of the Mahaparinirvan Express train by the Indian Railways in 2007. Modeled after luxury tourist trains such as the "Palace on Wheels," the Mahaparinirvan boasts of world-class facilities, providing seventeen special package trips over eight days during the pilgrimage season. These tours involve meals, guides, sightseeing, and luxury hotel accommodation that are connected with all the prominent Buddhist sites in India and Nepal—mainly Bodh Gaya, Nalanda, Rajgir, Kushinagar, Sarnath, Shravasti, and Lumbini. As a special Rajdhani-Express train, it is fully air-conditioned and is largely targeted at middle-class and higher-end Buddhist tourists, especially from Southeast Asia, China, and Japan. The prices can range from US$140 for AC (air-conditioning) I to US$80 for AC III per day, and fluctuate depending on the given time within the peak season months (Swaroop 2007).

The third initiative involves the acquisition of land in Bodh Gaya for an eighteen-hole golf course stretched over a two-hundred-acre plot of land. The proposal for a "golf resort" was submitted by the UK-based Professional Golfers' Association (PGA) in London, to include fifteen cottages and five villas, club facilities, an all-weather swimming-pool, and a state-of-the-art gymnasium (Pandey 2006). When I spoke with the secretary for the Bihar Tourism Development Corporation about the rationale behind the golf course, given the site's importance as a religious center, the surrounding abject poverty, and the likely depletion of groundwater, he replied that the main idea behind the golf course "is to preserve more green areas. This will enable two hundred acres to become green, but not only green alone, there will be two hotels and complexes that will be involved. There will also be golf cottages and some guesthouses." When pressed a bit further on this point, he added,

> We also want to bring more money into Bodh Gaya and we are certain the visitors from foreign Buddhist countries will use it. We want to enter Bodh Gaya into the global market. This is not to attract elite but to keep Bodh Gaya green. Otherwise there will be lots of construction. There is a new generation of Buddhists, so while those in South Korea are fading there is a revitalization in China. Japan also pays a lot of money for good infrastructure. So we see this as an opportunity to enter the international market. We also have envisioned floating a trophy for the Gautama Annual Tournament. People from all over will descend for a month to participate. So there are two reasons for the golf course; one is as an international market strategy and the other is to keep Bodh Gaya green. The golf course will also bring one to two hundred people employment. Horticulture can be improved. There can be lotus flower cultivation and the usual hotel cleaning. So there is scope for much more employment.[10]

At the time of fieldwork, the government had already transferred 137.51 acres of land to the tourism department for the eighteen-hole golf course and had received approval for the acquisition of 62.49 acres of land from the surrounding farmland. The estimated cost of the golf resort was Rs. 40 crore, and, not surprisingly, the government also sought private investment to help with construction. It was envisioned that several cottages would be sold to wealthy Buddhist interest groups in Japan, Thailand, South Korea, Taiwan, and Sri Lanka, where golf and meditation are prevalent.

As a consequence of these new tourism initiatives, synchronized with a glossy international marketing campaign, "backward" Bihar has been repositioned as "blissful" Bihar and a premier destination for tourism consumption. Ever since the bifurcation of Bihar in 2000 and the creation of mineral-rich Jharkhand to the south, tourism and pilgrimage circuits built around Buddhist heritage sites have been at the forefront of India's home-grown neoliberalism, which is aimed at building new networks of global capital and countering negative stereotypes that have long plagued the state's image. In this context of image building and the business of culture through recourse to the past, the branding of cities with UNESCO World Heritage can serve as a major marketing tool and central to new forms of governmentality.

THE UNESCO WORLD HERITAGE BRAND

World Heritage is arguably one of the most successful brand names in the international tourism market today. As a "prestige project" that confers value on cultural properties, the UNESCO brand has become a desirable icon of "world class" for many nation-states—an inter-referencing practice that puts into circulation a symbolic language of global significance (Ghertner 2011, Roy and Ong 2011). UNESCO branding also involves a process of meaning making that "not only identifies, but also *defines*, which heritage places are globally important" (Smith 2006, 99). This conflation is important as a critical place-making tool that helps to market tourist spaces and attracts investment for the state by invoking nostalgia within and against the formal city (Hancock 2008). In other words, heritage preservation and commodity consumption are tightly interwoven in the production of World Heritage, and World Heritage status can a have tremendous impact on the way urban environments are retooled for integration into the global economy.

Broadly speaking, a UNESCO World Heritage Site is a place of "cultural" or "natural" importance that ostensibly transcends the heritage sovereignty of the nation-state through its endorsement of "outstanding universal value" under the Convention concerning the Protection of World Cultural and Natural Heritage. Following its adoption during the General Conference of UNESCO on November 16, 1972, 192 state parties have ratified the convention, which provides a broad template for heritage governance around the world. As of July 2016, 1,052 sites are listed: 814 cultural, 203 natural, and 35 mixed properties, in 165 countries.

A natural or cultural heritage property must comply with two overarching conditions to qualify for inclusion on the World Heritage List. First, the site must be recognized as having "outstanding universal value" based on a set of evolving evaluation criteria defined by the World Heritage Centre.[11] Second, the country that nominates the site must demonstrate that management instruments are in place to ensure the long-term survival of values recognized by UNESCO. A central dilemma that underlies these conditions is that the preservation of cultural heritage is usually pitted against the pressures of urban development and the need to balance conservation with wider economic, social, and political goals of the state. To ensure that the proper heritage instruments are in place, an international advisory body evaluates the integrity of cultural value and provides technical advice to the state authorities on conservation management issues. These heritage advisors, who provide the voice of authority, are drawn from intragovernmental organizations such as ICOMOS (the International Council on Monuments and Sites), IUCN (the World Conservation Union), and ICCROM (the International Centre for the Study of Preservation and Restoration of Cultural Property).

In the case of Bodh Gaya, the Mahabodhi Temple Complex was first nominated and presented for evaluation by the Ministry of Tourism in 2001 but was not formally inscribed on the World Heritage List until June 26, 2002—the twenty-third Indian site to be included on the UNESCO list.[12] Lobbying for UNESCO's recognition was Ashwani Lohani, director of the Ministry of Tourism, and the main nomination dossier was drawn up by art historian and filmmaker Benoy K. Behl.[13] The application also required consensual support by members of the Bodh Gaya Temple Management Committee and other supporting agencies, such as the Archaeological Survey of India and the Bihar state government. In order to justify inclusion on the World Heritage List, the nominated cultural property had to meet at least one out of ten selection criteria. In addition, certain requirements of mass tourism had to be met, including a refinement of the archaeological-historical discourse to make it more consumer friendly and to clear up ambiguities and conflicting interpretations (Kinnard 2014). These requirements are reflected in the legislative discourse and categories that come to define World Heritage status as well as the accompanying spatial practices and zoning ordinances, which are designed to mark the boundaries of the heritage complex in space.

The technical advisors who provided the initial assessment identified a set of "pressures" around the Mahabodhi Temple that were likely to grow owing to further development of the site and the increasing number of visitors. The state government estimated that there were some four hundred thousand visitors per year (30% foreign and 70% domestic); and during the busy winter months, from November to February, there was an average of two thousand visitors a day. Linked to these rising numbers was the construction activity fast taking place in close proximity to the Mahabodhi Temple, including foreign nationals who had acquired land to build temples, monasteries, and accommodation for their visiting pilgrims. ICOMOS advised that the responsible authorities should "continuously monitor the impact that such challenges may have on the religious and spiritual significance of the place," *including* the "ambitious initiatives for the presentation of the site" by the state authorities themselves (UNESCO World Heritage Centre 2002, 8). Moreover, to resolve these pressures it was stressed that a "comprehensive management plan" needed to be developed that would account for the conservation needs and control the future impact of commercial and religious activities at the site.

We can see a delicate balancing act here between preservation and tourism development. Tourism is certainly one of the prime benefits deriving from World Heritage endorsement. Although the official mission statement by the World Heritage Convention does not explicitly highlight tourism or economic development as a direct consequence of World Heritage listing, there has long been an affinity between the two that is widely recognized by the states that ratified the convention. In fact, ever since the Mahabodhi Temple Complex entered the World Heritage List, its designation has been the primary basis for new financial arrangements involving public and private capital investment. Not surprisingly, many of the elite tourism initiatives discussed in the previous section, such as the eighteen-hole golf course and the Mahaparinirvana Express, overlapped with the recent World Heritage designation. Contrary to widespread belief, however, World Heritage inscription does not necessarily translate into direct financial support from the United Nations. Although UNESCO may provide some nominal monetary support under specific circumstances, this funding pales in comparison to the promotional benefits that derive from the World Heritage brand and its self-propagation as an object of tourism through international media circuits.

For example, in Feburary 2004, the International Conclave on Buddhism and Spiritual Tourism was held in New Delhi. The Buddhist summit was organized by the tourism and civil aviation ministries, and brought together several international Buddhist dignitaries, tourism ministers from over twelve counties, and prominent guest speakers, including then Indian president Dr. Abdul Kalam and the 14th Dalai Lama. In his keynote address, the president emphasized the importance of transforming religion into spirituality and finding strength in peace. "The religions are like exquisite gardens, places full of surpassing beauty and tranquility, like sacred groves filled with beautiful birds and their melodious songs," he said. "I truly think that religions are beautiful gardens. They are enchanting islands, a veritable oasis for the soul and the spirit. But they are islands nevertheless. How can we connect them so that the fragrance engulfs the whole universe?" he asked the audience.[14]

Taking heed of the president's advice, the Buddhist conclave concluded its deliberations by adopting a resolution to appoint a high-level commission to look into the Buddhist sites of India and recommend measures to rehabilitate them and bring them back to their former glory. This was followed by a post-tour "dedication ceremony" involving chartered flights from New Delhi to Bodh Gaya for the official inauguration of the Mahabodhi Temple Complex as a UNESCO World Heritage Site. Building on the enthusiasm, India's tourism minister, Jagmohan, announced plans to develop Bodh Gaya into an international destination and promised infrastructure and facilities to develop its tourism sector. "We are grateful to UNESCO that they responded to our request and have given the status of World Heritage to the Mahabodhi Temple. This has put Buddha Gaya on the world map," he announced (Maha Bodhi Society 2004, 4). When I met the joint secretariat of the Ministry of Tourism in New Delhi about the International Conclave and the prospects of Buddhism and spiritual tourism, she mentioned the recent developments in Bihar, noting that Bodh Gaya would become a "mega-destination" where one could have "a world-class spiritual experience of the Buddhist circuit."

The prospect of a "world-class spiritual experience" has been closely aligned with the resurrection of a master plan that both appeals to the recommendations by the World Heritage advisory body in terms of conservation management and incorporates the state's development agenda toward tourism promotion. The technical consultants who were entrusted by the Ministry of Tourism and Culture with the job of revising the master plan are from the Housing and Urban Development Corporation (HUDCO) with support from the Archaeological Survey of India (ASI). The recent ascendance of HUDCO and other public-private actors in shaping urban form and visioning urban futures is certainly not isolated to Bodh Gaya (Shaktin 2011, Roy 2011). Building directly on earlier data from previous master plans and incorporating a series of local stakeholder consultation meetings, surveys, and new satellite imagery, these agencies prepared three documents to meet the advisory recommendations.[15] A few years later, these documents were revised and synchronized into the comprehensive City

Development Plan under the Jawaharlal Nehru Urban Renewal Mission (JNNURM) that was launched in 2005.

This central government initiative and major urban redevelopment scheme selected Bodh Gaya and sixty-three other "priority" cities throughout India to encourage urban reforms and fast-track infrastructural development based on corporate-driven models.[16] Despite its homage to India's first postcolonial modernizer, according to Shaktin (2011, 89), the JNNURM scheme represents a turn away from "the pre-liberalization efforts at urban master planning and new town development, which articulated Nehruvian ideals of secularism, socialism, and modernism, to the aggressive espousal of a more entrepreneurial mode of governance." Through its market-oriented mode of planning, these reforms are meant to facilitate private-sector investment through the repeal of existing regulations and laws such as the Urban Land Ceiling and Regulation Act of 1976, to open up landholdings to encourage opportunities presented by liberalization (Roy 2011, Shaktin 2011). The rise of these public-corporate partnerships, as evidenced by the marriage between HUDCO, the ASI, and the Ministry of Tourism, has taken place alongside the formation of Special Economic Zones and other elite urban projects that incorporate large infusions of external loans by the World Bank and other major lending bodies. While the JNNURM national strategy promises services for all, it does so in a rather circumscribed language that promotes "consumer-citizens" and that can weaken the claims of the urban poor (Roy 2011, 261).

Bundled into the master plan for Bodh Gaya is an enormous amount of financing directed toward an extensive phasing in of specific heritage/tourism oriented projects and a powerful reformulation of space over the course of thirty years. Like other master plans that have gained currency in India under economic reform, the documents provide broad policy guidelines for development control and sustainable management, but now recast in terms of a model World Heritage city. Moreover, at the core of the master plan is a global ethical imperative to protect the heritage values associated with the site and to provide guidelines for developing Bodh Gaya into a "World Buddhist Centre" that offers glimpses of the land of enlightenment as it used to be during the time of the Buddha:

> The city of BodhGaya should have a serene, verdant ambience, the conceptualization of which was done by the Lord himself when he said "Lovely, indeed, O Venerable one is this spot of ground charming is the forest grove,

pleasant is the flowing river with sandy fords, and hard by is the village
where I could obtain food. Suitable indeed is this place for spiritual exer-
tion for those noble scions who desire to strive. (HUDCO 2006b, 4–5)

A 2006 HUDCO analysis of Bodh Gaya concludes that most of the developments specified in previous master plan documents have not taken place.
By contrast, Bodh Gaya has developed in "gross ignorance of the Master
Plan proposals," and there is a "significant increase in commercial activity
with a number of hotels, guesthouses and unauthorized shops coming up
in a haphazard way along the major road" (HUDCO 2006b, 88). The proliferation of multi-storied buildings and illegal encroachments—without any
architectural control—has greatly "devalued the aesthetics generated by
excellent monasteries and temples," including the Mahabodhi Temple (88).

In order to improve the positive urban imageability of Bodh Gaya and
protect its heritage values, the master plan spatially segregated the town into
four protective layers (initially three, but later expanded at the request of
the World Heritage Centre). These included the "World Heritage boundary
zone," which covers twelve acres of land enclosed by an outer boundary wall
that provides the primary unit of enclosure for the Mahabodhi Temple
Complex. This was followed by the "core zone," which includes a half-
kilometer radius around the Mahabodhi Temple and is modeled on Cunningham's 1892 excavation plan. The third and fourth layers were comprised
of a "buffer zone" consisting of a one-kilometer protection area and a
"periphery zone" of up to two kilometers from the World Heritage Site. The
one-kilometer radius buffer zone was collapsed into two "Special Areas"
intertwined with heritage bylaws designed to regulate height and urban
aesthetic control. In Special Area A, for example, there was a complete ban
on all further construction around the "core zone" that could disturb the
historical and visual presentation of the monument. This area was also
designated a "silence zone" to be traffic free and entirely pedestrianized to
limit noise pollution. In Special Area B, which encompassed the larger buffer zone, no new construction would be permitted unless for recreational,
cultural facilities and essential infrastructure. This was described as a
"cultural zone" where religious and related structures would be allowed but
would be limited to thirty-three feet in height. Finally, to further the goal
of having Bodh Gaya's heritage landscape "breath as a living city," extensive
agricultural greenbelts were planned—a new system of parks and a complete revitalization of traditional drainage systems that would function as
"city lung spaces" (HUDCO 2006b, 129).

The new meditation park inside the Mahabodhi Temple Complex. The temple management charges visitors Rs. 25 entrance.

These spatial tactics of segregation and the various layers of zoning protectionism can be seen as part of a new "aesthetic mode of governing" (Ghertner 2011). Wrapped in a political rhetoric of "world class," this aesthetic ordering is becoming widespread in many Indian cities and is central to the determination of new legalities and property relations. A growing scholarly literature critiques slum evictions in major cities such as Mumbai and Kolkata and points out problems with Special Economic Zones and new peri-urban enclaves (see Roy and Ong 2011). I argue here that UNESCO World Heritage can also provide new grounds for capital accumulation where certain "exceptions" and "special rules" are utilized by the state government to maximize profits. With culture reconfigured as a valuable substance and economic resource in the global tourism marketplace, heritage sites become vulnerable to processes of enclosure and containment (Collins 2011, Breglia 2006).

In other words, through a comprehensive reorientation of existing and future use values of public space, World Heritage provides a privileged platform for endorsing urban renewal projects that embodies global aspirations of both the state tourism officials and private agencies. Cloaked in a "beautification" garb and framed as an effort to enhance the city to attract tourists, heritage infused with global significance provides the justification to "clean up" the city, eliminate street vendors, demolish encroachments, and accelerate the formalization of a heritage-conscious cityscape for wider consumption (Rodriguez 2011). As an instance of what Harvey (2004) has termed "accumulation by dispossession," the master planning of the urban landscape in Bodh Gaya is not only about safeguarding the past but also about opening up new spaces of capital accumulation by marking these spaces with new juridical frameworks and bylaws.

In spite of these ambitious efforts to refurbish the city and create a "serene, verdant ambience" around the temple through buffer zones and surveillance mechanisms, tensions arose. Signs of discord had emerged within a few years of the site's inscription on the World Heritage List, when the United Nations committee received reports from local NGOs and other religious groups concerning increased tourism pressure, vandalism at the temple, proliferating court cases, and "conflictual relationships between the religious groups using the property and occasionally the local communities, which reportedly resulted in fires and riots" (State of Conservation Report 2003). Some groups were petitioning that the management of the property should be placed in the hands of Buddhists rather than the temple management committee. The UNESCO technical advisory committee also raised concerns regarding "the absence of a functioning comprehensive management plan" and expressed concern over conflicts between local stakeholders and religious groups (UNESCO World Heritage Centre 2003). The World Heritage Centre now asserted that city planners were "complicating the conservation process," skewing the process toward the development of tourism and pilgrimage-friendly facilities at Bodh Gaya (UNESCO World Heritage Centre 2004). To address these concerns, the World Heritage Centre and advisory body recommended an extension of the property to capture additional aspects of the cultural landscape that would enhance the "outstanding universal value" and ensure through legal mechanisms that the protective core and buffer zones would be meaningful and effective.

Shortly after the silent protest that took place in April 2005—where I began this chapter—I had a chance to interview several shopkeepers and concerned local citizens regarding these recent developments. While many of them embraced the World Heritage designation in its formative years, believing that it would bring economic prosperity to the town, as rumors of a revised master plan began to circulate through the bazaar, it was met with fierce opposition. Although stakeholder consultation meetings had been organized by HUDCO, some residents expressed frustration and resentment that they were not invited, did not have access to the master plan proposals, or found the material unclear.[17] The World Heritage designation was seen as a threat to local sovereignty and livelihood, spurring fears that local residents would be negatively affected by a master plan that privileged Asian Buddhist interests and entrepreneurial agendas of the state. With tourism and pilgrimage expenditures increasingly being absorbed by the Buddhist monastic community and the tourism department, there was wide agreement that outstanding universal value was being flouted to justify urban rehabilitation that sought to criminalize the poor and marginalize local Hindu and Muslim commercial interests. The recent construction of two standardized market complexes (Nodes 1 and 2) situated 1.5 kilometers from the town center and the demolishing of the high school building for the beautification of Maya Sarovar Park was seen as the beginning of the new aesthetic ordering of the city.

Symptomatic of "globally dominant models of value," these efforts to isolate and marginalize significant segments of the local population and disguise the messiness of everyday life that characterize market spaces is what anthropologist Michael Herzfeld (2006) refers to as "spatial cleansing." This involves the "conceptual and physical clarification of boundaries, with a concomitant definition of former residents as intruders (usually called 'squatters' or described with similarly demeaning language)" and relegates potentially "dangerous" populations to spaces where they can be subjected to increased surveillance and control (132). World Heritage in Bodh Gaya also brings into focus the ways in which struggles over urban social space can give rise to "differential groups" who seek to affirm their difference in relation to the universality of World Heritage. Local knowledge, Herzfeld (129) argues, "is resistant to the imperious claims of transcendence, universalism, and abstraction, but is instead rooted in lived experience" that also carries potential for subversion.

Many of Bodh Gaya's residents have witnessed the ebb and flow of master plan rhetoric in the past and are prepared to resist its latest incarnation, packaged under the sign of World Heritage. Following the April 2005 mission there have been several protests in response to the new set of urban policies designed to relocate shops and marginalize the informal sector through a process of spatial cleansing. Drawing comparison with the periodic "cleansing drives" that move through the town clearing informal shops and encroachments in anticipation of VIP guests, residents have become accustomed to these "ritualized civic spectacles" (Hancock 2008) of state power and aesthetic discrimination. They are also keenly aware of the empty promises and dismal record of state accountability toward rehabilitation and compensation, which is often much lower than the market price.

For example, when I spoke with Dilip, a concerned hotelier, he explained to me shortly after the silent march that "the main purpose of the master plan should be development, not destruction. We are not against development, but rehabilitation. If they would like to propose development they should confront the people of Bodh Gaya first. Not just papers. This place is not like Delhi," he argued.

> Many people here are illiterate. We understand leadership but we are not literate people. If you want to resettle us, there should be land for us, less taxes and necessary compensation. Otherwise it is not legal. The people who do not know the legal aspects are very scared. Only God knows . . . only Buddha knows when we will shift. Some hoteliers also do not have proper documentation of their construction permits. Here at Bodh Gaya, there is a long history of master plans. It was first made in 1966. It is now forty years later and what is the government doing?[18]

Various shopkeepers and business owners also made it clear that many of Bodh Gaya's residents have been shaped by the national and transnational heritage discourses and have developed a heightened sense of "locality" as a defense against political elites and state-imposed urban regimes. Under various grassroots organizations and civic associations that transcend class- and caste-based registers, such as the Citizens Development Forum (Nagrik Vikas Manch), the Hotel Association, the Shopkeepers and Footpath Union, and the Bodh Gaya Social Forum, these groups have brought their concerns into a transnational arena to assert their right to participate in the decision-making process, to highlight the inefficiencies within government, and to demand certain rights of livelihood and habitation from the state.[19] These local organizations have also leveraged the Buddha's message of tolerance and compassion in the news media, drawing attention to inherent contradictions within the government and their actions. Many have also found new grounds for political power by gaining a foothold in the *nagar panchayat* and other local village council groups, action that has enlarged their scope for democratic participation. In this way, many Bodh Gaya residents have also become implicated in worlding practices, and the mediating space of the bazaar becomes central to competing versions and expressions of World Heritage, especially when it threatens to undermine local economic livelihood and create an unequal playing field for business opportunities.

It should be clear at this point that the local business community is not the only stakeholder implicated in the master plan and its deployment of various heritage bylaws. Ever since the 2,500th Buddha Jayanti in 1956, several international Buddhist groups have acquired land to build monasteries and temples in what is now known as the "core zone." These Buddhist institutions continue to play an important role in mediating international pilgrimage activities and reinforcing the Buddhist memory of the site. In this respect, transnational Buddhism and World Heritage designation are complementary. However, under the inspection of the new international advisory body, many of these religious organizations are also concerned about the latest "construction freeze" and the imposition of a one-kilometer buffer zone around the temple if it affects their claims to land title. This has prompted municipal authorities to serve notice to several foreign monasteries about their alleged indulgence in illegal construction (Qadir 2013). The recent construction of the Wat Pa by the Thai Bharat Society is an example.

Under suspicious terms, the Thai Bharat Society acquired a large plot of land in 1997 in a prime real estate area directly south of the Mahabodhi Temple. During this period, permits for building were handled by civic authorities under the Gaya Regional Development Authority, which had a reputation for corrupt practices, especially under the chairmanship of Surendra Yadav—an RJD strongman and close ally of the then chief minister Lalu Prasad Yadav. When I first visited the Wat Pa campus in 2006, I was surprised by the sheer magnitude of construction work taking place. Under the watchful eyes of Thai monks in their saffron yellow robes was a long line of fifty to sixty laborers moving between residential buildings carrying metal bowls of freshly churned cement on their heads. Near one of the new meditational huts, the head monk of the Wat Pa mentioned that the Thai Buddhist organization had been ensnared in competing land claims by the land mafia and local vested interests ever since construction began. This led to several lengthy and costly court cases over the property, including a recent attempt by some Indian representatives of the society/trust to remove a founding Thai national member due to alleged involvement with a multi-crore land scam. To complicate matters, a portion of the Wat Pa campus sits directly on top of sensitive archaeological grounds in alleged violation of both the World Heritage guidelines and Archaeological Survey of India policies for protected monuments, which stipulate that there can be no construction within a hundred-meter radius of the Mahabodhi Temple. According to the head monk, when members of the World Heritage Committee visited the Thai monastery, "they demanded we stop building due to the archaeological importance and apparent violation of building laws. So, now we have to get construction permits from the World Heritage Committee and they won't let us. I argued that this was part of the system prior to its designation." Thus, rather than complying with the new building regulations under the city master plan, which still awaited formal approval by the state government, the Thai Buddhist community chose to expedite the building works. "I am not going to wait," he added. "These buildings are for the development of Buddhism here."

In view of the conjoining of international heritage bylaws and tourism development, several Buddhist groups, like the Thai Bharat Society, fear that the place of Buddha's enlightenment is fast becoming a spiritual Disneyland and heritage-themed environment that is also a threat to its contemporary vitality as an active religious complex. Initially, the announcement that the Mahabodhi Temple would become a UNESCO World Heritage Site was well received at first. Most Buddhists that I spoke with saw the international spotlight as an opportunity to move beyond the protests and conflicts that had characterized temple management since the early 1990s with the arrival of the Ambedkar Buddhists. This guarded optimism proved to be short-lived for many Buddhists as new conservation laws and restrictions were set in motion under the guise of a master plan.

Lama Choedon, the head monk of a Tibetan Buddhist temple, recalled a much quieter and peaceful place when he arrived in Bodh Gaya in the early 1980s. "There were few buildings at that time," he said. "It was really peaceful! The stupa was free to all the Buddhists. Even the Muslims would sit under the Bodhi tree," he said. "We were free to move around at night and do our meditation without any rules or restrictions. Nowadays we do not feel so free. There are lots of tourists coming." He feared that World Heritage would bring more changes and restrictions to the stupa. "They are just making a beautiful garden here. We are not free to light our lamps. More restrictions will follow. It has become a very limited space and more difficult to practice."

How does one speak to the importance of pilgrimage and religious practice without turning the Mahabodhi Temple into a fossilized artifact or museum? Can there be a practice-based design to heritage and conservation management that is sensitive to the multivalent forms of ritual behavior that foregrounds the performative, intangible, and process-oriented

The Mahabodhi Temple Complex as a living religious heritage site

aspects of utilizing the space, rather than the more concrete distinctions of place-making?

Approaching the Mahabodhi Temple Complex as living religious heritage may be an important step in transcending the physical orientation of the built environment and the Eurocentric assumptions that underpin the World Heritage designation process. But perhaps this also speaks to the limits of heritage when conservation and preservation practices enter into conflict with the embodied, sensory interactions that form the core of worship rituals. One might argue that the ongoing ritual activities—the embodied practices of remembrance and veneration dynamics—will keep the memory of this place alive and will (in all likelihood) outlive the World Heritage designation. As Kirshenblatt-Gimblett (2004, 56) reminds us, "a thing of vitality hardly needs safeguarding." For many pilgrims, the Mahabodhi Temple is not a fossilized artifact that can be "consumed," but rather, an affectively charged environment that is continuously produced and reproduced through devotional practice such as circumambulation, prostrations, chanting, and the rebuilding and/or renovation of stupas. The importance of these experiential and affective engagements with the built environment is also an integral part of the memory work that underlies the sites meaning and brings them to life.

As Amelia, an ordained Buddhist nun from Europe and a regular instructor in the Root Institute program, explained to me one afternoon, the Mahabodhi Temple has an inspirational quality and is ultimately a tool that helps direct one along the path. One of the things she really likes about Bodh Gaya, in comparison to other sacred sites, is that people coexist peacefully. "Unlike the Tushita Meditation Centre in McLeod Gangj," for example, "Bodh Gaya attracts a wide range of people and the focus is primarily pilgrimage. It is quite amazing to see everyone practicing at the temple. It is only the Westerners who have a difficult time meditating and finding peace here. They prefer silence and retreats." At the same time, she also noted that there is not much mixing going on, "which may not be such a bad thing. If there was more mixing it would probably lead to more disputes over who is practicing right and so forth. It is still quite segregated. But still it remains a place of purification, because of the power of the place. Pilgrimage has an effect on the mind. It is part of attaining a state that is beyond all suffering. We can't really grasp this with our own mind. Visiting these sites also reminds you that the Buddha was a living being and this can be inspiring."

Although much more could be said about the emerging discourse around living religious heritage and the phenomenological and ritual matrices in which pasts are conjured and lived (Hancock 2008, Nugteren 1995, 2014), for now, the balancing of the historical/original and contemporary/living dimensions (Kinnard 2014) of the Mahabodhi Temple largely resides in the hands of the temple management committee and advisory board. Although N. Dorjee, the current temple management secretary, has worked hard to balance these forces, increasingly, it would appear, there is greater pressure to strengthen the historicist/original view through the tourism-led aestheticization of cultural heritage. Even worse, these developments have the potential to exacerbate communal tensions that simmer beneath the surface of this historically contested sacred site. This has led many Buddhist leaders to ask, what are the benefits of World Heritage if it leads to more conflict? A prominent Rinpoche from the Tibetan Nyingma lineage asked me, "Why did the government choose to nominate a Buddhist site rather than a Hindu holy site? In 2002, the Mahabodhi Temple was nominated during BJP rule." Although I explained that the nomination came from the Ministry of Tourism in New Delhi, he remained suspicious, suggesting that there were ulterior motives behind World Heritage, fearing Hindu religious politics. "Until now it may seem good, but this place touches the very heart of Buddhist people. We need to be able to worship freely or else there will be strong resentment from Buddhists around the world," he commented. "Bodh Gaya is in the heart of Buddhists around the world and we are unhappy with the Indian government in how they are treating this place."

CONCLUSION

The state's territorial reach is produced and represented through the vehicle of the master plan, which has a complicated genealogy. Although one might interpret this genealogy as a familiar narrative of the postcolonial city and its failures, these proposals are still important because they chronicle the ways in which town planning authorities and political elites negotiate future images of the city. From the 2,500th Buddha Jayanti in 1956 to the 2002 Word Heritage designation, the state government sought to enhance its political legitimacy and boost economic growth through the formalization of the city as an emblem of "enlightened" stewardship designed to attract pilgrims and tourists. The deployment of these technocratic and rational-izing planning instruments has become even more salient in recent years as they mediate the aspirational economy of a "rising India." Rooted in national economic goals and ideological agendas in Delhi and Patna, the urban neoliberal turn builds on an entrepreneurial spirit that seeks to attract investment and strengthen consumer culture for international tour-ists and a growing middle-class population.

While considerable attention has been devoted to the profit-oriented spaces of Special Economic Zones and elite housing enclaves in the making of world cities (see Roy and Ong 2011), spaces of cultural and national pat-rimony, too, have become tools for place marketing and central to the image branding of cities and states. As an inter-referencing idiom that occludes a language of global transmission, the World Heritage brand—like metro systems, five-star hotels, international airports, and shopping malls—increasingly makes heritage sites desirable "world-class" icons that play a significant role in generating and harnessing global regimes of value. In this context, Buddhism provides a crucial resource for the state of Bihar that is part of an emergent "global nationalism" fast taking root in India as the nation attempts to redefine its place in the world (Haines 2011, 161). Using cultural heritage as a catalyst to shed its underdeveloped and back-ward image, Blissful Bihar helps to counter negative stereotypes and repre-sentations through its packaging of a world-class spiritual experience of the Buddhist circuit. The opportunity to sit beneath the tree of enlighten-ment affirms a certain global status that has become integrated into a broader strategy of transcendence that complements the state's new image campaign.

And like the Buddha, who in his quest for truth and emancipation sat beneath the Bodhi tree over twenty-five hundred years ago, the city becomes the site of diagnostic intervention and is posited as a space of salvation and future liberation through the master plan. At the heart of this planning imperative is the productive nostalgia that surrounds Bodh Gaya, as the seat of enlightenment, and the need to satisfy the tourist's desire to consume "authentic" landscapes. As critical geographer David Harvey (1996, 296) suggests, "Those who have invested in the physical qualities of place have to ensure that activities arise which render their investments profitable by ensuring the permanence of place." It is in this context that the World Heritage brand and its appeal to outstanding universal value can operate in a practical sense as it becomes retooled by the state to legitimize certain social and economic objectives. In other words, with universality conceived "as an important legal and moral ideology for protection" (Smith 2006, 110), the brand helps to naturalize a specific history and memory of the site, and through its universalizing abstraction make invisible the cultural and political work that the heritage process accomplishes.

At the same time, urban planning and city redevelopment have taken place in Bodh Gaya under conditions of great uncertainty. While many Hindu and Muslim residents are grateful for Lord Buddha in providing a livelihood, the promise of liberation and the image of development that the master plan promotes is one that many of these locals find difficult to accept. As with other ambitious development projects in the "new India," the increased market presence attached to Bodh Gaya's heritage landscape has given rise to an aesthetic mode of governance and new zoning ordinances that seek to marginalize street vendors and commercial activities, erasing them from the site. Under these conditions of marginalization and the continuing threat of displacement, the master plan has made attachments to place ever more antagonistic in recent years. It has also contributed to a reinvestment of the "local" as an important social and political register that now demands certain rights to habitation and public space before an international audience. Although it is tempting to read these forms of community activism through a familiar script of "local responses to global designs" or a case of the "heroic subaltern" against the juggernaut of planetary capitalism, they are also important struggles for imagining alternatives that are increasingly part of a wider demand for social justice and urban democracy around the world (Roy 2011, 327).

Although it is still early to tell how the latest master plan will unfold in Bodh Gaya, it appears that, as with its earlier antecedents, constraints in consolidating land and overcoming opposition to the city development plan have significantly stalled the plan, and it is likely that significant concessions will have to be made. Unless the state is willing to respond to these local demands and present a model of town planning that enhances the dignity and well-being of the residents who live there and those pilgrims who come for religious practice, the specter of communal violence and deep-seated opposition will continue to be a direct threat to the productive nostalgia that underlies the vision of Blissful Bihar.

Conclusion

ON THE EARLY MORNING OF JULY 7, 2013, BODH GAYA WAS ROCKED by a series of low-intensity timed explosions. The first bomb blast took place around 5:30 a.m. in the temple sanctuary, injuring two Buddhist monks from Myanmar and Tibet, with several explosions following in quick succession over the next hour. The additional blasts occurred within a five-hundred-meter radius of the Mahabodhi Temple, including three bombs at the Tibetan Tergar Monastery, the eighty-foot Buddha statue, and the nearby bus stand. Shortly after the attack, Indian president Pranab Mukherjee called the bombings a "senseless act of violence targeting innocent pilgrims and monks who had gathered to worship at this temple dedicated to the great apostle of peace—Gautama Buddha" (Anonymous 2013a). Indian prime minister Manmohan Singh was also quick to condemn the incident, saying that India's "composite culture and traditions teach us respect for all religions and such attacks on religious places will never be tolerated" (Anonymous 2013b). Although there was only peripheral damage reported to the structure of the world-famous Mahabodhi Temple, the ramifications have been far-reaching.

As a cultural anthropologist who has been working in Bodh Gaya since 2002, I could not help but feel during a short visit in 2013 that the recent turn of events was a setback to a town that is normally quiet and peaceful. Why target the Mahabodhi Temple and Bodh Gaya? Who was behind the serial bomb blasts? And, did the UNESCO World Heritage designation play a role in escalating the potential for religious conflict, including violence and terror?

In this book, I have shown how Bodh Gaya went from a relatively small town based on an agricultural economy to a rapidly urbanizing international destination that attracts tens of thousands of Asian Buddhist pilgrims and visitors each year. The recent designation of the Mahabodhi Temple Complex as a UNESCO World Heritage Site has also given rise to contestation and a new aesthetic politics in Bodh Gaya through its tourism-driven reformulation of space. As I demonstrate here, these changes to the public life of the Mahabodhi Temple have also intersected with the regional geopolitics surrounding the wider global War on Terror. Ironically, while one of UNESCO's main goals is to promote intercultural dialogue and build peace "in the minds of men," in the case of Bodh Gaya, its transformation into a global destination and place of outstanding universal value has also made it more vulnerable to the kind of identity politics the UNESCO Convention aims to transcend.

TEMPLE PUBLICS AND COMMUNAL CONFLICT IN MODERN INDIA

Since the late 1980s, spaces of religious heritage have become contentious grounds for defining national meaning among diverse communities of interest (Guha-Thakurta 2004). During this time, political claims on sacred space have been marred by two important developments: the ascendancy of Hindu nationalism and the accelerated processes of economic liberalization since the structural adjustments of the early 1990s (Hancock 2002, Appadurai 2000). These religio-political and economic changes have impacted urban temple landscapes in dramatic ways as both vectors of "popular anxiety over loss of cultural autonomy" and as keys to the advancement of the new economy, functioning as magnets for tourism revenue and development (Hancock 2002, 15). Using World Heritage and its international charisma as a proxy to legitimate state intervention through a comprehensive "master plan," we have seen how the Mahabodhi Temple has become subject to various conservation plans and new forms of legality designed to secure and strengthen the dominant values associated with its heritage identity and to displace those values deemed antithetical to its goal. It is precisely this globalizing production of place that makes them more vulnerable to communal sentiment and identity politics in the early twenty-first century.

Central to the renewed place of religion in the public and political sphere was the demolition of the Babri Masjid at Ayodhya in 1992, prompting one of India's worst bouts of nationwide religious rioting, resulting in over two thousand deaths. Among Hindus, the liberation of Hindu sacred space at Ayodhya was part of the reclamation of religious memory, a site that claims to have long-standing significance as the birthplace of Lord Rama (Ludden 1996). This cultivation of a public culture of Hindutva since the late 1980s is closely tied to the shifting ground of party politics that brought the Bharatiya Janata Party (BJP) forward as one of the leading national parties in India. The goal of replacing the sixteenth-century Babri Mosque with a

Hindu temple dedicated to Ram continues to be a cornerstone of the Hindu nationalist agenda and arguably has played a role in the BJP's rise as a major political party in the country.

The intensification of communal violence and religious nationalism in India has certainly heightened in the early twenty-first century as this conflict merges with the wider global politics around the War on Terror. Since 2002, there have been a series of violent outbreaks, such as the Gujarat riots and pogrom that led to the deaths of nearly 800 Muslims and 250 Hindus. There have also been numerous explosions on city buses, commuter trains, and public landmarks, many of them believed to be in retaliation for the destruction of the Babri Masjid in Ayodhya. In 2008, for example, India's financial urban center, Mumbai, was the target of coordinated bombing and shooting attacks that took place at more than ten city landmarks, including the opulent Taj Mahal Hotel. Often described as India's 9/11, the Mumbai attacks and other recent acts of violence have enlivened communal tensions as they merge with the wider global discourse surrounding the American-led War on Terror (Williams 2011). The media's rhetoric and foregrounding of "Islamic terror" and the notion of a "Muslim threat" have provided fertile ground for galvanizing political support among Hindu nationalist parties and legitimizing a number of Indian national and regional security measures, such as the implementation of new border policing and regulations (Williams 2011, 255).

As Williams (2011, 255) suggests, national and global discourses around the War on Terror interact and mutually reinforce conceptions of a Muslim "Other" that belies a more complex and nuanced history of Hindu-Muslim relations in India. The same can be said for the spatial politics that underlies Bodh Gaya as a UNESCO World Heritage Site today. Although there is a long history of contestation surrounding rites of worship and proprietorship of the Mahabodhi Temple that dates back to the late nineteenth century (and arguably much earlier), to a large extent Bodh Gaya has remained respectful of plurality and multi-religious uses throughout much of the twentieth and early twenty-first centuries. This is not to deny that a considerable transformation has taken place within the last 150 years that has greatly elevated the Buddhist history of the site at the expense of more fluid interpretations and overlapping pilgrimage traditions and narratives.

The Bodh Gaya Temple Act of 1949 stresses the dual identity of Bodh Gaya as a pilgrimage place that is under the protection of the state government of Bihar. Under this act, the Bodh Gaya Temple Management Committee (BTMC), first inaugurated in 1953, was established to make provisions for better management of the temple and properties near it. As the main executive body that looks after the daily affairs of the temple, the BTMC consists of eight elected members (four Buddhist and four Hindu) plus the chairman—the district magistrate of Gaya. As an important public institution, the temple also oversees a wide range of staff that look after the daily maintenance of the temple and ritual offerings, including local guards (*chowkidars*) and state police collaborators for protection. Providing additional support to the BTMC is an external advisory board under the governor of Bihar that consists of twenty to twenty-five members, with half of them (ideally) from foreign Buddhist countries.[1]

Under the Bodh Gaya Temple Act of 1949, the Bihar state government has played the role of adjudicator over the regulation of sacred space in Bodh Gaya and has reaped the benefits of situating its religious-cultural assets within a broader secular program of nation building, economic development, and heritage promotion. Through its legal-bureaucratic apparatus, the act provides an important mechanism for state legitimization that has repurposed religious difference to meet the civic and public life of the nation. Importantly, the Bodh Gaya Temple Act also represents an exception to the norm. The lion's share of restored Buddhist sites and monumental structures, such as Sarnath, Rajgir-Nalanda, Kushinagar, and Sanchi, have remained under the jurisdiction of the Archaeological Survey of India (ASI). Although the ASI remains an important consultant for renovations to the temple, it is largely confined to contract work such as special repairs and cleaning. Under the Bodh Gaya Temple Act and the protection of the Bihar state government, therefore, the Mahabodhi Temple has become a shared site of religious worship that infuses local configurations of management with extra-national forms of oversight. If Hindu temples, following the line of reasoning by Hancock (2008, 112), were reimagined by the postcolonial state as a "glue that would bind nation and state through virtue and through the shared past," then the Mahabodhi Temple became emblematic of India's secular commitment to religious pluralism and one that also contained a symbolic link with Asia.

Infused with tradition and charged with affective meaning among Buddhists around the world, the Mahabodhi Temple has become a magnet of international pilgrimage through the latter half of the twentieth century in a way that largely reflects the Buddhist values associated with the space. Although certain stipulations in the act continue to ensure that both Hindus and Buddhists have complete access to the temple land for the purpose of worship, including the *mahant*, who continues to control the small *panchapandav* complex located directly in front of the temple entrance, the vast majority of the built environment remains under the committee's full jurisdiction.

From the Burmese Muchalinda statue erected in the middle of the lotus tank to the various Tibetan prayer wheels installed along the circumambulation path, the elevation of a particular Buddhist narrative associated with the place of enlightenment is visible throughout the Mahabodhi compound. This is particularly evident among the seven stone signboards that are prominently displayed throughout the temple complex and relate what Shakyamuni did after he attained enlightenment. Despite the dubious ground of physical and historical certainty about some of the exact locations, a few influential Theravada monks were able to implement the signboards with little resistance. When Tara Doyle (1997, 2012) spoke with the superintendent of the Mahabodhi Temple at the time of installation, she was told that they were meant to educate the Hindu visitors, help direct the guides, and avoid "unnecessary confusion." Although Mahayana Buddhists, especially Tibetans, have added their own ritualized interpretations and understandings of the site, to a large extent, Theravada constructions of knowledge since the time of the Burmese envoys have had a tremendous influence on the discursive and physical development of Bodh Gaya as both a historical and living religious site (Doyle 1997).

This "absence of Hindu stories at the official level" (381) should not be surprising given the wider pan-Asian political, cultural, and economic factors that I have highlighted throughout this book. The same applies to the recent World Heritage designation, which almost exclusively presents the Mahabodhi Temple as a Buddhist site and masks the "larger complex, messy history and context of the temple and its environs," not to mention the more immediate renewed conflict under the Ambedkar Buddhists (Kinnard 2014, 136).

In recent years, the Mahabodhi Temple has also become a wealthy institution as a result of the ever-increasing donations made by pious Buddhist pilgrims and various Asian Buddhist dignitaries and elites who obtain merit for their contributions. When the first committee took charge of the temple in the 1950s, there was no fixed or permanent source of income, and the temple relied almost entirely on small offerings made in the charity boxes. These funds barely covered the cost of staff to ensure that the Mahabodhi Temple was clean, and the committee was always facing financial crisis (Sundrani 1986). By 2006–2007, following extensive renovations to the temple complex, the temple management committee had roughly Rs. 16–17 crore under its trust. This rising economic revenue has also correlated with the growing influence of the secretariat as a highly politicized position, with greater pressure from the district magistrate and state government officials.[2] Due to the surging influence of pious pilgrims and devotees contributing funds to the trust, and various conservation and beautification projects under way, any slippage of undocumented funds or signs of mismanagement has wider political ramifications for the ruling state party.

This was particularly evident in the aftermath of the bomb blasts in July 2013. Shortly after the blasts, the police cordoned off the area and a deluge of senior officials and politicians started looking into the matter, including the Central Industrial Security Force and the National Investigation Agency, which took over the investigation. Quickly arriving on the scene was the chief minister, Nitish Kumar, who vowed to strengthen security and resolve the crisis to ensure the continuing religious and economic patronage of Bihar's greatest cultural export. But despite a great deal of rumor and speculation circulating in the popular Indian news media, there was little progress, at least initially, in tracking the bombers. No group had claimed immediate responsibility for the gas cylinder bombs that exploded on the early morning of July 7.

The most promising lead was that the bombings were connected to the Indian Mujahideen (IM), a homegrown terrorist operation that some analysts contend is a front for the Pakistan based Lashkar-e-Tiaba (LET) and/or the militant branch of the Student Islamic Movement of India (SIMI). Beginning in 2010, the Delhi Police and Intelligence Bureau issued several warnings to the Bihar state government about a potential terrorist attack proposed by members of the Indian Mujahideen. In early 2013, for example, hackers gained access to the official Bihar state tourism website and threatened Hyderabad-like blasts, with messages like "Pakistan Zindabad," but these warnings did not appear to have been taken very seriously. Despite considerable media speculation around the various motivations behind the bomb blasts, the revelations following the arrest of four Muslim boys with links to the IM suggest that the bombing was retaliation for the massacre of Rohingya Muslim minorities in Myanmar by hardline Buddhist leaders.

Beginning in June 2012, a series of riots broke out after weeks of sectarian disputes and clashes in the northern Rakhine state in Myanmar, between the majority Rakhine Buddhists and minority Rohingya Muslims. These communal clashes left upward of two hundred dead and numerous people displaced by the violence, especially among the Rohingya minorities. Despite the Myanmar government imposing a state of emergency and deploying military troops in the region, the violence, especially toward the Muslim minority, has continued. Some organizations, like Human Rights Watch, have also criticized the Myanmar army and police for their lack of protection and for having played a leading role in targeting the minority Rohingya as "immigrants" that is part of several decades of systematic discrimination against the ethnic Muslims in the region.

Putting another twist on the unfolding mystery was a set of serial bomb blasts that exploded on October 27, 2013, in Bihar's capital city of Patna that were nearly identical to those in Bodh Gaya. The main target of the attacks was the recently elected prime minister Narendra Modi, who was there for a BJP election rally. Shortly after the bombings, the National Investigation Agency announced that they had tracked one of the suspected masterminds of the blasts to a small hotel in Ranchi, where they discovered explosives, incriminating evidence of a plot to bomb Buddhist pilgrimage sites, and the coded names of the attackers. After confirming that the Ranchi cell of the Indian Mujahideen was responsible for the blasts, the police arrested fourteen suspects with alleged links to the Indian Mujahideen in the Patna explosions and eight in the Bodh Gaya case; they remain in custody.

I made a short visit to Bodh Gaya for three weeks in December 2013. What came as a surprise when visiting friends and research informants was that a different narrative and set of stories attributed to the bomb blasts were in circulation than the one I had read in the Indian news. Despite the inconclusive evidence and speculation in the aftermath of the bombing, what did not receive international media attention was that the state government swiftly undertook a massive cleansing drive of the nearby bazaar, demolishing fifty-eight shops along the popular footpath shortly after the bomb blasts. Couched in rhetoric of security building (especially for the protection of VIP guests) and promoting serenity around the shrine, the demolition of shops that lined the temple premises was swift and substantive.

As I discussed in chapter 4, this popular marketplace and pedestrianized zone has long served as an extension, or at least an integral ancillary, to the ritual life of the temple. Through their servicing of devotion, the surrounding shops and economic lifelines that they support in Bodh Gaya provide an important sacral-commercial nexus that is crucial to the multi-religious ethos and civic harmony of the place. Longstanding residents of Bodh Gaya have built reputable businesses with repeat clientele over the years, specializing in goods that facilitate the pilgrims' goals, such as *malas*, souvenirs, statues, bodhi leaves, and postcards; there are also general stores, chai stalls, restaurants, and internet cafés. Not surprisingly, the bomb blasts and

Demolishing of the commercial business district in the bazaar following the July 2013 bombing. Photo courtesy of Matt Colaciello Williams.

the recent demolition drive have been devastating for several local shop-keepers and families that have long relied on sacred proximity to support their livelihoods.

Improved security is also part of the wider master plan vision that has been reenergized in the aftermath of the July 7 bomb blasts. During my 2013 visit, the government was in the midst of raising the height of the shrine boundary wall and former bazaar area to twenty feet, and talks are under way to hand the shrine security over to the Central Industrial Security Force (CISF). Additional checkpoints and "ultra sensitive" metal detectors have been introduced; there are also plans for the installation of guard houses and high-resolution CCTV, and there was a significant number of armed military personnel in army fatigues who now rubbed shoulders with mul-ticolor Buddhist robes en route to the temple. In other words, what was once a space of remarkable conviviality that helped foster a sense of civil society and community in an intensely socially heterogeneous place was now being replaced with surveillance, suspicion, and sadly, heightened communal polarization.

In this physical and social reengineering of the spatial environment, conspiracy theories are in wide circulation. Many shopkeepers who have been affected by the recent destruction of shops believe that politicians planted the bombs as a means of justifying the destruction of shops, bypassing tedious bureaucratic entanglements over compensation and local resistance. "Why bomb the Mahabodhi Temple in the off-season, the warm summer months, when few pilgrims are to be found?" asked one shopkeeper. "How is it that there were very few casualties and the temple was hardly damaged?" "How did the so-called 'terrorists' get access to the temple despite the presence of temple security personnel?"

When pressed about the Indian Mujahideen as the main suspect in the unfolding mystery, I was frequently told that "they simply do not exist" and that the recent "amateur firecrackers" at the temple were all part of a calculated strategy by the state government and district administration to push through their own economic agenda and eventually replace the shops with new private contracts. As with the recent ascendance of the Abraj Al-Bait Hotel Towers, just meters away from Islam's most sacred site, the Masjid al-Haram in Mecca, many fear that the removal of shops in the bazaar is part of a wider corporate takeover of the public commons that works productively with state government officials through the heritage brand. For some time, there have been rumors that politicians have been looking to build a VIP hotel at the former multimedia center (and Dak Bungalow) that is directed by the government and tourism department. Similarly, some have suggested political motives behind the bomb blasts in the capital city of Patna in early November during Modi's visit. Like the Ayodhya-Babri Masjid flare-up in the early 1990s, these "terrorist" attacks provided fertile ground for the BJP and the political arm of the RSS in the run-up to the 2014 general elections that brought Narendra Modi into power.

The destruction and cordoning off of shops by a twenty-foot cement wall outside the view of pilgrims and tourists is insulting and degrading. Several families from deprived sections of Bodh Gaya who struggle for a basic subsistence wage and require loans to survive during the summer months are at a crossroads. As Kinnard (2014, 188) writes in the context of Palestine, "A fence, a wall in this case, is also a walling out, a means of separating and defining—this is, after all, what definition is all about—and this separating is more often than not likely to give offense, likely to be perceived, by someone who finds themselves on the wrong side of the wall, or on any side at all, as aggressive." In other words, this form of prohibition and restriction, whether the Indian state government is conscious of it or not, has the effect of "othering," of producing an "us" and a "them" that can

Commercial shops behind the buffer zone

have serious repercussions in a multi-religious landscape with drastic inequalities like Bodh Gaya (Kinnard 2014).

When I visited the new commercial complex in Node 1 to speak with some of the former shopkeepers from the bazaar, the entire area was a ghost town. Despite its location adjacent to the bustling seasonal Tibetan Refugee Market, nearly all the shutters in the shopping complex were locked except for two to three travel agents and the popular local barbershop, Prince Saloon. There was little signage or advertising, trash and waste had begun to accumulate, cows meandered through grassy patches, and wild dogs frolicked on the dusty sandstone tiles. Sunil, a shopkeeper who chose to relocate his general store to the new complex after his was destroyed, expressed his disappointment with the government. "Unlike other shop-keepers who have been able to find a new location closer to the temple, I have not been so lucky. It is very difficult for me and my family," he said. "When we were on the footpath, I was paying the Nagar Panchayat Rs. 350 per month to rent the space. Now I am required to pay the tourism department close to Rs. 3,000 per month and there are no visitors. What am I to do?"

Although the bomb blasts on the morning of July 7 had no fatalities, the structural changes enforced by the state government in the surrounding area have been significant. Among several repeat visitors and families that I spoke with in the aftermath of the demolition drive, there is a growing sense of resentment toward the Nitish Kumar government and its handling of Bodh Gaya. "Since the bombing, I no longer go to the temple for *puja*," one shopkeeper said. "I used to go every morning and evening to feel the peace of Lord Buddha, but now I only feel anger." If security remains central to Nitish Kumar's response to the terrorist attack, the cleansing drive has deepened a climate of insecurity for many of Bodh Gaya's residents. "What is the cause of terrorism?" I was asked by one shopkeeper, "It is desperation and injustice! This is exactly what Nitish Kumar is sowing here in Bodh Gaya."

Adding salt to a fresh wound, in mid-November, the top of the vaulted spire of the Mahabodhi Temple was coated in 289 kilograms (660 pounds) of gold by former king of Thailand Bhumibol Atulaya and Thai Buddhist devotees. The gold plating of the temple structure, along with the new a high-tech lighting system, ensures that the glittering inlaid gold dome can be seen both day and night in the surrounding areas, where poverty is rampant and basic services like electricity (at the place of enlightenment no less) are scarce. How do the Buddhists feel about the recent turn of events? Many are concerned about the direction Bodh Gaya is going as a target of communal violence and terror. While some of the daily Buddhist devotees find the metal detectors and daily "frisks" a headache, for most pilgrims the Mahabodhi Temple Complex remains the same: a place of practice and an opportunity to move closer to the goal of enlightenment. In fact, some Buddhist pilgrims have welcomed the new security provisions, especially the banning of phone use at the temple.

Bhante Priyapal, from the Chakma Buddhist Temple, said to me, in his usual rhetorical manner, "Davidji, what is World Heritage? It is nothing. Buddhists come here for practice and reverence due to the memory of the Buddha . . . That is all. It is UNESCO that has glorified itself through the designation of the Mahabodhi Temple as a World Heritage Site."

HERITAGE FUTURES

A culturally open record of conflict, one that also shows clearly
how all preservation inevitably also entails selective destruction
and the displacement of living populations, might be distasteful
or embarrassing to state and international authorities, but, for the

same reasons, it would generate valuable lessons for future generations. A spirit of mutual generosity is one that encourages the
greatest possible array of distinctive voices. Such is the real challenge
of heritage. What national government will dare to break with the
prevailing, narrow vision and work to achieve a culturally pluralist
vision for the future of the past? (Herzfeld 2011, 19)

What will be the fate of Bodh Gaya and its World Heritage designation in
the years to come? Could the Mahabodhi Temple Complex be placed on the
World Heritage in Danger List, bringing shame upon the Indian government and perpetuating popular stereotypes of a corrupt and backward
Bihar? What will be the fate of the latest incarnation of the master plan?
Will Bodh Gaya be transformed into a Buddhist theme park, a kind of
spiritual Disneyland for mass tourism consumption? Or will the master
plan, like its antecedents, require further revisions at the cost of unyielding
urban construction and a complete breakdown of basic public and civic
amenities?

Since the early "discovery" of India's Buddhist past in the context of
British colonial rule, sites of religious memory like the Mahabodhi Temple
have become symbolic registers for enlivened debates over origins and
authenticity, rites of worship and competing claims of patrimony. These
debates have certainly expanded and multiplied in recent years under new
international frameworks such as the UNESCO Convention on World
Heritage. What makes World Heritage such a seductive force in our contemporary era is that its universalizing project, like the Declaration of
Human Rights, speaks to our global humanity and our common cultural
heritage. Herb Stovel, a former ICCROM advisor for UNESCO who had
recently returned from Bodh Gaya, explained to me that "it is a question of
asking, what sites do we have that tell stories of such profound and immense
importance that they should be shared beyond national boundaries . . . and
for which the international community should take responsibility, if necessary, for their long-term survival."

One of the great "ambiguities of preservation" in a place like Bodh Gaya,
according to Kinnard (2014, 142), is that while UNESCO creates a performance of equality through its discourse of outstanding universal value and
rhetoric of shared pasts and common futures, these new global configurations of space "may very well be at the expense of the very people who live
and worship in such sites." In myriad ways, pilgrims, shopkeepers, state
officials, and development planners seek opportunities, both spiritual and

material, through the emerging world prospects of Buddhism in North India. For many poor communities in contemporary India, like those in south Bihar, the resource of heritage and the regular influx of tourists provide a key source of livelihood offering income-producing opportunities to social groups that are often marginalized from the national and religious invocations of heritage.

This is not an argument for "elevating the local and/or global over the national," for this does not automatically resolve injustices and may contribute to more aggressive forms of spatial cleansing in the name of historic conservation (Herzfeld 2010, S259). Although there is no specific blueprint for a more equitable resolution to Bodh Gaya's ongoing contestation, what does seem crucial at this particular juncture is to work against the tendency to reinforce a singular and monolithic image that displaces the creative potential for collaboration that emerges from Bodh Gaya's dynamic social and spatial arena. Place and memory allow us to locate Bodh Gaya within a spatial environment that is more inclusive and integrates the social values of heritage among diverse publics, including those silenced or marginalized by the authoritative discourse of World Heritage.

Is it necessary that all heritage places require a singular definition, a buffer zone or clear decisive boundaries of what it represents? Is it possible to envisage an alternative interpretation of Bodh Gaya, one that is not restricted to an inward-looking history built on a nostalgia for origins, but that sees the multiple identities in relation to Bodh Gaya's spatial environment? Although UNESCO's vision of place is a restrictive one, the physical and discursive reimagining of Bodh Gaya as the place of Buddha's enlightenment has been under way since at least the late nineteenth century. For Buddhists around the world, Bodh Gaya will continue to be an active place of worship and sacred memory regardless of the World Heritage designation. For those Buddhist pilgrims who dream of prostrating before the central image of Shakyamuni or the Bodhi tree, the Mahabodhi *vihara* can be nothing but a Buddhist temple, but does this require buffer zones, and should it preclude the possibility of other forms of religious and recreational practice? As a sacred place with "multiple resonances" (Kinnard 2014), the temple will continue to inspire the place memory associated with the Buddha's awakening because there are so many stakeholders invested in its heritage.

Under new global declarations and mechanisms, there is still much debate about the meaning and potential value of World Heritage in a place like Bodh Gaya. These cultural debates are an essential part of what World

Heritage should be about. Perhaps, through unraveling some of the webs of meaning that constitute this living religious heritage site, Bodh Gaya and the Mahabodhi Temple Complex can provide a different model of World Heritage—a model that embraces the plurality of meanings found in place and uses heritage not as a mechanism for urban rehabilitation and spatial cleansing but as a creative arena where the past becomes crucial to dialogues about what is important in the present and future. This involves working against the temptation to filter its messiness at the expense of its current complexity and culturally diverse vitality. As Herzfeld (2010, S267) writes, it is important not only "to make such complexities accessible and interesting to multiple publics" but to illustrate how it also adds value to its potentiality "at a time when they are being cynically targeted for the seductive and perhaps irreversible addiction of false simplicities."

How, then, can the management of this sacred space reflect the participation of multiple publics? What is clear to me in my fieldwork over the last ten years, and in writing this book, is my own ambivalence toward the Bodh Gaya Temple Act of 1949. As Guha-Thakurta (2004, 298) writes, "The Bodh Gaya temple dispute found a legal solution . . . [and] the Mahabodhi Temple was able to find a renewed lease of life as both an archaeological and a sacred monument." In many ways this legislative act under the Bihar state government has supported the ritual life of the temple and provided a degree of elasticity that would likely have been endangered if the temple had been placed in the hands of the Archaeological Survey of India or a singular religious authoritative body. Although Buddhists continue to campaign for the "liberation" of the Mahabodhi Temple from the 1949 act, including a Supreme Court case still pending verdict, it is unclear how the Bihar government will address the complex fault lines of religious identity, not to mention the diverse expressions of Buddhism across traditions. At the same time, it well known that the multiple and competing management systems currently operating in Bodh Gaya impede the sustainable growth of this rapidly expanding urban-temple landscape. This lack of an integrated management system has also been an obstacle to strong collaboration between international Buddhist groups and prospective donors, who are keen to make broader financial contributions to city infrastructure such as a much-needed drainage system and hospital. It is hard to know at this juncture what effect these different voices on Bodh Gaya will have on its future governance. One proposal often suggested by shopkeepers and resident groups is to create a Bodh Gaya Development Association or World Heritage Management Authority, which would integrate management mechanisms that take into account the various stakeholder interests in the site. Among some of the state officials and World Heritage advisory bodies there have also been some suggestions that the four major Buddhist pilgrimage sites be reconceptualized as a cultural landscape and tourism zone, expanding the definition of World Heritage and UNESCO jurisdiction. The recent 2016 designation of Nalanda Mahavihara (University) archaeological site may be a step toward realizing this broader conception.

Although UNESCO, as a subsidiary of the United Nations, holds the sovereignty of member nations as a precondition for participation in the World Heritage Convention, this may soon be changing as heritage properties become aligned with a growing tourism industrial complex and are transferred to the private sector. As Lisa Breglia (2006, 53) shows in her work on Chichén Itzá, the most profound transformations in the production of space occurring around the globe are those of the cultural commons under neoliberal agendas and how "the cartography of heritage" is no longer confined to national borders. Although this does not appear to be taking place in Bodh Gaya at the moment, the state has begun to outsource the management of prominent cultural festivals such as the Buddha and Rajgir Mahotsav to private event management groups (Anonymous 2012). This is part of much broader trend in Indian tourism toward PPPs (Public Private Partnerships), which have been used in several Indian states to improve tourist sites and amenities, including temples.

At a religious site of "outstanding universal value," how might the demands of Asian Buddhists articulate with international judicial laws that challenge national claims to cultural patrimony? Whatever direction future management and governance may take in Bodh Gaya, it seems unlikely that the surge of Asian Buddhist pilgrimage and influence will halt any time soon. Reminiscent of Edwin Arnold's provocative plea in "East and West: A Splendid Opportunity," Bodh Gaya and Bihar's cultural heritage has become a central node in the creation of a global Buddhist ethnoscape that has far-reaching implications for a "rising Asia" in the early twenty-first century. On a recent trip to the Nalanda International University, Amartya Sen noted: "Bihar is not only for Biharis; it is for the world. . . . Why can't we overcome the disadvantages and build a glorious future? We should learn a lesson from the achievements of Bihar and seek inspiration from the past. It will help us address and conquer the persistent disadvantages" (Ahmad 2009).

As a fitting destination for the prospect of an enlightened future, the return of Buddhism in the land of its origin is also located in what some still regard as India's heart of darkness. If Bodh Gaya presents a "splendid opportunity," in the words of Edwin Arnold, it will likely depend more on its relationship with other Asian Buddhist countries than patronage from the West. Moving beyond its earlier colonial invocation as the "Jerusalem of the Buddhists," in Bodh Gaya today, East is meeting East in creative and unexpected ways. Although Buddhism continues to grow in the West, the Buddhist pilgrims from China, Tibet, Taiwan, Myanmar, and Thailand have the most significant cultural and economic influence in Bodh Gaya today. Like the recent resuscitation of nearby Nalanda University and its pan-Indo-Asian character, Bodh Gaya (and other Buddhist sites) lies at the political matrix of growing inter-Asian networks of aid and transnational capital that will inevitably affect decisions on future management and governance, but it remains unknown whether they will be willing to work together and see beyond their own immediate interests.

Although there has been a great deal of media interest and attention in the revival of Nalanda University and the prospect of a rising Asia, ongoing religious conflict and political fault lines continue to cast a shadow over the prospects of an Asian future. In several parts of the Asian world, religious violence and communal conflict have increased, especially in light of the wider global discourse on terror. Whether its Buddhist-Muslim conflict in Myanmar and its ripple effect in Bodh Gaya or frequent surges of communal riots between Hindu and Muslims in India, acts of violence have invigorated religious differences in ways that presuppose and reinforce the idea of cohesive "communities" (Williams 2011). Despite the suspected complacency of Narendra Modi during the Gujarat riots in 2002, the landslide victory of the new controversial prime minister speaks to the fragile commitment to the protection of religious and ethnic minorities that underscores the "idea of India" (Khilnani 1999). If the main axes of identity surrounding a national imaginary continue to hinge on religious ones, what role can heritage, especially global heritage that transcends national boundaries, play in mediating these ruptures in the national body politic?

On September 5, 2015, Prime Minister Modi visited Bodh Gaya along with a hundred delegates as part of the Hindu Buddhist Conference on Conflict Avoidance and Environmental Consciousness, organized by the Vivekananda International Foundation in partnership with the Tokyo Foundation and International Buddhist Confederation. As part of the concluding ceremonies, he promised that his government would develop the site into a "spiritual capital" that would serve as a "civilizational bond between India and the Buddhist world." "I recognize how Buddhists all over the world revere Bodh Gaya as a place of pilgrimage," he said, after visiting the Mahabodhi Temple (Anonymous 2015). "On the issue of conflicts—most of which are driven by religious intolerance," he said, "the participants of the conference seem to have agreed that while there is no problem about the freedom to practice one's religion, it is when radical elements try to force their own ideologies on others, that the potential for conflict arises." Describing Buddha as a "crown jewel" of India and a reformer of not only Hinduism but also the world, Modi offered prayers in the Mahabodhi Temple sanctum and spent time in meditation under the Bodhi tree.[3]

Notes

Introduction

1 Bodh Gaya is a municipality in the Gaya District of south Bihar, comprising twenty-two villages, including the nearby Magadh University campus. In the Buddha's time, Bodh Gaya was known as "Uruvela"; the modern designation, recognized by the Indian state government, is a contraction of "Buddha Gaya," a designation used to distinguish Bodh Gaya from the district headquarters, Gaya, and from the popular Hindu pilgrimage site Vishnupad Temple (Asher 2008). According to Bihar government tourism figures, 1,647,701 domestic and 225,668 foreign tourists visited Bodh Gaya in 2014 (www.bihartourism.gov.in/data/2010%20&%202011&2012.pdf).

2 "Opening of the Nalanda Multimedia Museum," YouTube video, 7:42, posted by pracinbarat, August 20, 2009, www.youtube.com/watch?v=idHWFsRDaAQ.

3 One example is the International Institute for Asian Studies (IIAS) in Leiden, Netherlands, which offers research fellowships to scholars working on Asian heritage and publishes a number of critical commentaries and articles through its newsletter.

4 Throughout, I have provided pseudonyms for the majority of research participants or refer to them in a general way to protect their anonymity. There are also a number of readily identifiable individuals in Bodh Gaya to whom I refer with their consent.

1. The Light of Asia

1 This abridged account comes from a translation of Manuscript No. 217, kept at the Bernard Free Library, Rangoon, in the custody of the Honorary Keeper of the Manuscripts. It was reprinted as a pamphlet (Maha Bodhi Society 1907).

2 From the late eighteenth and early nineteenth centuries on, Bodh Gaya was also visited by many travelers, surveyors, and artists, such as William Daniel and his nephew Thomas, who painted the ruins of the Mahabodhi Temple and Bodhi tree in 1790.

3 For more on Buchanan's account of the Gaya region, see James (1934).

4 Captain Markham Kittoe's (1808–1853) archaeological inquiries in Bodh Gaya actually predated those of Cunningham (see Kittoe 1854–1855).

5 As Doyle (1997) shows, delegations of Burmese Buddhists had made repeated visits to Bodh Gaya in 1795, 1811, 1823, 1833, and 1867.

6 Although Cunningham's voice dominates discussion of the archaeology and conservation of the site, especially with the publication of his 1892 monograph, it is not entirely

clear if he was directly involved with the on-site reconstruction itself (Asher 2004, 63). Beglar began work in January 1879 and continued until August 1884.

7 These 1889 letters between G. A. Grierson and the superintendent engineer were reprinted in a pamphlet entitled *Rescue Buddha Gaya: Rescue the Great Maha Bodhi Temple Buddhists of Asia! Wake Up from Your Sleep* (Dharmapala 1923).

8 As Huber (2008, 251) points out, these pronouncements that the "Buddhists" had "forgotten" their holy land was an unfair accusation to level at Tibetans, who had at least since the seventeenth century undertaken pilgrimage to India.

9 Sir Edwin Arnold's *Light of Asia*, subtitled *The Great Renunciation*, was a highly acclaimed "biblicized" Buddhist epic chronicling the life of the Buddha. It became one of the most widely read English texts ever published on Buddhism, selling almost one million copies. Translated into dozens of languages, it was also made into an opera and a Broadway play.

10 Arnold's account is reproduced as an appendix in Dharmapala (1900).

11 The Panadura debate was a significant event in the nineteenth-century revival of Buddhism in Ceylon. The famous two-day debate against Christian missionaries took place in Panadura, on the outskirts of Colombo, in 1873. On this occasion, the monastic leaders Sumangala and Gunandanda defended the Buddha *dhamma*, and particularly Sinhalese Buddhism, as more rational, ethical, and tolerant than Christianity, winning over the audience, including a young Dharmapala.

12 The Theosophical Society was founded in New York in 1875 with the objective of investigating mediumistic phenomena and advancing the spiritual principles and search for truth known as Theosophy (Greek: *theo*, "of Gods"; *sophia*, "wisdom"). It was held by the Theosophists that all religions are both true in their inner teachings and problematic or imperfect in their external conventional manifestations. The main founders of the organization were Henry Steel Olcott and the Ukranian mystic Madame Helena Petrovna Blavatsky; they moved to India in the 1880s and established their international headquarters at Adyar, Madras (Chennai).

13 Shaku Kozen was a disciple of the Shingon priest and Buddhist reformer Shaku Unsho. At the request of Shaku Unsho, Kozen went to Ceylon in 1886 to study Pali and take precepts from the high priest, Hikkaduwa Sumangala. Under the name Gunaratana, he became one of the first Japanese-born Theravada Buddhist monks.

14 The four young monks were Dunuville Chandrajoti, Anuradhapura Pemananda, Galle Sudassana, and Matale Sumangala. The former three left soon after they were assigned to Bodh Gaya. Sumangala was alone for most of the thirteen years he spent in Bodh Gaya and had a reputation for misbehavior (Kemper 2015).

15 The International Buddhist Conference was attended by Y. Ato, C. Tokuzawa, and Kozen Gunaratne of Japan; Sumangala of Ceylon; Lama To-Chiya of the Yung-ho-kung Temple in China, and Krishna Chandra Chaudhury and Girish Chandra Dewan, of Chittagong Hill Tracts, among others (Maha Bodhi Society of India 1952).

16 As noted later in this chapter, proprietorship of the temple was contested. Clearly, the Japanese saw the *mahant* as the "owner."

17 Hem Narayan Giri, whom Dharmapala described as a "kind hearted man," died in December 1891. With the arrival of the new *mahant*, Dharmapala experienced, in his own words, "oppression, persecution, spurious worship, [and] attempt[s] to eject the Buddhist monks from the Burmese resthouse" (Dharmapala 1923).

18 The phrase "and the United Buddhist World" disappeared without explanation from the journal's masthead in 1924 (Kemper 2015, 27).

19 Mary Foster was Hawaiian by birth, of a royal family, and had married a wealthy North American banker. From 1902 onward, she became a steady supporter of Dharmapala and the Maha Bodhi Society, especially his educational works in India and Ceylon, various publication projects, and the institutional growth of several Maha Bodhi branches. One of Mary Foster's legacies is the Foster Botanical Garden in Honolulu, which is the oldest botanical garden in Hawaii and listed on the National Register of Historic Places. Among other things, the garden contains a Bodhi tree cutting from Anuradhapura that was gifted by Dharmapala.

20 The Japanese image of Buddha Amitabha was made by the famous Buddhist sculptor Sadatomo of Nanto (Nara) in Yamato province and enshrined by Minamoto Yoritomo in 1200 CE. With changes to the Court of Kamakura, the image was taken to a faraway mountain valley, after which it was given to the chief priest of Kwomyogi, where it was enshrined in a temple. In 1890, the image was placed in a newly built temple, Kai-ko-ji, in Sangami province, until it was gifted to Dharmapala in the third year of Meiji, in 1893. After the fallout with the *mahant* in Bodh Gaya, the image was moved to Calcutta, where it is enshrined at the Mulagandhakuti Vihara (Mahabodhi Society 1907).

21 This was the second time Dharmapala sought to install the Japanese image in the temple. In 1894 the *mahant* had prevented its installation, and the image was kept at a rented house in Gaya and later placed in the Burmese Rest House, which gave rise to a trail of litigation (Kemper 2015).

22 Following the second partition of Bengal in 1911, the British authorities made one final push to place the disputed Mahabodhi Temple under the Ancient Monuments Preservation Act of 1904, but fear of "complications" once again prevailed, with the Commissioner of Patna, W. A Oldham, suggesting that "things had much better be left as they are." The move to place the Mahabodhi Temple under the Ancient Monuments Act was initiated by J. F. Blakiston, who provided an inventory of archaeological sites and monuments that could be enlisted as protected properties under the Archaeological Survey of Bihar and Orissa (Trevithick 2006, 174).

23 For example, the well-known Burmese monk and leader of the independence movement from British colonial rule, U Ottama (1879–1939), led a delegation of Indian, Japanese, and Burmese Buddhists to the All India Hindu Mahasabha Conference at Kanpur in 1935. Although conference attendees expressed support for the bill before the Legislative Assembly, it was shot down by some influential supporters of the Bodh Gaya *mahant*.

24 To complicate matters, following a Ceylonese delegation to India led by Dr. Pereira during this time, Rajendra Prasad was inundated with letters from Hindu groups in Ceylon under the banner "Buddha Gaya Defense League" belittling the work of the Maha Bodhi Society and claiming that the temple at Katagarama had been taken over by Buddhists.

25 Azad Hind was a provisional Indian government established in occupied Singapore in 1943 and supported by Japan and Nazi Germany.

26 In 2013 the Bihar government amended the Bodh Gaya Temple Act, removing the provision that empowers the state government to nominate a Hindu as chair of the management committee if the district magistrate is not a Hindu.

27 After the bill was passed, a management committee was formed. The five Hindu members were K. N. Sinha, (ex-officio chair), Kumar Ganga Nand Singh, R. L. Nandakeolyar, Brij Kishore Narain Singh; and Mahant Harihar Giri. The four Buddhist members were Devapriya Valisinha, Jinaratana Bhikshu of Assam, Bhikshu Jagadish Kashyap, and Arabinda Barua. The first superintendent of the Mahabodhi Temple was Anagarika Munindra, from the Chittagong region (Maha Bodhi Society of India 1952, 128).

28 At the first formal meeting of the Bodh Gaya Temple Management Committee (BTMC), held at Gaya on April 26, 1953, a caretaker was appointed to look after the affairs of the temple; two Buddhist *bhikkhus* (monks) were appointed to conduct worship in the temple (one of whom was to be maintained by the Maha Bodhi Society); a charity box was placed inside the temple to facilitate offerings; and a thorough cleaning of the temple and surrounding area was arranged.

2. Rebuilding the Navel of the Earth

1 This vision of a revived international landscape of Buddhist cottages was not limited to Bodh Gaya or Dharmapala. For example, see the Japanese Buddhist Okakura and his view of Bodh Gaya as "little colonies of devotees" (Kemper 2015, 228–231). In Sarnath, as well, Dharmapala had circulated a proposal to Maha Bodhi Society members in 1933 suggesting that Japanese, Siamese, Burmese, Ceylonese, Chinese, Tibetan, and Nepalese cottages be built at a cost of Rs. 7,000; the cottages would form the nucleus of an international Buddhist institute along the lines of the former Nalanda University (Maha Bodhi Society of India 1952, 109).

2 The information in this chapter comes from several primary and secondary sources. Most of the information pertaining to specific monasteries and temples derives from interviews and surveys conducted in 2005–2007 and 2011 with the head monks, nuns, and caretakers of the various centers in Bodh Gaya. I also gathered supplementary data from monastery articles, newsletters, and publications, along with Buddhist journals such as the the *Journal of the Maha Bodhi Society*, *Sambodhi*, and *Prajna*.

3 The Indian State Railways exhibited several attractive posters of the Buddhist holy places; they also ran full-page advertisements promoting organized rail pilgrimages on the back covers of the Maha Bodhi Society's monthly international journal (Huber 2008, 304).

4 Although there is little consensus among historians and Buddhist sects around the specific date of the birth, enlightenment, and *parinirvana* of the Buddha, among Theravada Buddhists this date is often associated with *vesak purnima*, a full moon that falls in late April or May.

5 On several occasions in official correspondence letters printed in the *Selected Works of Jawaharlal Nehru*, Nehru refers to the Buddha as "one of India's greatest sons" and one of "the greatest historical figures that India has produced."

6 The Buddha Jayanti Celebrations Committee, headed by Indian vice president S. Radhakrishnan, led to several important developments, such as physical improvements made at Buddhist sites; the publication of government-sponsored books and pamphlets on Buddhism and Buddhist places (e.g., *2500 Years of Buddhism*); the

broadcasting of numerous features, talks, and dramas about Buddhism by All India Radio; the convening of the International Buddhist Conference; the erection of the Buddha Jayanti Monument in Delhi; the creation of GB (Gautama Buddha) roads in several metropolitan centers; a Buddhist art exhibition; the issuing of a special commemorative stamp; the making of a government-sponsored film on the life of the Buddha; the translation and publication of the complete Pali Tipitaka in Devanagari and Bengali; the declaration of the Buddha Jayanti day—the *vesak purnima*—as a public holiday for the whole of India; and the organization of thousands of Buddha Jayanti cultural events and programs on the life and teachings of the Buddha. Generous concessions were also given by the Indian railways to encourage travel to the different Buddhist sites. For more details on the Buddha Jayanti celebrations in India and abroad see Maha Bodhi Society (1956).

7   The first meeting of the Bodh Gaya Temple Advisory Board was held on March 17, 1956, although it was not until 1959 that the governor of Bihar formally established its rules and regulations. The primary task of the board, which is required to meet at least every two years, is to advise the Indian government on the development aspects of the temple and Bodh Gaya in general. The board is to consist of no fewer than twenty members, of which two-thirds should be Buddhist, with at least half of them foreign citizens. All members of the board are appointed by the government of Bihar.

8   Shortly after his mass conversion, Ambedkar traveled to Kathmandu in Nepal to attend the Fourth World Buddhist Conference. He then undertook pilgrimage to Bodh Gaya, Sarnath, and Kushinagar before dying on December 6, 1956.

9   From Bodh Gaya, the Burmese U Chandramani (1875–1972) moved to Kushinagar (alongside Indian Buddhist Mahavira), where he established a Burmese *vihara*. He was also active in Sarnath, Balrampur, Rajgir, Calcutta, Sravasti, and Lumbini, where several Burmese *viharas* and *dharmashalas* were erected for the convenience of Buddhist pilgrims. U Chandramani also presided as the lead *dhamma*-guru figure over Dr. B. R. Ambedkar's *diksha* ceremony on October 14, 1956.

10 According to head monk Sayadaw U Nyaneinda, the Burmese *vihara* was built on land acquired by the Tekari Raj, and the first abbott of the *vihara* was U Nandumala. During this period the Burmese monks had come to stay in Varanasi and were provided support from a Burmese British assistant, U Ba Be, who helped with the acquisition of land at various Buddhist sites. Following the departure of U Nandumala, the head abbot was U Dhammetsara, who remained in Bodh Gaya until 1943. He was then replaced by U Otdama, who was head abbot from 1943 to 1966; U Tilawka was head abbot from 1966 to 1976. Prior to settling in Bodh Gaya, U Nyaneinda had spent over a decade in the Ledo region of Assam at the request of Prime Minister U Nu as part of a government exchange program between India and Burma.

11 This did not stop General Ne Win from making his own pilgrimage to Bodh Gaya in January 1968, accompanied by his wife and an entourage of twenty (Maha Bodhi Society 1968a, 86).

12 The Samanvay Ashram was established in 1954 by Vinoba Bhave. It is a charitable trust run by Dwarko Sundrani that aims to uplift the scheduled castes and scheduled tribes in the Bodh Gaya area. The ashram is based on Gandhian values and is a center for research and training in education and development.

13 These teachers include Michael Kewlay, a former Theravada Buddhist monk and a disciple of the late Sayadaw Rewata Dhamma. In 1986, Andrew Cohen visited Bodh Gaya and participated in a *vipassana* retreat held by Christopher Titmuss. Later, Cohen had a life-transforming encounter with the Indian master of Advaita Vedanta H. W. L. Poonja and decided to teach under the guidance of his guru (with whom he later parted ways philosophically). Between 1990 and 1996, Andrew Cohen ran a number of popular meditation retreats that were held at the Bihar State Tourist Bungalow near the Royal Wat Thai.

14 Although I do not know how many Indian students have gone to Myanmar as part of this program, Dr. Tulku, former head of the Buddhist Studies Department at Magadh University, told me that since the early 1990s, several foreign monks have been enrolled in the Buddhist studies graduate program at Bodh Gaya, largely from Myanmar, Bangladesh, Cambodia, Vietnam, Laos, and Sri Lanka.

15 As early as 1947 the Siamese government sent a formal request to the Ministry of External Affairs requesting to build a rest house in Bodh Gaya with the purpose of strengthening cultural ties between India and Siam. See Ministry of External Affairs (1956).

16 The Buddha statue is 3.60 meters in height and was cast in brass at Wat Benchamabopit in Bangkok on May 4, 1966. A team of forty-five guests from Thailand, including the mother-in-law of the Thai prime minister, attended the Golden Buddha installation.

17 The Kalachakra is a complex and advanced form of Vajrayana Tantric practice that aims to empower the initiate in the service of attaining Buddhahood. The Sanskrit word *kalachakra* means "time-wheel" or "time-cycles" and refers both to a Tantric deity of Vajrayana Buddhism and to the philosophies and meditation practices contained within the Tantra and its many commentaries. The 14th Dalai Lama is regarded as the most prominent Kalachakra lineage holder alive today, having performed over thirty initiations around the world.

18 More recently, both Urgyen Trinley Dorje Rinpoche and Trinley Thaye Dorje Rinpoche have independently performed ceremonial duties in the role of Karmapa at Bodh Gaya, even though they have never met. In the 2010–2011 winter season at Bodh Gaya, for example, both leaders were using the seat of Buddha's enlightenment to stage their celebration of the nine-hundred-year anniversary of the first Karmapa Dusum Khyenpa.

19 *Gompa*, or *dgon-pa*, is a Tibetan term that is used in the Himalayan region to describe a center of learning, monastery, or university complex.

20 According to interviews with senior resident monks from the Gelug Tibetan Temple, Lama Ngawang Samten was originally from Ladakh but also spent time as the abbot of a monastery in Tibet. The land was donated by the Maha Bodhi Society and later offered to the Tibetan government. Under the Tibetan government, Dam Doe Rinpoche (or Dhamgto Rinpoche) was the first head lama, or abbot, and under his management the guesthouse was constructed in 1952. After Dam Doe Rinpoche, the temple was gifted to the 14th Dalai Lama, who directed Ling Rinpoche to become the Head Lama after 1959.

21 Since the 2,500th Buddha Jayanti ceremonies, these include the Urvela Zangskar Ladakh Temple (or Bakroar Tibetan Monastery), the Sakya Monastery, the Royal

Bhutanese Monastery under the Royal Government of Bhutan, the Root Institute for Wisdom Culture (affiliated with the Foundation for the Preservation of the Mahayana Teachings) under Lama Zopa and Lama Yeshe, the Karma Tharjay Chokhorling, the Kagyupa Vajrayana Buddhist Monastery (known locally as the "Karma Temple") under Rinpoche Beru Khyentse, the Maitreya Project, the Duidal Jyangchub Choling Monastery of the Nepal Tamang Buddhist Association from Darjeeling, the Asian Buddhist Cultural Centre, the Nyingma Monlam Institute, the Shechen Tennyi Dargyeling–Nyingmapa Buddhist Monastery, the Druk Ngawang Thubten Choling of Bhutan, the Sikkim Temple Guest House, the Amitabha Meditation Centre, the Battsagaan Mongolian Temple, the Manang Social Development Committee Meditation Centre, and the Palyul Thupten Choskhor Dhargyeling (a unit of the Penor Rinpoche Foundation).

22 It is difficult to find reliable information on the origins of the Chinese temple. For example, the 1991 "A Buddha Gaya Tourist Guidebook" cites Si-Tingchen as the original founder, but scholars date the origins of the temple to either 1935 or 1945. The growing number of Chinese delegates and goodwill missions to India in the mid-1940s suggests that it was established during that time and grows out of ties with the Chinese community in Calcutta.

23 For more on the biography of Tan Yun-Shan see Menon (2013). The Mahabodhi Chinese Monastery and Temple also underwent major renovations in 1997, led by the head Chinese monk Wuqian, a prominent English-speaking Fo Guang Shan missionary and abbot of the Xaunzang Temple in Calcutta.

24 Another significant Japanese Buddhist traveler who played a leading role in the propagation of Buddhism throughout the twentieth century in India is Nichidatsu Fujii, known popularly as Fujii Guruji (1885–1985). Throughout his life, and after his death in 1985, Fujii Gurujii erected over fifty stupas, or peace pagodas, around the world.

25 Managal Subbha passed away on April 15, 2006, at the age of fifty-seven. He was replaced by Kiran Lama, who is the manager of the Daijokyo Buddhist Temple and current general secretary for the International Buddhist Council in Bodh Gaya.

26 The Bhikshuni *sangha* is believed to have disappeared from India around the tenth century and from Sri Lanka in the eleventh century.

27 For a recent review of Sakyadhita and its links with Bodh Gaya and Taiwan, see Yu-Ling Chang (2017).

28 The Maha Bodhi Rest House remained under dual control with the Gaya District Board until June 24, 1968.

29 Another key supporter who contributed significant financial resources to the building of Maha Bodhi Society *dharamshalas* was Jugal Kishore Birla (1883–1967), noted industrialist from the Birla family.

30 Devapriya Valisinha was born in the village of Apalatotuwa in the Sabaragamuwa Province near Kandy on February 10, 1904. He was sixth child of a family of seven brothers and sisters, and lost both his parents at a young age. For a biographic overview see Maha Bodhi Society (1968b).

31 The All India Bhikkhu Sangha (Akhila Bharata Baudha Bhikkhu Sangha) first met from July 3 to July 6, 1970, and decided to establish a *sangha*. The *sangha* was registered

on October 15, 1971; the first attempt at systematically training the new Buddhist monks took place from November 1 to November 30, 1972 (Kantowsky 2003, 152).

32 Arya Nagarjuna Surai Sasai was born Minoru Sasai in Okayama, Japan, in 1934. He was ordained as a Buddhist monk within the Nichiren order and studied *vipassana* in Thailand at the request of his teacher. He first went to India in 1966, when he met Nichidatsu Fujii, the founder of the Nipponzan Myohoji. After a falling out with Fujii, Surai Sasai had a vision that compelled him to visit Nagpur, where his affiliation with Dalit Buddhists began. For more biographic details on Surai Sasai, see Doyle (1997, 410-411).

33 As Tara Doyle (1997) points out, almost all of the Buddhist members of the temple management committee since 1953 came from a Theravada Buddhist background and maintained ties with the Maha Bodhi Society.

3. The Afterlife of *Zamindari*

1 According to Balindralal Das (1936), the monastery was originally built by Mahadeva Giri (and his successors) but was demolished and rebuilt several hundred years later, under the supervision and planning of Goswami Ramsahay Giri and Krishnya Dayal Giri.

2 According to Singh Bahadur's 1893 *Brief History of Bodh Gaya Math*, the lineage of *mahants* is as follows: Ghamandi (1590–1615), Chaitanya (1615–1642), Mahadeva (1642–1682), Lal (1682–1720), Keshava (1720–1748), Raghava (1748–1769), Ramhit (1769–1806), Balak (1806–1820), Shiva (1820–1846), Bahipat (1846–1867), Hem Narayan (1867–1892), Krishna Dayal (1892–1932), and Itarihar Giri (1932–1958).

3 For more on the prevailing customs of the Math, see Das (1936, 143–144).

4 This Settlement, also referred to as the Cornwallis Code, was an agreement between the British East India Company and Bengali landlords that fixed revenues to be raised from agricultural land. This comprehensive land management system laid the groundwork for uniting India into a single economic field based on a common currency and various policies that were gradually introduced across the subcontinent.

5 In *A Statistical Account of Bengal*, W. W. Hunter (1877) writes that the Bodh Gaya Math was one of three major religious endowments in the District of Gaya.

6 Annapurna is considered the sustainer of prosperity. In Sanskrit language the word *anna* means "food and grains" and *purna* means "full" or "complete." Many devout Hindus believe that by worshipping this goddess one will never be without food.

7 The charitable distribution of food was a special feature of the Math; the monastery was also widely famed for a special healing elixir known as *sankharab*. Manufactured by the *mahant* and freely distributed to the poor, this medicine, made of a special lemon preparation, was designed to cure liver and stomach ailments.

8 Rajendralala Mitra, who visited the Math in mid-nineteenth century, held a less flattering view of the monastic community: "The monks lead an easy, comfortable life, feasting on rich cakes (*malpuya*) and pudding (*mohanbhog*), and freely indulging in the exhilarating beverage of bhanga. Few attempt to learn the sacred books, and most of them are grossly ignorant" (1878, 6).

9 The Telangana uprising was a communist-led peasant rebellion that was followed by

a series of violent clashes against the landlords of the Telangana region in Andhra Pradesh and later against the princely state of Hyderabad between 1946 and 1951.

10 Under the 1950 Bihar Land Reforms Act, for example, there were certain government exemptions such as private lands, privileged lands, and lands used for agricultural and horticultural purposes in possession of the proprietor (*zamindar*). In Bihar there was no imposed limit on the size of lands that could be declared under "personal cultivation," and as a result it became possible for those who supervised the land (or did so through a relative) to call themselves cultivators.

11 According to Arun Sinha (1991), the Bihar government ordered an inquiry into the Bodh Gaya monastery at this time, but the state eventually gave up after covering 108 villages in the Gaya district where the monastery "allegedly" owned land. Beyond this point no further official inquiries were made until the late 1970s and early 1980s under the K. P. Saxena Commission report. The commission report, from what I understand, was never formally published.

12 This is probably why the Bihar state government decided to dissolve the State Bhoodan Committee in 1999 for its inability to distribute even half the *bhoodan* land available over the preceding thirty-eight years (Chandra et al. 2000).

13 Influenced by his education in the United States and by Gandhi, Jayaprakash Narayan (1902–1979) was a freedom fighter and popular socialist leader whose activism involved a combination of democratic socialist ideals based on Marxist theory and a firm commitment to the use of *satyagrahas*, or nonviolent resistance. He was also involved in the *bhoodan* campaign for several years prior to his leadership in the student movement.

14 For more on Krishnammal and Sankaralingam Jagannathan, see Land for the Tillers' Freedom, http://www.lafti.net/.

15 For a more detailed account of the resulting clash, see Sinha (1991) and Prabhat (1999).

16 Yadav has been one of the strongest supporters and benefactors of the Mandal commission. Born in a peasant household to a traditional farm-herder caste family, he became politically active as a student leader during the JP movement and joined the Janata Dal Party after the Emergency. Through his strategic appropriation of votes from both the Yadav and Muslim communities in Bihar, Lalu assumed state leadership in 1990, first as the chief minister of the Janata Dal Party and later as the leader of his own party, the Rashtriya Janata Dal, which forged an alliance with the Congress Party in the 1998 elections.

17 From the late 1970s until his death in 2005, Kumar's main competitor was the long-standing Communist Party of India leader Balikram (also from the Paswan caste). Over the course of two decades the two leaders swapped positions of political influence as Members of the Legislative Assembly (MLA) for the Bodh Gaya constituency. During this time "caste" supplanted "class" in the battleground for votes and the Communist Party of India began to lose its traditional base of support among some peasant communities in south Bihar. Although Rajesh Kumar was arguably the undisputed leader of Bodh Gaya from the late 1990s onward, when he was reelected as MP, his controversial political maneuvering (some suggest) eventually led to his demise; he was murdered on January 23, 2005, in the Imamganj area just outside Bodh Gaya.

18 Linked to the laws and regulations governing the Societies Registration Act (1860) is the Religious Endowment Act (1863), the Indian Trust Act (1882), and the Charitable and Religious Trust Act (1920). Registering a "trust" requires a minimum of three trustees with a majority of Indian citizens, while registering a "society" requires a minimum of seven members, at least four of whom must be Indian.

19 In the case of donations provided by foreign patrons, these institutions are legally bound to the Foreign Exchange Management Act (1999) and the Foreign Contribution Regulation Act (1976). All earnings must be declared as part of the Indian Income Tax Act (1961).

20 A forty-two-member hotel association was established in Bodh Gaya in 2002 to serve the needs of pilgrims and tourists and present a united voice before the state and municipal government regarding their concerns with the expanding monastic community.

21 Although some of the Buddhist monasteries have begun to pay the "holding taxes" in recent years, these matters are far from resolved and have recently been taken up in the High Court in Patna.

22 The Buddhist monasteries are also contesting their recent categorization as commercial enterprises by the Bihar State Electrical Board, which has led to a significant hike in electrical tariffs. This contentious issue reached a boiling point in February 2002, when the Bihar State Electrical Board disconnected the power supply at thirty-four monasteries. The monasteries threatened to close until matters were resolved at the state and municipal levels. According to an online article, the cost of electricity collectively runs around Rs. 2.5 million (www.rediff.com/news/2002/jan/31soroor.htm).

23 Monasteries are not the only targets of extortion in Bodh Gaya. For example, the successful Sujata Hotel, one of the first hotels in Bodh Gaya, has also been subject to similar land claim disputes.

24 In late January 2011 a large amount of foreign currency was seized by the Indian government during raids at a transit home for the 17th Karmapa Ugyen Trinley Dorje, near Dharamsala.

4. Tourism in the Global Bazaar

1 In 2005, the Ministry of Tourism adopted the tagline *atithi devo bhavah* as part of a social awareness campaign to improve the treatment of tourism providers in India.

2 A detailed survey of income levels conducted as part of a city development plan (Housing and Urban Development Corporation 2006a, 2006b) revealed that nearly 70% of the population had an income level below Rs. 2,500 (US$52) per month, with many relying upon seasonal work. The survey indicated that while agriculture remained the primary source of income in the surrounding area, the service industry at Bodh Gaya was growing.

3 These shops were under the jurisdiction of three administrative bodies—the tourism department of the Bihar state government, the Bodh Gaya Temple Management Committee, and the Nagar Panchayat. In addition, a handful of shops near the Samadhi graveyard are managed by the Bodh Gaya Math. Nearly all of these shops were demolished in 2013 following the bomb blasts (see conclusion).

4   The market is run by a committee of ten members consisting of six Tibetans and four Indians. It costs roughly Rs. 3,000 to rent a space for the entire season and Rs. 2,800 to 3,000 for electricity.

5   Some of the organizations behind the campaign to make Bodh Gaya a vegetarian zone are Tibetans for a Vegetarian Society (T4VS), Spitians for a Vegetarian Society (S4VS), Tibetan Homes Vegetarian Society (THVS), and the Sakya College Loving Kindness Vegetarian Committee.

6   Commercial lodging was relatively scarce in Bodh Gaya until the early 1990s. During the Buddha Jayanti festival in 1956, for example, accommodation was restricted to a few Buddhist monasteries and *dharamshalas* like the Maha Bodhi Society, the Burmese Vihara, the Birla Dharamshala, the Samanvay Ashram, and a small guesthouse and dormitory run by the Indian central government (later remodeled by the Indian Tourism Development Corporation (ITDC) and named Ashok's Travelers Lodge). There were also a few small family-run hotels along the Gaya riverside road. These included the Hotel Amar, the Hotel Shashi, the Hotel Archana, and later, the Hotel Cantica.

7   In response to the exorbitant rates being charged by the Mala Photo Association, the Buddhist monk Bhante Pannarama of the Maha Bodhi Society established a canteen restaurant and souvenir shop on the campus grounds in order to control prices.

8   Yuki developed an interest in Buddhism, especially as a member of Happy Science, which she joined in 1992. Founded in 1986, Happy Science is a growing worldwide movement initiated by Master Ryuho Okawa (b. 1956), who is believed to be the carrier of El Cantare, the Eternal Buddha, which resides in his core consciousness. As a nonprofit organization, Happy Science has several branches and charitable projects throughout the world, including Bodh Gaya.

9   See Huberman (2012) for a discussion of informal guiding in Banaras.

10 The etymology of the word *tout* derives from the Middle English *tuten,* meaning "to protrude or peer." When applied as a verb, according to the Oxford dictionary, it generally refers to two prominent actions: (1) the process of selling something, typically by a direct or persistent approach with an attempt to persuade people of the merits of purchasing an item in order to obtain some profit or commission, often more than the original production cost; and (2) the frequenting of heavily tourist areas and presenting oneself as a guide—particularly to those who do not speak the local language.

11 For a short documentary film on Bodh Gaya's "charity" industry, see *Destination: Tourism,* produced by Dafna Kory (2007).

5. A Master Plan for World Heritage

1   The Ashokan pillar was originally part of the Sujata Stupa complex, located on the eastern banks of the Niranjana River. In the early 1800s, the local district collector mined the stupa for building materials and moved the pillar to Gaya city, where it remained at the Gol Pather intersection until it was brought to Bodh Gaya in 1956.

2   The only copy of the 1973 Revised Master Plan that I could find was located in the Archaeological Survey of India Library in Patna, Bihar. The master plan was approved in 1973 by the Town Planning Organization, Local Self-Government Department,

and the government of Bihar for the Bodh Gaya Town Planning Authority (Bodh-Gaya Town Planning Authority 1973).

3   On July 7, 1977, a town meeting was held to explore the question of resettlement. Attendees included the district magistrate of Gaya, P. P. Sharma, state regional and local authorities, and over two hundred "awardees" connected with the proposed program. During the meeting, R. J. Sinha detailed the proposed benefits, such as road, water, light, park, school and market improvements. Taradih residents also requested that the government provide employment opportunities to affected family members and share some of the responsibility in constructing their new homes. Little appears to have been done following the initial meeting, and many residents grew skeptical of the resettlement plan, fearing inadequate compensation and a lack of commitment by the housing board.

4   Although the Gautam Van project was never implemented, a corridor of enclosed green space called the Jayprakash Udayan now lies to the west of the Mahabodhi Temple, maintained by the Forest and Environment Department, government of Bihar, and the Gaya Forest Division. The Jayprakash Udayan, despite its direct association with the popular political leader of Bihar, features a prominent statue of B. R. Ambedkar in the east corner of the park.

5   A major turning point in the evolution of Indian tourism was its formal recognition as an industry by the National Development Council in 1984. Such changes in state economic policy are certainly noticeable in the Seventh Five-Year Plan (1985–1990), with its allocation of over Rs. 68 crore to be used for various tourist development schemes and promotional activities throughout the county. For more on the institutional history of India's Ministry of Tourism, see Hannam and Diekmann (2011).

6   The Task Development Force led to several Department of Tourism documents in the late 1980s, such as the Action Plan for the Development of the Buddhist Sector (1986) and the Report on Area Development of the Buddhist Centres in Uttar Pradesh and Bihar (1988).

7   According to a former state government tourism official in Patna, a soft loan of Rs. 143.17 crore was provided by the OECF for the development of several important Buddhist sites in Bihar during this time.

8   The annual three-day Buddha Mahotsav (festival) could also be added to this list. The first Mahotsav was launched in Bodh Gaya in 1994; it relies heavily on spectacle and incorporates dance performances, Bollywood singers, craft exhibitions, and hand-picked artists from the state tourism department. These events have been known to attract opposition because they sometimes overlap with prominent religious gatherings in Bodh Gaya (e.g., the Tibetan Monlams) and lack religious content.

9   The original airstrip was built in 1937 and was used for military purposes. According to Robert Pryor, the airstrip was used as an American refueling site for DC-3s in the 1940s. During WWII the United States was providing assistance to the British, and several thousand US soldiers were stationed in the area.

10 Interview with Secretariat of the Bihar State Tourism Development Corporation, February 14, 2006. In 2013 and 2016, I was told by people in Bodh Gaya that the Bihar government was having difficulty acquiring land, so the plans for the eighteen-hole golf course were temporarily on hold.

11   The criteria for selection can be found at http://whc.unesco.org/en/criteria/.

12   Initially, ICOMOS officials raised concerns during their assessment of the Mahabodhi Temple that the Indian management plan lacked a clear sense of boundaries pertaining to the "core" area and how the designation would impact the spiritual and historical values of the site (see Kinnard 2014 for further analysis). As a result, revisions to the nomination dossier were required before the Mahabodhi Temple Complex could be formally inscribed on the World Heritage List.

13   Benoy K. Behl is a New Delhi–based filmmaker, photographer, and art historian. He is particularly well known for his photographs of the Ajanta caves, which were published in *National Geographic*.

14   The speech is available at http://www.presidentofindia.nic.in, accessed December 12, 2006.

15   These documents were as follows: Mahabodhi Temple Complex World Heritage Property: Site Management Plan; Heritage Led Perspective Development Plan for BodhGaya, Vision 2001–2031: The Plan; and Heritage Led Perspective Development Plan for BodhGaya, Vision 2001–2031: The Work Studies.

16   The City Development Plan was meant to complement the Site Management Plan under HUDCO and was finalized in September 2006 by the Department of Urban Development, Government of Bihar. It is the principal document that I refer to in this section and builds upon the consultative data provided by the Housing and Urban Development Corporation. For Bodh Gaya, an amount of Rs. 434.63 crore had been sanctioned under this JNNURM scheme.

17   For example, the entire village of Bakroar was incorporated into the master plan, but no prior orders were issued, and local representatives were not consulted.

18   This hotelier is referring to an incident in 2006 in which the Gaya Regional Development Authority demolished the fourth floors of two hotels, the Prince Hotel and the Jeevak Hotel, without any forewarning at the beginning of the tourist season. The GRDA argued that the hotels did not have permission to construct a fourth floor, which was against the town height restriction policies. Immediately following the demolition, a press conference was held by the hotel association, and a peace march against the master plan occurred on November 22, 2006.

19   In view of the resistance to the master plan and concerns raised by the UNESCO authorities, the government of Bihar organized several high-level committees in 2008 to look into the objections raised by the Nagrik Vikas Manch and others.

Conclusion

1   Despite provisions that Asian Buddhist delegates should constitute over 50% representation on the advisory board, the reality over the last few decades has been that most representatives are Indian government officials. The meetings are also held less frequently than in the past.

2   The income tax department issued its first notice to temple management in 2013. This was likely due to the fact that Buddhist devotees had donated over Rs. 6 crore, including cash, to the BTMC in the 2012–2013 year.

3   This was followed by a short presentation to the conclave participants in which the prime minister and a government official shared a fifteen-minute film on the rich Buddhist heritage of Gujarat, especially near Modi's hometown Vadnagar. Taking inspiration from Bihar and the place of Buddha's enlightenment, Modi emphasized the vital prospects of renewing Buddhist ties with Gujarat and developing it as a future pilgrim destination.

Glossary

adda. The practice of "hanging out," drinking tea, watching, commenting, and debating, which reflects a particular way of dwelling in modern India.

avatar (or avatara). Manifestation of a deity or released soul in bodily form on earth; an incarnate divine teacher.

basti. Village of huts.

benami. Made, held, done, or transacted in the name of another person; in Hindu law, designates a transaction, contract, or property transfer.

bhandara. Grand feast.

bhikku/bhikkuni. Ordained male and female monastic (monk/nun) in Buddhism.

bhoodan andolan. Land-gift movement.

Bhotia. Term encompassing several Tibetan-language groups of the Himalayas.

charpoy. A traditional Indian woven bed.

chowkidar. Local guard.

crore. Ten million; one hundred lakhs, especially of rupees, units of measurement, or people.

dacoity. (from Hindi, *ḍakaitī*) Act of violent robbery committed by an armed gang.

dalali. Brokerage, commission, procuration.

dalit. "Oppressed"—a self-chosen political name of the lowest caste groups in India.

dana. Virtue of generosity, charity, or giving of alms.

deva/devi. Term used for *deity* in Hinduism.

dhamma/dharma. Basic principles of cosmic or individual existence: divine law as applied to the teachings of the Buddha.

dhammaduta/dharmaduta. Ambassador of the dharma/messenger of truth.

dhamma-raja. Dharmic kingship based on the Ashokan ideal of a galactic polity.

dharmashala. A religious sanctuary or rest house for pilgrims and travelers.

dhyana mudra. Meditation gesture with hands placed on lap, right hand over left, palms facing upward and fingers stretched in a relaxed pose.

firman. Deed of agreement.

goonda. Hired thug or leader of a gang; both a colloquial term and defined and used in laws, generally referred to as Goonda Acts.

itihasa. Religious story that tells about what happened in the past, often in the form of epic poems.

jagir. A type of feudal land grant common in South Asia that developed during Islamic rule beginning in the early thirteenth century.

kamia. Caste/tribe laborers who tilled the land through a system of debt servitude prevalent in Bihar. This system of debt servitude is known as *kamiauti.*

kutcherie. Landlord's farmhouse turned office/court.

lakh. Unit in the Indian numbering system equal to one hundred thousand.

Majjhimadesa. (Middle Land) Ancient name of the north-central region of India, the valley of the Ganges and Yamuna Rivers, and the birthplace of Buddhism.

mahant. Main abbot or head of a religious order.

maidan. An open space in or near a town, used as a parade ground or for events such as public meetings.

mala. A bead or a set of beads commonly used by Hindus and Buddhists for keeping count while reciting, chanting, or mentally repeating a mantra or the name or names of a deity.

mukarrari. Form of lease held at a fixed and permanent rent.

nikaya. Pali word meaning "volume," used like the Sanskrit word *āgama* to mean "collection," "assemblage," "class," or "group" in both Pali and Sanskrit. Most commonly used in reference to the Buddhist texts of the Sutta Pitaka but can also refer to the monastic divisions of Theravada Buddhism.

ofuro. Japanese soaking bathtub.

padayatra. Pilgrimage on foot, especially one made for religious purposes, or expressing charitable, social, or political concerns; a protest march or political campaign tour.

panchasila. The five Buddhist rules of conduct, calling for peaceful coexistence between people, nations, and ideologies.

panchayat. Assembly (*ayat*) of five (*panch*), the oldest system of local government in the Indian subcontinent.

parikrama. Circumambulating path.

parinirvana. (Sanskrit: *parinirvāṇa*; Pali: *parinibbāna*) Nirvana-after-death, which occurs upon the death of the body of someone who has attained nirvana during his or her lifetime; implies a release from the cycle of Samsara, karma, and rebirth.

peepal. Sacred fig, a species of fig native to the Indian subcontinent, and Indochina (also known as Bodhi tree).

pindadana. Offering of balls of rice, wheat, or barley (*pindas*) as oblations to one's ancestors and carried out by the devotee at various sacred sites.

posadha. (Pali; Sanskrit: *uposatha*) Buddhist day of observance; cleansing of the defiled mind resulting in inner calm.

puja. Acts of worship and prayer showing reverence to a god, spirit, or another aspect of the divine through invocations, songs, and rituals.

purnima. (Sanksrit: *pūrṇimā*) Full moon.

sadhu. A Hindu ascetic or holy person.

samadhi. Shrine or tomb that commemorates the saints or gurus in Hindu religious traditions.

samanera. (Pali; Sanskrit: *śrāmaṇera*) Buddhist rite of ordination by which a layman becomes a novice.

samsara. The cycle of death and rebirth to which life in the material world is bound.

sangha. Association of Buddhist monks, nuns, novices, and lay followers of Buddhism.

sannyasin. Hindu mendicant.

sasana. (Sanskrit: *śāsana*; Pali: *sāsana*) Usually refers to the Buddha's teachings but has a range of translations and meanings across cultures and denominations.

sepoy. Indian soldier serving under British colonial orders.

Shaivites/Shaivas. Hindu sect that reveres the god Shiva as the Supreme Being.

sraddha. Ritual that one performs to pay homage to one's ancestors, especially to one's dead parents.

Upasampada. Literally, "approaching or nearing the ascetic tradition." In Buddhism, it is the rite of ordination by which one embraces the monastic life.

Vaishnava. Hindu tradition that considers Vishnu as the Supreme Lord.

vajrasana. "Diamond throne"; the exact place where the Buddha sat when he was enlightened.

Vesak. (Pali: Vesākha; Sanskrit: Vaiśākha) Buddhist holiday that celebrates three major events in the Buddha's life: his birth, enlightenment, and death.

vihara. Buddhist monastery.

vipassana. A form of meditation in which mindfulness of breathing and thoughts, feelings, or actions is used to gain insight into the true nature of reality.

zamindar. Aristocratic landowner, especially one who leases land to farmers. *Zamindari* refers to the system under which such landownership patterns occur.

References

Ahir, Diwan Chand. 1989. *Pioneers of Buddhist Revival in India*. New Delhi: Sri Satguru.
———. 1994. *Buddha Gaya through the Ages*. New Delhi: Sri Satguru.
Ahmad, Faizan. 2009. "Fight Caste System: Amartya." *Times of India*, February 22.
Aitken, M. E., ed. 1995. *Meeting the Buddha: On Pilgrimage in Buddhist India*. New York: Riverhead Books.
Allen, Charles. 2003. *The Buddha and the Sahibs: The Men Who Discovered India's Lost Religion*. London: John Murray.
Almond, Philip C. 1988. *The British Discovery of Buddhism*. Cambridge: Cambridge University Press.
Ambedkar, B. R. 2011 [1959]. *The Buddha and His Dhamma: A Critical Edition*, edited by Aakash Singh Rathore and Ajay Verma. New York: Oxford University Press.
Anjaria, Jonathan Shapiro. 2011. "Ordinary States: Everyday Corruption and the Politics of Space in Mumbai." *American Ethnologist* 38 (1): 58–72.
Anonymous. 1923–1926. "Bodh Gaya Temple: Concerns of Burmese Buddhists regarding the Control of the Buddha Gaya Temple by Non-Buddhists." Pamphlet titled "Rescue Buddhagaya." IOR/L/PJ/6/1858. File 3933. July 1923–April 1926. British Library.
———. 1944. "Restoration of Bodh-gaya to Buddhist Hands." IOR/R/8/27: 24. File 9C20/PA44. May–August 1944. British Library.
———. 2006."Special Train to Buddhist Sites." *Hindustan Times*, December 23.
———. 2012. "Private Agency to Organize Bihar Tourism Festivals." *Times of India*, November 7.
———. 2013a. "President Condemns Bodh Gaya Blasts as Senseless Terror Act." *DNA India* (New Delhi), July 7.
———. 2013b. "Suspected IM Member Arrested in Kolkata for Bodh Gaya Terror Attack." *India Today*, July 7. http://indiatoday.intoday.in/story/serial-blasts-bodhgaya-in-bihar-mahabodhi-temple/1/287300.html.
———. 2015. "Bodh Gaya to Be Developed as a Spiritual Capital: Modi." *Hindu*, September 5.
Appadurai, Arjun. 1988. "Putting Hierarchy in Its Place." *Cultural Anthropology* 3 (1): 36–49.
———. 1991. "Global Ethnoscapes: Notes and Queries for a Transnational Anthropology." In *Recapturing Anthropology: Working in the Present*, edited by R. G. Fox, 191–210. Santa Fe: School of American Research Press.
———. 2000. "Spectral Housing and Urban Cleansing: Notes on Millennial Mumbai." *Public Culture* 12 (3): 627–651.

Arnold, Edwin. 1879. *Light of Asia: The Great Renunciation*. New York: Rand McNally.

Asher, Frederick M. 2004. "The Bodhgaya Temple: Whose Structure Is It?" *Religion and the Arts* 8 (1): 58–73.

———. 2008. *Bodh Gaya: Monumental Legacy*. New Delhi: Oxford University Press.

Banerjee, Naresh. 2000. *Gaya and Bodh Gaya: A Profile*. New Delhi: Inter-India.

Barnes, Nancy J. 1996. "Buddhist Women and the Nuns' Order in Asia." In *Engaged Buddhism: Buddhist Liberation Movements in Asia*, edited by C. S. Queen and S. B. King, 259–294. Albany: SUNY Press.

Bartwal, H. S. 2006. "Rlys Plans More Trains of Buddhist Circuit." *Hindustan Times*, November 28.

Bayly, C. A. 1983. *Rulers, Townsmen and Bazaars: North Indian Society in the Age of British Expansion, 1770–1870*. Cambridge: Cambridge University Press.

Beltz, Johannes, and Surendra Jondhale, eds. 2004. *Reconstructing the World: Dr. Ambedkar and Buddhism in India*. Oxford: Oxford University Press.

Bodh-Gaya Town Planning Authority. 1973. *Revised Master Plan*. Bihar: Superintendent Secretariat Press of Patna.

———. 1966. *Draft Master Plan*. Bihar: Superintendent Secretariat Press of Patna.

Bond, George D. 1992. *The Buddhist Revival in Sri Lanka: Religious Tradition, Reinterpretation and Response*. New Delhi: Motilal Banarsidass.

Borchert, Thomas. 2007. "Buddhism, Politics, and Nationalism in the Twentieth and Twenty-First Centuries." *Religion Compass* 1(5): 529–546.

Bornstein, Erica. 2009. "The Impulse of Philanthropy." *Cultural Anthropology* 24(4): 622–651.

———. 2012. *Disquieting Gifts: Humanitarianism in New Delhi*. Stanford: Stanford University Press.

Brass, P. R. 1990. *The Politics of India since Independence*. Cambridge: Cambridge University Press.

Breglia, Lisa 2006. *Monumental Ambivalence: The Politics of Heritage*. Austin: University of Texas Press.

Brennan, Denise. 2004. *What's Love Got to Do with It?: Transnational Desires and Sex Tourism in the Dominican Republic*. Durham: Duke University Press.

Brown, Rebecca M. 2009. "Reviving the Past: Post-independence Architecture and Politics in India's Long 1950s." *Interventions* 11 (3): 293–315.

Carrette, Jeremy R., and Richard King. 2005. *Selling Spirituality: The Silent Takeover of Religion*. Hove, UK: Psychology Press.

Chakrabarty, Dipesh. 1999. "Adda, Calcutta: Dwelling in Modernity." *Public Culture* 11 (1): 109–145.

Chambers, Erve. 2010. *Native tours: The Anthropology of Travel and Tourism*. 2nd ed. Long Grove: Waveland Press.

Chandra, Bipan. 2003. *In the Name of Democracy: JP Movement and the Emergency*. New Delhi: Penguin.

Chandra, Bipan, M. Mukherjee, and Aditya Mukherjee. 2000. *India after Independence, 1947–2000*. New Delhi: Penguin.

Cohn, Bernard S. 1964. "The Role of the Gosains in the Economy of Eighteenth and Nineteenth Century Upper India." *Indian Economic and Social History Review* 1 (4): 175–182.

———. 1996. *Colonialism and Its Forms of Knowledge: The British in India*. Princeton: Princeton University Press.

Cole, Jennifer, and Deborah Durham, ed. 2008. *Figuring the Future: Children, Youth, and Globalization*. Sante Fe: School for Advanced Research Press.

Coleman, Simon. 2002. "Do You Believe in Pilgrimage? Communitas, Contestation and Beyond." *Anthropological theory* 2 (3): 355–368.

Collins, John F. 2008. "But What if I Should Need to Defecate in Your Neighborhood, Madame?": Empire, Redemption, and the "Tradition of the Oppressed" in a Brazilian World Heritage Site." *Cultural Anthropology* 23 (2): 279–328.

———. 2011. "Culture, Content, and the Enclosure of Human Being UNESCO's "Intangible" Heritage in the New Millennium." *Radical History Review*, no. 109: 121–135.

Comaroff, Jean, and John L. Comaroff. 2000. "Millennial Capitalism: First Thoughts on a Second Coming." *Public Culture* 12 (2): 291–343.

Connerton, Paul. 1989. *How Societies Remember*. Cambridge: Cambridge University Press.

Copeman, Jacob. 2011. "The Gift and Its Forms of Life in Contemporary India." *Modern Asian Studies* 45 (5): 1051–1094.

Copland, Ian. 2004. "Managing Religion in Colonial India: The British Raj and the Bodh Gaya Temple Dispute." *Journal of Church and State* 46 (3): 527–559.

Crick, Malcolm. 1989. "Representations of International Tourism in the Social Sciences: Sun, Sex, Sights, Savings, and Servility." *Annual Review of Anthropology* 18: 307–344.

Crowther, G. 1985. *India Travel Survival Guide: Lonely Planet Travel Survival Kit*. Melbourne: Lonely Planet.

Csordas, Thomas J., ed. 2009. *Transnational Transcendence: Essays on Religion and Globalization*. Berkeley: University of California Press.

Dalai Lama. 1990. *Freedom in Exile: The Autobiography of His Holiness the Dalai Lama of Tibet*. London: Hodder and Stoughton.

Das, Arvind N. 1992. *The Republic of Bihar*. New York: Penguin Books.

Das, Balindralal. 1936. *A Hindu Point of View on the Bodh-Gaya Temple: With Some Reference to the Bill regarding the Same Pending in Assembly*. Calcutta: Author.

Dazey, Wade. 1992. "Tradition and Modernization in the Organization of the Dasanami Sannyasins." In *Monastic Life in the Christian and Hindu Tradition*, edited by Austin Creel and Vasudha Narayanan, 281–321. Lewiston: Edwin Mellen Press.

Del Marmol, C., M. Morell. and J. Chalcraft, eds. *The Making of Heritage: Seduction and Disenchantment*. Routledge, 2014.

Department of Tourism, Government of India. 1986. "Action Plan for the Development of the Buddhist Sector." New Delhi: A. F. Ferguson.

———. 1988. "Report on Area Development of the Buddhist Centres in Uttar Pradesh and Bihar." New Delhi: A. F. Ferguson.

———. 1992. "Development of the Buddhist Sector for the Japanese Market." New Delhi: Pacific Consultants International in Tokyo and Consulting Engineering Services.

Dhammika, Shravasti. 1996. *Navel of the Earth: The History and Significance of Bodh Gaya*. Singapore: Buddha Dhamma Mandala Society.

Dharmapala, Anagarika. 1900. *History of Maha-Bodhi Temple at Bodh Gaya*. Calcutta: K. P. Mokkerjee. British Library.

———. 1923. *Rescue Buddha Gaya: Rescue the Great Maha Bodhi Temple Buddhists of Asia! Wake Up from Your Sleep.* Calcutta: Maha Bodhi Society. British Library.

———. 1925. [Oppression and Tyranny at Buddha Gaya. Buddhist Pilgrims Forcibly Ejected from the Great Temple by the Menials of the Saivite Mahant. The Visit of the Lieutenant Governor of Bengal to the Temple on December 3rd, 1909. (With Illustrations.)] Calcutta: Maha Bodhi Society. British Library.

Dhawan, Himanshi. 2011. "Bihar More Happening Tourist Spot Than Goa?" *Times of India*, January 5.

Dirks, Nicholas B. 1993. *The Hollow Crown: Ethnohistory of an Indian Kingdom.* Ann Arbor: University of Michigan Press.

Doyle, Tara. N. 1997. "Bodh Gaya: Journeys to the Diamond Throne and the Feet of Gayasur." PhD diss., Harvard University.

———. 2003. "'Liberate the Mahabodhi Temple!' Socially Engaged Buddhism, Dalit-Style." In *Buddhism in the Modern World: Adaptations of an Ancient Tradition*, edited by S. Heine and C. S. Prebish, 249–280. Oxford: Oxford University Press.

———. 2012. "'Why Cause Unnecessary Confusion?': Re-inscribing the Mahabodhi Temple's Holy Places." In *Cross-Disciplinary Perspectives on a Contested Buddhist Site: Bodh Gaya Jataka*, edited by David Geary et al., 119–138. London: Routledge.

Eade, John, and Michael J. Sallnow. 1991. *Contesting the Sacred: The Anthropology of Pilgrimage.* Champaign: University of Illinois Press.

Favero, Paolo. 2003. "Phantasms in a 'Starry' Place: Space and Identification in a Central New Delhi Market." *Cultural Anthropology* 18 (4): 551–584.

Foucault, M. 1991. "Governmentality." Translated by Rosi Braidotti and revised by Colin Gordon, in *The Foucault Effect: Studies in Governmentality*, edited by G. Burchell, C. Gordon, and P. Miller, 87–104. Chicago: University of Chicago Press.

Geary, David. 2008. "Destination Enlightenment: Branding Buddhism and Spiritual Tourism in Bodhgaya, Bihar." *Anthropology Today* 24 (3): 11–14.

Geary, David. 2012. "World Heritage in the Shadow of Zamindari." In *Cross-Disciplinary Perspectives on a Contested Buddhist Site: Bodh Gaya Jataka*, edited by David Geary et al., 141–152. London: Routledge.

———. 2013a. "The Decline of the Bodh Gaya Math and the Afterlife of Zamindari." *South Asian History and Culture* 4 (3): 366–383.

———. 2013b. "Incredible India in a Global Age: The Cultural Politics of Image Branding in Tourism." *Tourist Studies* 13(1): 36–61.

———. 2014. "Rebuilding the Navel of the Earth: Buddhist Pilgrimage and Transnational Religious Networks." *Modern Asian Studies* 48 (3): 645–692.

Geary, David, Matthew R. Sayers, and Abhishek Singh Amar, eds. 2012. *Cross-Disciplinary Perspectives on a Contested Buddhist Site: Bodh Gaya Jataka.* London: Routledge.

Ghertner, D. A. 2011. "Rule by Aesthetics: World-Class City Making in Delhi." In *Worlding Cities: Asian Experiments and the Art of Being Global*, edited by A. Roy and A. Ong, 279–306. Malden: Wiley-Blackwell.

Goldberg, Kory. 2011. "Buddhists without Borders: Transnational Pilgrimage, Social Engagement, and Education in the Land of Enlightenment." PhD diss., University of Quebec, Montreal.

Grierson, George Abraham. 1893. *Notes on the District of Gaya*. Calcutta: Bengal Secretariat Press.

Guha, Romit. 2013. "Bihar Enters the Fast Lane." *Wall Street Journal,* February 21.

Guha-Thakurta, Tapati. 2004. *Monuments, Objects, Histories: Institutions of Art in Colonial and Postcolonial India*. New York: Columbia University Press.

Guichard-Anguis, Sylvie, and Okpyo Moon, eds. 2008. *Japanese Tourism and Travel Culture*. New York: Routledge.

Gupta, Akhil. 1998. *Postcolonial Developments: Agriculture in the Making of Modern India*. Durham: Duke University Press.

Guruge, Ananda, ed. 1965. *Return to Righteousness: A Collection of Speeches, Essays and Letters of the Anagarika Dharmapala*. Colombo: Department of Government Printing.

Guy, John. 1991. "The Mahābodhi Temple: Pilgrim Souvenirs of Buddhist India." *Burlington Magazine* 1059: 356–367.

Haines, Chad. 2011. "Cracks in the Façade: Landscapes of Hope and Desire in Dubai." In *Worlding Cities: Asian Experiments and the Art of Being Global,* edited by A. Roy and A. Ong, 160–181. Malden: Wiley-Blackwell.

Halperin, Rhoda H., and Suzanne Scheld. 2007. "Introduction: Youth Engage the City and Global Culture." *City and Society* 19 (2): 169–178.

Hamilton, Francis. 1925. "Journal of Francis Buchanan (afterwards Hamilton) Kept during the Survey of The Districts of Patna and Gaya In 1811–1812: Edited with Notes and Introduction by VH Jackson." Patna: Superintendent, Government Print., Bihar and Orissa.

Hamilton-Buchanan, F. 1937. *An Account of the Districts of Bihar and Patna in 1811–1812*. Calcutta: Bihar and Orissa Research Society.

Hancock, Mary E. 2002. "Modernities Remade: Hindu Temples and Their Publics in Southern India." *City and Society* 14 (1): 5–35.

———. 2008. *The Politics of Heritage from Madras to Chennai*. Bloomington: Indiana University Press.

Hannam, K., and A. Diekmann. 2011. *Tourism and India: A Critical Introduction*. London: Routledge.

Hannerz, Ulf. 1998. "Other Transnationals: Perspectives Gained from Studying Sideways." *Paideuma* 44: 109–123.

Harvey, D. 1996. *Justice, Nature and the Geography of Difference*. Oxford: Blackwell.

———. 2004. "The 'New' Imperialism: Accumulation by Dispossession." *Socialist Register,* no. 40: 63–87.

Hefner, Robert W. 1998. "Multiple Modernities: Christianity, Islam, and Hinduism in a Globalizing Age." *Annual Review of Anthropology* 27: 83–104.

Herbert, Tony. 2010. *A Cultural Journey: With the Bhuiyas of Central East India*. New Delhi: Indian Social Institute.

Herzfeld, Michael. 2006. "Spatial Cleansing, Monumental Vacuity and the Idea of the West." *Journal of Material Culture* 11 (1–2): 127–149.

———. 2010. "Engagement, Gentrification, and the Neoliberal Hijacking of History." *Current Anthropology* 51 (S2): S259–S267.

———. 2011. "European Lessons for Asian Heritage Studies." *International Institute for Asian Studies Newsletter,* no. 57: 19.

Hirsch, Eric, and Michael O'Hanlon. 1995. *The Anthropology of Landscape: Perspectives on Place and Space*. Oxford: Oxford University Press.

Holt, John. 2004. *The Buddhist Visnu: Religious Transformation, Politics, and Culture*. New York: Columbia University Press.

Housing and Urban Development Corporation (HUDCO). 2006a. *City Development Plan for Bodh Gaya*. New Delhi: Author.

———. 2006b. *City Development Plan for Bodhgaya under the JNNURM: Final Report*. Bihar: Department of Urban Development, Government of Bihar.

Huber, Toni. 2008. *The Holy Land Reborn: Pilgrimage and the Tibetan Reinvention of Buddhist India*. Chicago: University of Chicago Press.

Huberman, Jenny. 2012. *Ambivalent Encounters: Childhood, Tourism, and Social Change in Banaras, India*. New Brunswick: Rutgers University Press.

Hunter, William Wilson. 1877. *A Statistical Account of Bengal*. Vol. 20. London: Trübner.

Inden, Ronald. 1995. "Embodying God: From Imperial Progress to National Progress In India." *International Journal of Human Resource Management* 24 (2): 245–278.

Ivy, Marilyn. 1995. *Discourses of the Vanishing: Modernity, Phantasm, Japan*. Chicago: University of Chicago Press.

Jaffe, Richard M. 2004. "Seeking Śākyamuni: Travel and the Reconstruction of Japanese Buddhism." *Journal of Japanese Studies* 30 (1): 65–96.

Jain, Kajri. 2007. *Gods in the Bazaar: The Economies of Indian Calendar Art*. Durham: Duke University Press.

James, John, ed. 1934. *An Account of the Districts of Bihar and Patna in 1811–1812*. Patna: Bihar and Orissa Research Society.

Jeffrey, Craig. 2010. "Timepass: Youth, Class, and Time among Unemployed Young Men in India." *American Ethnologist* 37 (3): 465–481.

Jha, Sanjay K. 2003. "Knot Uncommon." *India Today*, March 31.

Kalam, Farhana. 2005. "Shrine to Keep Heritage Tag." *Telegraph*, April 26.

Kantowsky, Detlef. 2003. *Buddhists in India Today: Descriptions, Pictures, and Documents*. New Delhi: Manohar.

Kelkar, Govind, and Chetna Gala. 1990. "The Bodhgaya Land Struggle." In *A Space within the Struggle: Women's Participation in People's Movements*, edited by I. Sen, 82–110. New Delhi: Kali for Women.

Kelsky, Karen. 2001. *Women on the Verge: Japanese Women, Western Dreams*. Durham: Duke University Press.

Kemper, Steven. 2005. "Dharmapala's Dharmaduta and the Buddhist Ethnoscape." In *Buddhist Missionaries in the Era of Globalization*, edited by Linda Learman, 22–50. Honolulu: University of Hawai'i.

———. 2015. *Rescued from the Nation: Anagarika Dharmapala and the Buddhist World*. Chicago: University of Chicago Press.

Khilnani, Sunil. 1999. *The Idea of India*. New Delhi: Penguin.

King, R. 1999. *Orientalism and Religion: Postcolonial Theory, India and "The Mystic East."* London: Routledge.

Kinnard, Jacob N. 1998. "When is the Buddha not the Buddha? The Hindu/Buddhist Battle over Bodhgayā and Its Buddha image." *Journal of the American Academy of Religion* 66 (4): 817–839.

———. 2014. *Places in Motion: The Fluid Identities of Temples, Images, and Pilgrims.* Oxford: Oxford University Press.

Kirshenblatt-Gimblett, Barbara. 2004. "Intangible Heritage as Metacultural Production." *Museum International* 56 (1–2): 52–65.

Kittoe, Markham. 1854–1855. "Request for Aid in Archaeological Enquiries at Gya and Convict Labour Refused." IOR/Z/E/4/25/K181: 1854–1855. British Library.

Kunnath, George J. 2009. "Smouldering Dalit Fires in Bihar, India." *Dialectical Anthropology* 33 (3–4): 309–325.

Leoshko, Janice. 1996. "On the Construction of a Buddhist Pilgrimage Site." *Art History* 19 (4): 573–597.

———, ed. 1988. *Bodhgaya, the Site of Enlightenment.* Bombay: Marg.

LeVine, S., and D. N. Gellner. 2005. *Rebuilding Buddhism: The Theravada Movement in Twentieth-Century Nepal.* Cambridge: Harvard University Press.

Ling, Trevor. 1968. *A History of Religion East and West: An Introduction and Interpretation.* London: Palgrave Macmillan.

Lopez Jr., Donald S., ed. 1995. *Curators of the Buddha: The Study of Buddhism under Colonialism.* Chicago: University of Chicago Press.

———. 2006. *The Madman's Middle Way: Reflections on Reality of the Tibetan Monk Gendun Chopel.* University of Chicago Press.

Louis, Prakash. 2002. *People Power: The Naxalite Movement in Central Bihar.* Delhi: Wordsmiths.

Ludden, David. 1996. "Ayodhya: A Window on the World." In *Contesting the Nation: Religion, Community, and the Politics of Democracy in India,* edited by D. Ludden, 1–23. Philadelphia: University of Pennyslvania Press.

Maha Bodhi Society. 1891. "The Maha-Bodhi Society: Its Constitution, Rules and List of Officers." Calcutta: Maha-Bodhi Society.

———. 1907. "Buddha Gaya, etc." [A petition to the viceroy, and other documents relating to the Buddhist rest-house at Buddha Gaya]. Calcutta: Maha Bodhi Society. British Library.

———. 1922. "Reply to Dharmapala." *Journal of the Maha Bodhi Society* 30: 242.

———. 1924. "Sarnath: A site for a Buddhist Vihara and University." Calcutta: Maha Bodhi Society. British Library.

———. 1947. "Notes and News." *Journal of the Maha Bodhi Society* 55 (5–6): 150–151.

———. 1948a. "Correspondence." *Journal of the Maha Bodhi* Society 56 (5–6): 203–204.

———. 1948b. "The Maha Bodhi Temple Bill." *Journal of the Maha Bodhi Society* 56 (9): 342–344.

———. 1952. "Management of Buddha Gaya Temple Transferred." *Journal of the Maha Bodhi Society* 60 (6): 249–256.

———. 1956. "Notes and News." *Journal of the Maha Bodhi Society* 64 (7): 368–369.

———. 1957. "Notes and News: His Holiness the Dalai Lama and His Holiness the Panchen Lama at Buddha Gaya." *Journal of the Maha Bodhi Society* 65 (1): 27–28.

———. 1961. "Notes and News: Historic Event at Buddhagaya." *Journal of the Maha Bodhi Society* 69 (1): 22–23.

———. 1967. "Notes and News: Golden Buddha Image Installed at Buddha Gaya." *Journal of the Maha Bodhi Society* 75 (7): 273.

———. 1968a. "Notes and News: General Ne Win Visits Buddha Gaya." *Journal of the Maha Bodhi Society* 76 (4): 86.

———. 1968b. "Devapriya Valisinha (A Biographical Sketch)." *Journal of the Maha Bodhi* Society 76 (8–9): 233–240.

———. 1972. "Notes and News: Initiation Ceremony at Buddha Gaya." *Journal of the Maha Bodhi Society* 80 (4): 311.

———. 1973. "Notes and News: Sacred Relics of Lord Buddha to Japan." *Journal of the Maha Bodhi Society*" 81 (11–12): 460.

———. 1987. "Notes and News: First International Conference of Buddhist Nuns." *Journal of the Maha Bodhi Society* 95 (1–3): 28–30.

———. 2004. "Notes and News." *Journal of the Maha Bodhi Society* 111 (1): 4.

Maha Bodhi Society of India. 1952. *Diamond Jubilee Souvenir, 1891–1951*. Calcutta: Maha Bodhi Society.

———. 1994. *Ven. B Pannarama Nagrick Abhidnandan Samaroh Samiti*. Calcutta: Maha Bodhi Society.

Martin, Robert Montgomery. 2012 [1838]. *The History, Antiquities, Topography, and Statistics of Eastern India*. Cambridge: Cambridge University Press.

Masuzawa, Tomoko. 2005. *The Invention of World Religions: Or, How European Universalism Was Preserved in the Language of Pluralism*. Chicago: University of Chicago Press.

Matthews, Bruce. 1999. "The Legacy of Tradition and Authority: Buddhism and the Nation in Myanmar." In *Buddhism and Politics in Twentieth-Century Asia*, edited by I. Harris, 26–53. London: Continuum.

McKeown, Arthur Philip. Forthcoming. *Guardian of a Dying Flame: Sariputra (c. 1335–1426) and the End of Late Indian Buddhism*. Cambridge: Harvard University Press.

McMahan, David L. 2008. *The Making of Buddhist Modernism*. Oxford: Oxford University Press.

Menon, K. P. S. "My Tribute to Tan Yun-Shan." Accessed May 6, 2013. //www.ignca.nic.in /ks_40016.htm//.

Meyer, Karl E., and Shareen Blair Brysac. 1999. *Tournament of Shadows: The Great Game and the Race for Empire in Central Asia*. New York: Basic Books.

Ministry of External Affairs, Government of India. 1956. File no. 242-M.E. (1947) and 40(2)–BC(B)/56(S) or 40/2/BC/B/56 (1956). National Archives, Delhi.

Mitra, Rajendralala. 1878. *Buddha Gaya: The Hermitage of Sakya Muni*. Calcutta: Bengal Secretariat Press.

Moran, Peter, ed. 2004. *Buddhism Observed: Travellers, Exiles and Tibetan Dharma in Kathmandu*. London: Routledge.

Morean, Brian. 2004. "Rereading the Language of Japanese Tourism." In *Tourists and Tourism: A Reader*, edited by Sharon Bohn Gmelch, 111–125. Long Grove: Waveland Press.

Morris, Brian. 2006. "Buddhism and Spirit-Cults." In *Religion and Anthropology: A Critical Introduction*. Cambridge: Cambridge University Press.

Nehru, Jawaharlal. 1948. "Revolutionizing the Political Vision."*Selected Works of Jawaharlal Nehru* 8: 5.

———. 1949a. "The Message of the Buddha." *Selected Works of Jawaharlal Nehru* 9 (January 14): 102.

———. 1949b. "The Bodh Gaya Temple." Note to Principal Private Secretary, February 15, 1949. File No. 2(271)/48-PMS.10. *Selected Works of Jawaharlal Nehru* 9: 607.

———. 1952. "To Sri Krishna Sinha." File No. 2(271)/48-PMS. *Selected Works of Jawaharlal Nehru* 20 (November 27): 204–205.

———. 1955a. "To Chief Ministers." JN Collection. *Selected Works of Jawaharlal Nehru* 28 (March 25): 450–451.

———. 1955b. "Beautifying the Sacred Place." *Selected Works of Jawaharlal Nehru* 27 (April 10): 452.

———. 1955c. "To Krishna Sinha," JN Collection. *Selected Works of Jawaharlal Nehru* 28 (May 25): 453–454.

———. 1956. "The Way of the Buddha." Speech at a Public Meeting on the Occasion of the Two Thousand Five Hundreth Birth Anniversary of Gautama Buddha, New Delhi. *Selected Works of Jawaharlal Nehru* 33 (May 24): 20.

———. 2004a [1946]. *The Discovery of India*. New Delhi: Penguin.

———. 2004b [1936]. *Autobiography*. New Delhi: Penguin.

———. 2012 [1934]. *Glimpses of World History*. New Delhi: Penguin.

Nugteren, Albertina. 1995. "Rituals around the Bodhi-Tree in Bodhgaya, India." In *Pluralism and Identity: Studies in Ritual Behavior*, edited by J. Platvoet and K. van der Toorn, 145–165. Leiden: E. J. Brill.

———. 2014. "Rites of Reverence, Ways of Worship." In *Objects of Worship in South Asian Religions: Forms, Practices and Meanings*, 200–215. London: Routledge.

O'Malley, L. S. S. 2007 [1906]. *Bengal District Gazetteer: Gaya*. Delhi: Logos Press.

Pandey, Jai Narain. 2006. "Now, Tee Off on Pilgrimage to Bodh Gaya." *Hindustan Times*, December 18.

Parry, Jonathan. 1986. "The Gift, the Indian Gift and the 'Indian gift.'" *Man* 21 (3): 453–473.

———. 1989. "On the Moral Perils of Exchange." In *Money and the Morality of Exchange*, edited by J. Parry and M. Bloch, 64–93. Cambridge: Cambridge University Press.

Pinkney, Andrea. 2015. "Looking West to India: Asian Education, Intra-Asian Renaissance, and the Nalanda Revival." *Modern Asian Studies* 49(1): 111–149.

Prabhat, Kumar. 1999. *Zamin Kiski, Jote Uski: Bodhgaya Bhumi Andolan*. Patna: Kisan Vikas Trust.

Prakash, Gyan. 1990. *Bonded Histories: Genealogies of Labor Servitude in Colonial India*. Cambridge: Cambridge University Press.

Prasad, Rajendra. 1957. "Buddha Gaya Temple." In *Rajendra Prasad: Autobiography*, 232–234. Bombay: Asia Publishing House.

Prost, Audrey. 2006. "The Problem with 'Rich Refugees' Sponsorship, Capital, and the Informal Economy of Tibetan Refugees." *Modern Asian Studies* 40 (1): 233–253.

Pryor, C. Robert. 2006. "Anagarika Munindra and the Historical Context of the Vipassana Movement." *Buddhist Studies Review* 23: 241–248.

Qadir, Abdul. 2007a. "CJM Takes Cognizance against Chief Priest." *Times of India* (Patna), December 7.

———. 2007b. "11 Child Labourers Rescued in Gaya." *Times of India* (Patna), February 8.

———. 2013. "Are Foreign Monasteries Misusing Bodh Gaya Hospitality?" *Times of India* (Patna). December 22.

———. 2016. "Bodh Gaya Monasteries Decry Land Lease Charges." *Times of India* (Patna), November 9.

Queen, Christopher S., and Sallie B. King. 1996. *Engaged Buddhism: Buddhist Liberation Movements in Asia*. Albany: SUNY Press.

Rabinow, Paul. 1982. "Ordonnance, Discipline, Regulation: Some Reflections on Urbanism." *Humanities in Society* 5 (3–4): 267–278.

Rajagopal, Arvind. 2001. "The Violence of Commodity Aesthetics: Hawkers, Demolition Raids, and a New Regime of Consumption." *Social Text* 19 (3): 91–113.

Ramagundam, Rahul. 2006. *Pausing Poverty: Gaya in Bihar*. Delhi: GrassRootsIndia.

Ray, Himanshu Prabha. 2014. *The Return of the Buddha: Ancient Symbols for a New Nation*. New Delhi: Routledge.

Rodman, Margaret C. 1992. "Empowering Place: Multilocality and Multivocality." *American Anthropologist* 94 (33): 640–656.

Rodriguez, Jason A. 2011. "Translating Desires in Bodhgaya: Buddhism and Development in the Land of Buddha's Enlightenment." PhD diss., University of California, Santa Cruz.

Roy, Ananya. 2011. "The Blockade of the World-Class City: Dialectical Images of Indian Urbanism." In *Worlding Cities: Asian Experiments and the Art of Being Global*, edited by A. Roy and A. Ong, 259–278. Malden: Wiley-Blackwell.

Roy, Ananya, and Aihwa Ong, eds. 2011. *Worlding Cities: Asian Experiments and the Art of Being Global*. Malden: Wiley-Blackwell.

Roy Choudhury, Pranab Chandra. 1957. *Bihar District Gazetteers*. Vol. 14. Bihar: Superintendent, Secretariat Press.

Said, Edward W. 1979. *Orientalism*. New York: Vintage.

Sangharakshita, Bhikshu. 1980. *Flame in Darkness: The Life and Sayings of Anagarika Dharmapala*. N.p.: Trinatha Grantha Mala.

———. 1988. *The History of My Going for Refuge: Reflections on the Occasion of the Twentieth Anniversary of the Western Buddhist Order*. Cambridge: Windhorse Publications.

School of Planning and Architecture. 1991. *Tourism Development Plan for Bodh Gaya, Nalanda and Rajgir*. New Delhi: Author.

Sen, Tansen, ed. 2014. *Buddhism across Asia: Networks of Material, Intellectual and Cultural Exchange*. Vol. 1. Singapore: Institute of Southeast Asian Studies.

Shaktin, Gavin. 2011. "Planning Privatopolis: Representation and Contestation in the Development of Urban Integrates Mega-Projects." In *Worlding Cities: Asian Experiments and the Art of Being Global*, edited by A. Roy and A. Ong, 77–97. Malden: Wiley-Blackwell.

Singh Bahadur, Ram Anugrah Narayan. 1893. *A Brief History of Bodh Gaya Math, District Gayá*. Compiled by Rai Ram Anugrah Narayan Singh Bahadur under the orders of G. A. Grierson. Calcutta: Bengal Secretariat Press.

Singh, Upinder. 2010. "Exile and Return: The Reinvention of Buddhism and Buddhist Sites in Modern India." *South Asian Studies* 26 (2): 193–217.

Sinha, Arun. 1991. *Against the Few: Struggles of India's Rural Poor.* London: Zed Books.

Sinha, Ashish. 2006. "Little Hopes Drown in Country's NGO 'capital.'" *Telegraph,* September 26.

Sinha, Manoranjan. 1921. *Gaya and Bodh Gaya.* Calcutta: R. Cambray.

Smith, Laura J. 2006. *Uses of Heritage.* London: Routledge.

Smith, Michael Peter, and Luis Eduardo Guarnizo, eds. 1998. *Transnationalism from Below.* Vol. 6. New Brunswick: Transaction.

Stoddard, H. 1985. *Le Mendicant de l'Amdo.* Paris: Société d'Ethnographie.

Sundrani, Dwarko 1986. "Maha Bodhi Temple, Buddhagaya: Some Aspects of Management (from 1953 to 1986)." Report. Varanasi: Buddhagaya Temple Management Committee.

Swaroop, Vijay. 2007. "Around the Buddhist Circuit in $80!" *Hindustan Times,* March 27.

Tambiah, Stanley Jeyaraja. 1976. *World Conqueror and World Renouncer: A Study of Buddhism and Polity in Thailand against a Historical Background.* Cambridge: Cambridge University Press.

Tanner, Evelyn Lloyd. 1919. *Final Report on the Survey and Settlement Operations in the District of Gaya (1911–1918).* Patna: Superintendent, Government Print., Bihar and Orissa.

Thakur, Sankarshan. 2000. *The Making of Laloo Yadav: The Unmaking of Bihar.* Uttar Pradash: HarperCollins Publishers India.

———. 2006. *Subaltern Saheb: Bihar and the Making of Laloo Yadav.* London: Picador.

Timothy D. J., and D. H. Olsen, eds. 2006. *Tourism, Religion and Spiritual Journeys.* New York: Routledge.

Trevithick, Alan. 2006. *The Revival of Buddhist Pilgrimage at Bodh Gaya (1811–1949): Anagarika Dharmapala and the Mahabodhi Temple.* New Delhi: Motilal Banarsidass.

Tsing, Anna Lowenhaupt. 2005. *Friction: An Ethnography of Global Connection.* Princeton: Princeton University Press.

Tsomo, Karma Lekshe. 2007. "Sakyadhita Pilgrimage in Asia: On the Trail of the Buddhist Women's Network." *Nova Religio: The Journal of Alternative and Emergent Religions* 10 (3): 102–116.

Turner, Victor. 1973. "The Center Out There: Pilgrim's Goal." *History of Religions* 12 (3): 191–230.

Turner, Victor, and Edith. Turner. 1978. *Image and Pilgrimage in Christian Culture.* New York: Columbia University Press.

UNESCO. 2010. UNESCO Initiative on Religious Heritage and Statement on the Protection of Religious Properties within the Framework of the World Heritage Convention. Accessed July 28, 2015. http://whc.unesco.org/en/religious-sacred-heritage/.

UNESCO World Heritage Centre. 2002. "Mahabodhi Temple Complex at Bodh Gaya." Advisory Body Evaluation. Accessed July 7, 2013. //whc.unesco.org/en/list/1056.

———. 2003. "State of Conservation Report." Accessed July 7, 2013. //whc.unesco.org/en/list/1056.

———. 2004. "State of Conservation Report." Accessed July 7, 2013. //whc.unesco.org/en/list/1056.

Vij-Aurora, Bhavna. 2011. "The Buck Stops Here." *India Today,* February 14.

Werbner, Pnina. 1996. "Stamping the Earth with the Name of Allah: Zikr and the Sacralizing of Space among British Muslims." *Cultural Anthropology* 11 (3): 309–338.

Williams, Phillipa. 2011. "Hindu–Muslim Relations and the "War on Terror." In *A Companion to the Anthropology of India*, edited by I. Clark-Decès, 241–259. Oxford: Wiley-Blackwell.

Witsoe, Jeffrey. 2011. "Corruption as Power: Caste and the Political Imagination of the Postcolonial State." *American Ethnologist* 38 (1): 73–85.

Wong, Edward. 2012. "China Said to Detail Returning Tibetan Pilgrims." *New York Times*, April 7.

Yadav, Kripal Chandra. 2001. *The Laloo Phenomenon: Paradoxes of Changing India*. Bihar: Hope India.

Yang, Anand A. 1989. *The Limited Raj: Agrarian Relations in Colonial India, Saran District, 1793–1920*. Berkeley: University of California Press.

———. 1998. *Bazaar India: Markets, Society, and the Colonial State in Gangetic Bihar*. Berkeley: University of California Press.

Yu-Ling Chang, C. 2017. "When Buddhist Women Meet: Sakyadhita and the International Buddhist Women's Movement." Dharma Library. http://dharmalib.net/when-buddhist-women-meet-sakyadhita-and-the-international-buddhist-women-s-movement.

Index

A

abolition of cow-killing and beef-eating, 36

abolition of *zamindari*, 84–85, 93–97

"accumulation by dispossession" (Harvey), 172

adda, 139–40. *See also* timepass

adivasi (tribal groups in India), 85

Advani, L. K., 76

"aesthetic mode of governing" (Ghertner), 171

aesthetic politics, 182

Ahir, D. C., 75–76

Ajanta-Ellora temple cave complex, 160, 211n13

Akihito, Crown Prince, 66–67

All India Bhikkhu Maha Sangha, 78

All India Bhikkhu Sangha, xiv–xv*map*, 75–78

All India Kisan Sabha, 94

All-Indian Congress. *See* Indian National Congress

All-Indian Hindu Mahasabha, 36–37, 201n23

Almond, Philip C., 5, 20

Amaravati, Andhra Pradesh, 110

Ambedkar, B. R., Dr., 47–48, 72, 75, 78, 203nn8,9

Ambedkar Buddhists, 47–48, 75–79, 176, 186

"ambiguities of preservation" (Kinnard), 193

Amitabha Buddha statue, 31, 201n20

Anand, Bhadant, 77–78

Ancient Monuments Preservation Act

(1904), 33, 201n22. *See also* Curzon, Lord (viceroy)

Antioch University (Carlton-Antioch) Buddhist Studies Program, 10, 51, 61, 119, 121

Appadurai, Arjun, 9, 146, 183

archaeological museum, xiv–xv*map*, 150

Archaeological Survey of India (ASI), 21–23, 73, 147, 166, 168–69, 175, 185, 195, 201n22, 209n2

archaeology, 5–7, 18–24, 34, 150–52, 157*fig.*, 157–58, 195, 199n6

Arnold, Edwin, 26–28, 30, 38, 42, 196–97, 200nn9,10

Ashoka, Emperor, 4, 38–39, 48, 71, 150, 209n1

Ashoka-Mauryan past, 4, 39, 71

Ashokan pillar, 38, 150, 209n1

Ashok's Travelers Lodge, 175, 209n6

Asher, Frederick, 19–21, 68, 71, 199n1, 200n6

Asian Relations Conference (New Delhi), 39–40

atithi devo bhavah (guest is god), 114, 208n1. *See also* Indian tourism

Autobiography (Nehru), 38

Ayang, Rinpoche, 61

Ayodhya, 76, 78, 183–84, 190

B

Babri Masjid Mosque, 76, 183–84, 190

backward castes, 101, 128, 130, 151. *See also* caste

Ba Khin, Sayagyi U, 50

GLOBAL
SOUTH
ASIA

Padma Kaimal
K. Sivaramakrishnan
Anand A. Yang
SERIES EDITORS

GLOBAL SOUTH ASIA takes an interdisciplinary approach to the humanities and social sciences in its exploration of how South Asia, through its global influence, is and has been shaping the world.

CPSIA information can be obtained
at www.ICGtesting.com
Printed in the USA
BVHW03s1507011018
528829BV00003B/5/P